Legal Publishing in Antebellum America

Legal Publishing in Antebellum America presents a history of the law book publishing and distribution industry in the United States. Part business history, part legal history, part information history, M. H. Hoeflich's book shows how various developments such as printing and binding, the introduction of railroads, and the expansion of mail service contributed to the growth of the industry from an essentially local one to a national scale. Furthermore, the book ties the spread of a particular approach to law, that is, the "scientific approach" championed by northeastern American jurists, to the growth of law publishing and law bookselling, and shows that the two were critically intertwined.

M. H. Hoeflich is Kane Professor of Law at the University of Kansas. He is the author of *Roman and Civil Law and the Development of Anglo-American Jurisprudence* as well as articles in various journals, including the *Journal of Legal History*, *American Journal of Legal History*, *Law and History Review*, and *Law Library Journal*. Professor Hoeflich is also a Fellow of the Royal Historical Society and member of the American Law Institute.

Legal Publishing in Antebellum America

M. H. HOEFLICH
University of Kansas

CAMBRIDGE
UNIVERSITY PRESS

CAMBRIDGE UNIVERSITY PRESS
Cambridge, New York, Melbourne, Madrid, Cape Town, Singapore,
São Paulo, Delhi, Dubai, Tokyo

Cambridge University Press
32 Avenue of the Americas, New York, NY 10013-2473, USA

www.cambridge.org
Information on this title: www.cambridge.org/9780521192064

First published 2010

Printed in the United States of America

A catalog record for this publication is available from the British Library.

Library of Congress Cataloging in Publication Data
Hoeflich, Michael H.
Legal publishing in antebellum America / M. H. Hoeflich.
p. cm.
ISBN 978-0-521-19206-4
1. Legal literature – Publishing – United States – History – 18th century. 2. Legal literature – Publishing – United States – History – 19th century. I. Title.
Z480.L44H64 2010
070.509′033–dc22
2009053585

ISBN 978-0-521-19206-4 Hardback

Additional resources for this publication at www.antebellumlegalpublishing.org

In memory of my grandparents Harry & Gertrude Junger

and

In gratitude to my doctor and my friend Mary Frank, M.D.

Contents

Preface

This book's life began in 1973 when, as a newly arrived Fulbright Scholar at Cambridge, I became friends with three men. One, a contemporary and Fulbright like myself, Tony Grafton, already possessed the love of books and broad and deep knowledge of book history that has led him to both a distinguished chair at Princeton and rightful acknowledgment as one of the founders of the scholarly study of the history of the book. The second person to whom I owe a great debt of gratitude for starting me on the long road to this book was Tim Munby, one of twentieth-century England's greatest book men, who opened his library and his own vast store of knowledge to me. The third great influence on me in this subject was Sir Geoffrey Elton, Regius Professor of History at Cambridge, Fellow of Clare College, and historian extraordinaire. The many nights I sat with him drinking Glenfiddich and talking history and books were the richest intellectual experiences of my life. In the intervening years I have been fortunate to have benefited from the advice and assistance of countless scholars, librarians, and booksellers. I would be ungracious not to mention specifically Steve Sheppard, Rob Meade, Jim Brundage, Carolyn Clark, Mary Bilder, Alfred Murphy, Joe McKnight, Joel Fishman, Roy Mersky, Mike Widener, David Warrington, Karen Beck, Rick Surles, James Green, Douglas Osler, Steve Epstein, Jonathon Clark, Bill Wiecek, Ken Pennington, Joe Levine, Dan Hulsebosch, Bill Nelson, Amanda Zagnoli, and many others to whom I apologize for failing to name. And then, of course, there is Morris Cohen, the iconic figure to all who study the history of the American law book, without whose pioneering work and magisterial *Bibliography of Early American Law* this book could not have been written. Christine Sheppard read through and edited this book in an exemplary manner.

I owe her a great debt. Dan Ernst spent countless hours editing and improving this book. My gratitude for his help is unbounded. Also, many thanks to Kathleen Levy, who created the index.

I also owe a great debt of gratitude closer to home. My colleagues Sid Shapiro and Ellen Sward, who have served admirably as Associate Deans for Research, have been a source of great support. Professor Joyce McCray Pearson, director of the University of Kansas Law Library; Joe Custer, Associate Director; and Rob Mead, Pam Tull, Katherine Greene, Gale Troth, and Chris Steadham, all University of Kansas law librarians, as well as Carolyn Clark, have also aided me well beyond the call of duty. I must also mention the enormous help provided to me by my research assistants, Scott Rice, Jennifer Haaga, Carol Liang, Slade Bond, Ryan Schwarzenberger, and Jessie Mickloski.

I must also gratefully acknowledge the funding provided to me to do this book. First and foremost I want to thank the Kane family for the financial assistance provided to me by the endowment that they created and the chair in their name that I hold. Second, I wish to acknowledge the American Philosophical Society; the American Antiquarian Society, especially William Reese, who is a member thereof; and the Massachusetts Historical Society for providing me with research fellowships. The Delmas Foundation, and its trustee David Stam; and the William Nelson Cromwell Foundation, particularly its trustees Conrad Harpur, Esq., and Henry Christiansen, Esq., were immensely generous in providing grants for this work and the digitization of the sources underlying this work. The John H. & John M. Kane Endowment at the Kansas University Endowment Association has provided incredible financial support since 1997. Finally, I must also acknowledge grants from the Graduate Research Fund at the University of Kansas, which, over the years, have supported my summer research activities.

Several pages in Chapter 2 first appeared in *The Green Bag*. An early version of Chapter 3 appeared in the *Proceedings of the American Antiquarian Society*. An early version of Chapter 5 appeared in the *American Journal of Legal History*. A version of Chapter 4 was delivered as the first Tarlton Law Library Lecture at the University of Texas School of Law and was published by the Tarlton Law Library in that form. I thank the editors and the publishers of these journals for permission to include these materials in this book.

This book is the product of ten years of visiting libraries and archives, both famous and obscure. I have benefited enormously from the care, advice, and ministrations of hundreds of librarians in these marvelous places. For me, like Borges, if there is a Heaven, then it shall indeed resemble a library. In many ways, the writing of this book has been like a decade-long sojourn in an earthly, albeit often dusty, paradise. Finally, it could only have been paradise because of the presence of my wife and life partner Karen, an engineer who learned to love books and libraries out of her love for her bibliomaniac husband; and of my dogs, George, Dudley, Barney the Wonder Dog, Cocoa, and Niobe, who are now waiting for me, I hope, in that heavenly library (complete with soft chairs and plenty of toys and treats), and Callie, Augie, Archie, Victoria, Josephina, Buster, and Pete, who surround and comfort me each day as I do my work.

Bibliographical Note

In this book I have used books, periodicals, and ephemera in two ways. The first – and more conventional – was as a source of content to inform my narrative. The second – and less conventional – was as artifacts whose printing, binding, bibliographical, and codicological details helped me to understand the underlying industry that produced and sold them. Many of the volumes that I used for this second purpose have had little value to readers for decades, if not centuries. These were working books and periodicals designed to be used hard and then, once obsolete, discarded. Many were not collected by libraries or individuals. As a result, many of these volumes have become exceedingly rare. In some cases they are known today only in a small number of copies. Because of the difficulty of accessing these books and ephemera, I have chosen to make use of Web technology rather than include a traditional bibliography. This enables me to reproduce in digital form all of the important sources cited in this book and make them easily available to readers. While I realize that eliminating the conventional printed bibliography at the back of this volume and, instead, creating a digital repository of the sources themselves on the Web may be considered inconvenient by some readers, overall, I think that the gains from this method far outweigh the inconveniences.

With the financial assistance of the William Nelson Cromwell Foundation, I have established a Web site: www.antebellumlegalpublishing.org. On this site will be found detailed bibliographies of both primary and secondary sources used in this volume, digital reproductions of many of these sources, and comments about these sources including, where useful, location information. It is my intention that, unlike printed bibliographies and illustrations that once printed cannot be supplemented except by new printings, this Web site will be continuously updated with new entries to the secondary literature bibliographies as they are printed and reproductions of new documents to the primary sources bibliographies as they are discovered.

Because the field of "book history" is, itself, in its early years and the subfield of the history of law books in its infancy, I have chosen to include on the Web site links to other Web pages that may be of interest to readers of this book as well as a "wiki" feature that permits readers to post comments on the subjects covered. I look forward to hearing from you and beginning a discussion on the history of the law book trade in the United States.

Introduction

Today Auburn, New York, is a sleepy upstate town most notable for its prison. But in the antebellum period, Auburn was a bustling mercantile center built astride the Erie Canal and a convenient stop en route from Syracuse to Buffalo. It was a town served by newspapers, publishers, a variety of retail businesses, and, of course, a thriving professional community. In the early years of the nineteenth century, one of the most respected members of the Bar was Judge Elijah Miller, who built a splendid mansion on one of Auburn's wide, tree-lined avenues. In 1823 Judge Miller took as his partner a young lawyer fresh from New York City: William Henry Seward.[1] In 1824 Seward married Judge Miller's daughter, Frances, whom he had met several years earlier. From this time until his death, Seward made Judge Miller's house his home. Over the next half century, Seward led a distinguished career as a lawyer and politician holding the office of Governor of New York, U.S. Senator from New York, and Secretary of State in the administration of President Abraham Lincoln. Travel as he may, however, Seward always returned to the house in Auburn, where he died in 1870.

The house in which Seward spent his life still stands on its quiet street in Auburn and has changed very little over the past century and a half.[2]

[1] Biographical details on Seward are taken from John Grant Wilson and John Fiske, *Appleton's Cycolpedia of American Biography* (New York: Appleton, 1898), v. 5, 470–73.

[2] The Seward House is now maintained as a museum; its Web site is www.sewardhouse.org/house/.

One enters through a grand entry and is confronted by a majestic staircase that leads up to the second floor. The furniture is high Victorian, and the walls are covered with portraits of the great and good of nineteenth-century America, portraits that once hung in Seward's Washington residence. But what strikes the visitor to Seward house immediately and forcefully are the books, row upon serried row in virtually every room. In some of the rooms they fill whole walls from floor to ceiling; in other rooms they are contained in bookshelves that stretch from one wall to another. Up the stairs and in the main upper hall, one walks between gorgeous glass-fronted cases that reach to the high ceilings. These are filled with thousands of leather-bound volumes.

Visitors to the Seward house are surrounded by not only the tools of trade of several generations of lawyers but also one essential tangible manifestation of antebellum American legal culture: books. Without books, American law and the American legal profession could not have developed as it did. Books were the medium by which the various legislatures, judges, lawyers, and others concerned with the law shaped the Bar and the legal system itself.

For nearly two millennia, the relationships among lawyers, the law, the producers of law books, and the distributers of law books has been exceptionally close. One may fairly say that this relationship has been symbiotic; lawyers and judges needed books, and law publishers and sellers needed lawyers and judges. In late Antiquity, when the world of written communication underwent the shift from scroll to codex in copies of the Christian Bible, it was the lawyers who embraced the format shift and championed the new mode.[3] In the high Middle Ages, when the faculties of law came to dominate universities around Europe, one could always find booksellers, many of whom owned scriptoria to mass produce legal texts in affordable format, close by the lecture halls.[4] In the late fifteenth century, when Johann Gutenberg introduced the art of printing from moveable type to the West, first it was the Bible and related theological texts that poured from the new presses; but soon, it was law books that dominated the trade for the next

[3] See Franz Wieacker, *Textstufen klassiker Juristen* (Gottingen: Van den Hoeck & Ruprecht, 1975), 93–119.

[4] See Frank Soetermeer, *Utrumque Ius in Peciis: Aspetti della Produzione Libraria a Bologna Fra Due e Trecento* (Milan: Giuffre, 1997).

half-century.[5] For the past two thousand years, where one found lawyers, one found law books and those who produced and sold them.

This book cuts across disciplinary lines. As I sat in my study over the past ten years writing it I often wondered how some anonymous cataloguer deep within the bowels of the Library of Congress would deal with the dilemma this work poses: is it a work of legal, business, or book history? The answer, I fear, is not one that fits within the Library of Congress cataloging categories. To my mind, this is a book about the co-evolution of the law, the legal profession, and one of the principal ancillary support and communication networks, which together combined to make the development of American law and the American legal profession possible. It is not a traditional book about legal doctrine or about legal institutions. It is not a compilation of biographical stories of great men and women. The heroes of the story I tell in this book are, for the most part, humble and obscure people whose professions were to make and sell law books. Some achieved wealth and notoriety in their time. Most did not. Even those who did, like John Livingston or Hocquet Caritat, are now forgotten even among historians. But without them, there would be no history of American law because they were enablers. These obscure printers, binders, and booksellers provided the means by which great men like Joseph Story and James Kent could disseminate their ideas and achieve greatness. When we think today of a Story or a Kent, we seldom think of all those forgotten people and of the long-vanished mercantile infrastructure on which the great jurists depended. It has been my self-appointed task over the past decade to try to write the history of that long forgotten and neglected world.

[5] See the monumental work of Douglas Osler, *Bibliographica Iuridica: Catalogue of Books Printed on the Continent of Europe from the Beginning of Printing to 1600 in the Library of the Max-Planck Institut fur Europaische Rechtsgeschichte, Frankfurt am Main* (Frankfurt: Klostermann, 2000), 2 vols.

Chapter 1

A Bookish Profession

In 1848 Rufus Choate made a motion before the Massachusetts Supreme Court for the admission of his student and protégé, Matthew Hale Carpenter.[1] Carpenter was duly admitted and began his preparations to leave Boston for Wisconsin in the hopes of building a professional and personal life in this frontier state. Upon learning of his student's decision, Choate's first question to Carpenter was whether he had enough money to equip himself with an adequate professional library to bring with him to his new home.[2] When Carpenter replied that he had not and that "the idea of going to a new country as an attorney with no books" had been a great worry, Choate immediately told Carpenter to go to Little, Brown & Co., establish a credit line, which Choate himself would guarantee, and buy a library.[3] Delighted with this offer, Carpenter did so and soon returned to Choate with a list of the books he had purchased. Choate looked at the list and scolded Carpenter that he had been too parsimonious. He sent Carpenter back, and this time Carpenter spent almost $1,000 on his new professional library.[4]

In December 1825, Charles Augustus Dewey, a young lawyer and Harvard graduate living in Williamstown, Massachusetts, wrote a letter to I. L. Bangs, proposing that they consider becoming law partners.

[1] Frank Flower, *Life of Matthew Hale Carpenter* (Madison, WI: David Atwood, 1883), 52.
[2] Ibid., 52. [3] Ibid., 53.
[4] Ibid., 53. Within a short time, Carpenter paid his debt in full to Little, Brown & Co. and became a lifelong customer; Ibid., p. 54.

His greatest concern in forming this union was the question of offices. He wrote:

I would enter into the concern with no view less than that of having a business office where clients could be as well served as in any of the western counties – to effect this your own personal attention will be requisite – *so too should there be a very extended and perfect library, which can easily I believe be made out from ours united – I have more than 300 vols.*[5]

Joseph Story, Associate Justice of the Supreme Court of the United States and Dane Professor of Law at Harvard, devoted his life to the law and to books; he collected books,[6] he read books constantly, he wrote books from an early age. Books were at the center of his life. According to his son William, every morning Story would awaken and, if breakfast was not immediately available, hasten to his library. He spent much of the day reading and writing among his books, except when he was in the classroom.[7] Indeed, so important was constant access to the library to Story that he arranged his books and papers so that he might be able to find them even at night in the darkness.[8] Thus, it is not surprising that William Story found the following notation of advice for ambitious lawyers in his father's memorandum book for 1831–1832: "Books should be read."[9]

James Kent, the great Chancellor of New York, first law professor at Columbia University, and author of the first great American institutional legal work, the *Commentaries on American Law*, also built up a large library.[10] He expressed his devotion to his books and his library in the strongest terms: "next to my wife my library has been the solace of

[5] This manuscript letter is contained in the Dewey-Bliss Collection at the American Antiquarian Society in Worcester, Massachusetts; emphasis added.

[6] According to his son William, "His library was very select and extensive. It had been collected with great care, and at a large expense, and was precisely adapted to his wants," quoted in W. W. Story, *Life and Letters of Joseph Story*, vol. 2 (Boston: Little, Brown & Co. 1851), 40.

[7] Ibid., 102. [8] Ibid., 604.

[9] Ibid., 90. The fact that this note was written in the book in which Story kept his case notes may well indicate his dissatisfaction with the level of learning displayed by some counsel before the court. The full couplet reads: "Books should be read; but if you can't digest, The same's the surfeit, take the worst or the best."

[10] See William Kent, *Memoirs and Letters of James Kent, LLD* (Boston: Little, Brown & Co. 1898).

my greatest pleasure and devoted attachment."[11] At least he put his wife first.[12]

All of these anecdotes provide a very different view of lawyers and the legal profession from the popular image of lawyers today as oral advocates who vanquish their opponents by the strength of their rhetoric in court. In fact, even the most skilled litigator must know the law and argue from legal principles. To do otherwise is to risk the displeasure of the court and almost certain defeat to an opponent who does know the law. The law in Western society for the past millennium has been acquired by its students through tedious reading in often dry and bloated tomes that embody the sum total of legislative, court, and private literature, which together make up the law. Thus, though a lawyer might well have practiced on horseback, as did Lincoln 150 years ago, or out of the back of a minivan, as some do today, all still have needed and continue to need access to the books and documents that contain the accumulated law and legal wisdom with which they must be familiar.[13] Choate's assistance to his young student simply testifies to the continuity over centuries of this connection between lawyers and books.

In the period from the founding of the new republic to the beginning of the Civil War, American law and the American legal profession underwent profound changes.[14] This was a period of extensive legal syncretism of American and English law. English law was neither wholly rejected nor wholly accepted, and every lawyer during this period had to know something of English statutes and cases as well as the great treatise literature that had dominated English legal thought,

[11] Quoted in Dan Hulsebosch, *Constituting Empire: New York and the Transformation of Constitutionalism in the Atlantic World, 1664–1830* (Chapel Hill, NC: University of North Carolina Press, 2005), 285.

[12] Every bibliophile should ponder carefully the scene from Umberto Eco's *Name of the Rose* in which the master, in the face of a devastating fire in the library, chooses to save the most precious books, leaving his apprentice to save himself, if he could. My wife has chided me more than once that were such a choice to be mine, I too would save the books and leave her to fend for herself.

[13] See Henry C. Whitney, *Life on the Circuit with Lincoln* (Boston: Estes & Lauriat, 1892), for an excellent evocation of the life of a circuit-riding lawyer in antebellum Illinois.

[14] See M. Bloomfield, *American Lawyers in a Changing Society, 1776–1876* (Cambridge, MA: Harvard University Press, 1976); G. W. Gawalt, *The Promise of Power: The Emergence of the Legal Profession in Massachusetts 1760–1840* (Westport, CT: Greenwood Press, 1979), 81–128.

particularly the works of Coke and Blackstone.[15] At the same time each of the new American states and the new federal government were developing legal literatures of their own, in courts, in legislatures, and in law offices and law schools. No antebellum American lawyer could risk not knowing his own state's and nation's laws. Finally, American lawyers of this period were cosmopolitan in their thinking and writing. If they could not find relevant English or American law they would gladly look to the law of ancient Rome, and of contemporary France or Germany, among others.[16] The new nation in its formative period offered lawyers unparalleled freedom to look widely for their authorities.

In practice this broadly syncretic approach to legal sources meant that lawyers needed to aspire to have access, either through proximity or ownership, to a major law library, one that could indeed offer the full range of legal sources that lawyers of the period used in drawing their arguments and documents. Many were not satisfied simply with a few reports of local cases and a dog-eared Blackstone. Instead they longed for copies of Pothier on contracts and Vattel on natural law, of Vinnius on Justinian's *Institutes*, and Littleton on the English law of tenures.[17]

As the economists have taught us, when one finds a conjunction of demand with the ability to pay for the goods demanded, a market to supply such goods will inevitably result. This is precisely what happened in the first decades of the new United States. Prior to the Revolution, a number of booksellers offered law books, mostly imported from England, and a few even issued catalogues or held the occasional auction

[15] See, esp., A.W.B. Simpson, "The Rise and Fall of the Legal Treatise: Legal Principles and the Forms of Legal Literature," in *Legal Theory and Legal History*, ed. A. W. B. Simpson (London: Hambledon Press, 1987), 273–320. See also Michael Lobban, "The English Legal Treatise and English Law in the Eighteenth Century," *Iuris Scripta Historica* 13 (1997): 69–88; and M.H. Hoeflich, "American Blackstones," in *Blackstone Studies*, ed. Wilfred Prest (London: Hart, 2009).

[16] See M. H. Hoeflich, *Roman and Civil Law and the Development of Anglo-American Jurisprudence* (Athens, GA: University of Georgia Press, 1997); see also Peter Stein, "The Attraction of the Civil Law in Post-Revolutionary America," *Virginia Law Review*, 52 (1966): 403–34; R.H. Helmholz, "Use of the Civil Law in Post-Revolutionary American Jurisprudence," *Tulane Law Review*, 66 (1992): 1649–84.

[17] See, for example, the comments of Daniel Mayes, a professor at the Transylvania Law School, *An Address to the Students of Law in Transylvania University* (Lexington, KY, 1834), reprinted in M.H. Hoeflich, ed., *The Gladsome Light of Jurisprudence* (Westport, CT: Greenwood Press, 1988), 145–64.

of a private library. A few law libraries of the colonial period were notable for the breadth and depth of their holdings. There were not a great number of such libraries. Thomas Jefferson, for example, built up a respectable legal collection, which eventually became the foundation for the Library of Congress.[18] Edwin Wolf has shown how readily available English law books were in colonial cities such as Philadelphia.[19] The Loganian Library there is one such example.[20] John Adams, too, built up a substantial law library in Boston. But the colonial law book trade and the demand for law books in colonial America were far less significant and far smaller than that which grew up in the first seventy-five years after independence. It was in the antebellum period that the American legal profession saw its first dramatic increase in size and prestige, soon eclipsing, as Perry Miller has demonstrated, at least in prestige, the American clergy.[21] And all of these lawyers needed books. Thus, we find the growth of the law book trade in every major city during this period: Little, Brown in Boston; Banks in Albany; Johnson in Philadelphia; and Voorhies and Livingston in New York City are just a few of those that prospered during this period.[22]

The complete history of the trade in law books in the antebellum United States has still to be written. But even preliminary research shows that the law booksellers of this period carried on a sophisticated trade, importing books from both England and the Continent (and pirated English editions from Ireland) as well as printing, publishing,

[18] See, above all, M. Sowerby, ed., *Catalogue of the Library of Thomas Jefferson* (Charlottesville, VA: University of Virginia Press, 1983).

[19] Edwin Wolf II, *The Book Culture of a Colonial American City* (Oxford: Clarendon Press, 1988), 131–63.

[20] See *Catalogue of the Books Belonging to the Loganian Library* (Philadelphia: Z. Poulson, Jr., 1795).

[21] Perry Miller, *The Life of the Mind in America from the Revolution to the Civil War* (New York: Harcourt, Brace, 1969); see also Samuel Haber, *The Quest for Authority and Honor in the American Professions. 1750–1900* (Chicago: University of Chicago Press, 1991), esp. 91–116; Samuel Haber, "The Professions," in *Encyclopedia of American Social History*, vol. 2, ed. Mary K. Cayton, Elliot J. Gorn, and Peter W. Williams (New York: Scribner, 1992); Bruce Kimball, *The True Professional Ideal in America* (Cambridge, MA: Blackwell, 1992), 106–97.

[22] The standard work on the history of American law publishing is Edwin Surrency, *A History of Law Publishing* (New York: Oceana, 1990). Surrency does not deal with either auctions or retail sales in any detail. H. Amory and D. Hall, *The Colonial Book in the Atlantic World* (2000) only touches on the period covered in this present work and is little concerned with law publishers and bookselling.

and selling American-produced translations of foreign works and texts and reports of American origin. Most of the major law booksellers and publishers also sold books by catalogue through the newly created and often unpredictable United States Postal Service, when it became possible to do so.[23] Finally, a number of booksellers, both those in general trade and those specializing in legal materials, began to hold auctions of notable law libraries and collections of law books.

Legal historians have paid too little attention to the law book trade in antebellum America.[24] There are a number of reasons for this. First, traditional legal history has been doctrinal history, interested in the contents of books, not in the more mundane matters of how such doctrines were, in fact, made known to lawyers and the public. The assumption has been that a doctrine in print was a doctrine of importance, particularly if it was incorporated into a court report or legislative text. The "new" legal history has broken from the doctrinal focus of the traditionalists to explore such issues as race and gender, but it too has been more concerned with the substance of the law than with the vectors by which legal doctrines became known. It is only within the past decade that a few hardy legal historians such as Richard Ross, Ann Fidler, Mary Bilder, and Al Brophy have attempted to combine the new field of book history with legal history.[25]

[23] Books could not be sent securely or inexpensively through the U.S. Postal Service until 1851; see Richard R. John , *Spreading the News* (Cambridge, MA: Harvard University Press, 1995), 39; see also R. B. Kielbowicz, *News in the Mail: The Press, Post Office, and Public Information, 1700–1860s* (Westport, CT: Greenwood Press, 1989); R. B. Kielbowicz, "Mere Merchandise or Vessels of Culture? Books in the Mind, 1792–1942," *Papers of the Bibliographical Society of America*, 82 (1988): 169–200.

[24] Historians of European law have done far better in this regard; see the works cited in notes 3–5.

[25] See Ann Fidler, "'Till You Understand Them in Their Principal Features': Observations on Form and Function in Nineteenth-Century American Law Books," *Papers of the Bibliographical Society of America* 92, no. 4 (1998): 427–42; Richard Ross, "The Memorial Culture of Early Modern English Lawyers: Memory as Keyword, Shelter, and Identity, 1560–1640," *Yale Journal of Law and the Humanities* 10, no. 2 (1998): 229–326; Mary Bilder, "The Lost Literates: Early American Legal Literates and Transatlantic Legal Culture," *Yale Journal of Law and the Humanities* 11, no. 1 (1999): 231–85; Alfred Brophy, "The Rule of Law in Antebellum College Literary Addresses: The Case of William Greene," *Cumberland Law Review* 31, no. 2 (2000/2001): 231–85; see also M.H. Hoeflich, "Legal History: A History of the Book: Variations on a Theme," *University of Kansas Law Review* 46 (1998): 415ff.; M.H. Hoeflich and Steve Sheppard, "Disciplinary Evolution and Scholarly

A second reason the history of law books and the law book trade has not been written is because of the difficulty of finding the sources with which to write such a history. There are very few remaining business records of antebellum law booksellers and publishers. These were lost long ago as have most mundane business records. The printed remains of these businesses, their catalogues, can still be found; but they have, for the most part, suffered the fate of most printed ephemera. They have not been preserved by institutional libraries precisely because they are ephemera. Indeed, book catalogues are usually at a particular disadvantage in regard to library preservation. Librarians are inundated by such catalogues; once they have been perused they are disposed of. To do otherwise requires an institutional preservation vision of the greatest rarity.

Happily, a few institutions have had such a rare vision. Among such libraries, first rank must be given to the New York Public Library, the Athenaeum in Boston, the Harvard Law Library, and the library of the American Antiquarian Society. Other institutional libraries that had substantial collections of these materials, such as the New York State Historical Library, have sold off many of their holdings, but this, too, has served a purpose in that it has permitted these items to enter the current market to be purchased by other libraries and private collectors.

Although American legal historians generally have not paid adequate attention to the history of the American law book trade, such attention is necessary and long overdue. Indeed, despite some legal historians' resistance to the introduction of the methodologies and techniques of the emerging field of the history of the book, these methodologies and techniques have much to offer American legal historians.[26] Indeed, a merging of the two fields will produce a richer and more expansive view of American legal history, especially of the antebellum age. Let me explain why.

The antebellum lawyer's "lust" for books, as illustrated in the anecdotes at the beginning of this chapter, was one of the central facts of

Expansion: Legal History in the United States," in *American Law in the 21st Century: U.S. National Reports to the XVIIth International Congress of Comparative Law*, ed. John C. Reitz and David Clark (Ann Arbor, MI: American Society of Comparative Law, 2006), 23–44.

[26] See Hoeflich, "Legal History and the History of the Book."

legal culture in the emerging nation.[27] Lawyers trade in information, and in the antebellum period, the most important means of acquiring specialized information was through books and professional periodicals. But books do not simply appear like manna from heaven. They must be written, printed, marketed, and distributed. This requires the development of a complex industry of printers, binders, publishers, and booksellers, and the means to transport and advertise the books. The anecdote involving Rufus Choate and Matthew Hale Carpenter with which this chapter began is emblematic of why the history of the antebellum law book trade is so important. Not only does the anecdote highlight the practical importance of possessing a good law library, but it also demonstrates that by 1848 acquisition of such a library had become relatively easy, even for a lawyer moving to the frontier. One could go to a major law bookseller and purchase literally every book one desired if one had the means to do so. Further, one could purchase these books on credit, albeit sometimes with a friend's guarantee. And even when a lawyer had moved westward, away from the centers of law publishing and bookselling, one could still obtain law books by ordering them from a catalogue.[28] The lifelong business relationship between Carpenter and Little, Brown & Co. was not at all atypical of this period.

In fact, the development of the American law book trade in the latter years of the eighteenth and the first half of the nineteenth centuries played a crucial role in the growth of the American legal profession and of university-affiliated law schools like Harvard and Transylvania. Indeed, one might argue that the rise in prestige of both the legal profession as a whole and university-trained lawyers in particular was made possible, in part, because of the rise of the American law book trade and the wide and easy circulation of law books that resulted. It also played a crucial role in the spread of the political and legal ideologies of the Eastern, Federalist legal elite, who came to dominate both

[27] Not everyone was happy about this; see R. Kent Newmyer, "Harvard Law School, New England Legal Culture and the Antebellum Origins of American Jurisprudence," *Journal of American History* 74, no. 3 (1987): 814–35, esp. p. 821 and n. 14; C. Clark and M.H. Hoeflich, "Oceana Juris" (lecture, University of Edinburgh, March 2007).

[28] For a brilliant, albeit rather lengthy, narrative of the transformative effect of new modes of transportation and communication on the antebellum United States, see Daniel Walker Howe, *What Hath God Wrought* (New York: Oxford University Press, 2007); see also M.H. Hoeflich and Robert Mead, "Law, Lawyers and Books in Early Kansas," *University of Kansas Law Review* 50, no.5 (2002): 1051–72.

the organized Bar and the elite law schools throughout the eastern United States.

Perry Miller's insight, that the key to establishing the law as a prestigious profession lay in making lawyers learned, lies at the heart of why the history of the production and distribution of law books is so crucial.[29] Put simply, in this period books were the repositories and the material evidence of learning. As Charles Augustus Dewey realized in 1825, a substantial law library was not only a resource on which lawyers could depend for learning the law necessary for their practice, but also the visible means by which they could impress clients with their learning and knowledge. It was both a basic information resource and a stage prop. This is precisely why so many antebellum lawyers had themselves portrayed by artists of the day with law books and papers in hand.[30] If the profession was to become actually learned and to appear learned to the rest of American society, it had to become bookish. The clergy had their bibles and their volumes of theology. The lawyers needed their statutes, reports, and treatises. Only the growth of an extensive domestic law book trade could make this possible.

There was another, sociological, side to this growth as well. The American legal profession experienced unprecedented growth in the antebellum period.[31] In part, this was attributable to the growing commerce of the new nation, which created opportunities for legal practice, but it was also partly a result of the growing democratization of American society, which found its keenest expression in the populist reforms of the Jacksonian period. The number of lawyers practicing in the United States increased dramatically during this period.[32] This dramatic rise came about as the movement toward increasing the qualifications of lawyers begun in the eighteenth century was reversed. Stricter admissions requirements for admission to the Bar were

[29] Miller, *Life of the Mind in America*.

[30] M. H. Hoeflich, "Lawyers, Books and Papers, *The Green Bag*, 2d ser., 5 (2002): 163–71.

[31] Lawrence Friedman, *A History of American Law*, 2d. ed. (New York: Simon & Schuster, 1985), 304–05.

[32] According to Friedman, *A History*, 304, the number of lawyers in Massachusetts, for example, increased from 15 in 1740 to 112 in 1790 to 200 in 1800 to 492 in 1810 and 640 in 1840, an increase in terms of lawyers per non-lawyers in the population of 1,000 percent. Friedman relies for these figures on Gerald Gawalt, *The Promise of Power: The Emergence of the Legal Profession in Massachusetts, 1760–1840* (Westport, CT: Greenwood Press, 1979), 14.

abolished.[33] Attempts to create gradations in the Bar based on experience and learning were swept away.[34] Many of the Jacksonians argued for a system in which anyone of "good character," regardless of learning or accomplishments, could be admitted to practice in the courts.[35] At the same time, the popular image of lawyers and the legal profession was quite negative.[36] Although many saw this expansion and democratization of the law as a positive development, more traditional members of the legal elite were not so sure. They feared that the development of the Bar as a cohesive, elite profession, dating back to the eighteenth century, would soon be lost.[37]

The democratization movement, which threatened to overtake and dilute the quality of the Bar in the early decades of the nineteenth century, and the fear that the image of the profession, already negative among the general populace, might decline further led to the elite

33 Friedman, *A History*, 315–18. 34 Ibid.

35 The most famous example of this is the process by which John Dean Caton was admitted to the Bar in Pekin, Illinois. Caton and a local judge had a long walk by the river in which they discussed various points of law. Caton's answers revealed that he was a man of good character but little learning in the law; however, this was enough to satisfy the judge that he should become a lawyer; see John Dean Caton, *Early History of the Bench and Bar of Illinois* (Chicago: Chicago Legal News, 1893), pp. 170–71, cited in Friedman, *A History*, p. 317. Although Caton may not have known much law, he became one of the leading American experts on antelope and other American game; see John Dean Caton, *The Antelope and Deer of America* (New York: Hurd & Houghton, 1877). On the often controversial history of the "good character" requirement for Bar admission, see Keith Swisher, "The Troubling Rise of the Legal Profession's Good Moral Character," *St. John's Law Review* 82 (2008): 1–54.

36 See Maxwell Bloomfield, *American Lawyers in a Changing Society: 1776–1876* (Cambridge, MA.: Harvard University Press, 1976), pp. 32–57; Haber, *Authority and Honor*, pp. 104–5. An amusing example of this is an anecdote, published in the *Nebraska Adventurer* on 25 October 1856, relating the story of a woman who brought her seven-year-old son to a lawyer's office to be apprenticed. When the lawyer asked her why she thought so young a boy was ready to train for the law, she replied that at five "he had lied like the devil," at six "he was sassy and impudent," and that at seven "he would steal everything he can lay his hands on." The lawyer agreed that he was already fairly far along on the path toward admission to the Bar; quoted in Charles M. Haar, *The Golden Age of the Law* (New York: George Brazziller, 1965), 94–95.

37 For evidence of this early development of the Bar's self-image as a cohesive elite, see Eben Moglen, "Considering *Zenger*: Partisan Politics and the Legal Profession in Provincial New York," *Columbia Law Review* 94 (1994): 1495–1524. Not everyone viewed this emerging social coherence positively; see the comments of Frederick Robinson to Rufus Choate criticizing the "secret, powerfully organized fraternity" of the Essex Bar Association, which he believed "would crush him"; excerpted in Charles M. Haar, *Golden Age*, 90.

members of the profession reacting and pushing toward making the law a "learned profession." In practical terms, this meant a reinstitution of standards for admission and a reconceptualization of the very idea of what it took to be a lawyer. Books and education lay at the heart of this reconceptualization. Even if every lawyer could not be learned, every lawyer could aspire to learning.[38]

At the time of the Revolution, there were few law books available to American lawyers. For several subsequent decades, the growth of the law book trade was slow, and it impeded the growth of the legal profession as a learned one. In August 1813 Justice Joseph Story sent a letter to Nathaniel Williams, enclosing a copy of his opinion in the "Case of the Julia."[39] He had to send the case report to his colleague, because, as he complained, it was extremely difficult to get it printed:

> A volume of my reports is prepared by the reporter, but he finds here no person willing to print them and pay any value for the copyright. *Our booksellers are poor, and law reports are not esteemed of so quick a sale as to induce a strong attachment to them.*[40]

Nineteen years later the situation had changed drastically. Once the law book trade had grown, not only did Story no longer have to complain of the difficulty of getting his opinions printed, but instead he could boast that he had already sold two-thirds of the edition of 1,500 printed copies of his *Equity Pleadings*.[41] Twenty years before few booksellers would have taken the financial risk of so large an edition, and few law books would have sold so many copies.[42]

The growth of the law book trade in the antebellum period did more than simply provide lawyers with more books from which they could learn more law, thereby increasing the prestige of the American legal

[38] This also led to the ancillary movement among elite lawyers that a lawyer should know not only the law but general literature, science, and so on; see, above all, Robert Ferguson, *Law and Letters in American Culture* (Cambridge, MA: Harvard University Press, 1984) and Miller, *Life of the Mind in America*. A good account of the general culture within which this movement flourished is provided by Catherine O'Donnell Kaplan, *Men of Letters in the Early Republic* (Chapel Hill, NC: University of North Carolina Press, 2008) and Robert Ferguson, *The American Enlightenment, 1750–1820* (Cambridge, MA: Harvard University Press, 1997).

[39] Story, *Life and Letters*, vol. 1, pp. 246–48.

[40] Story, *Life and Letters*, p. 248; emphasis added.

[41] Story, *Life and Letters*, 297.

[42] One exception to this was the edition of Blackstone's *Commentaries on English Law* published by Robert Bell by subscription; see Chapter 5.

profession. The growth of the law book trade in antebellum America also was intimately tied to and enabled the growth of university-affiliated law schools, a growth that eventually transformed American legal education in the latter part of the nineteenth century.[43] The founders of university-based law schools, men such as Joseph Story and Simon Greenleaf at Harvard, David Hoffman in Baltimore, Daniel Mayes at Transylvania, and James Kent at Columbia[44] also recognized that for American lawyers to transform themselves into a true learned profession, they would have to transform the method by which lawyers were trained.[45] They recognized that the apprenticeship system of instruction was simply too haphazard to ensure the growth of a learned, elite in the law.[46] A good apprenticeship served with a serious jurist, such as that which John Quincy Adams undertook with Theophilus Parsons, would be one in which the pupil learned substantial amounts of law by reading and observation.[47] But few apprenticeships were of this caliber.[48] Story and his colleagues realized that the

[43] See K. Newmyer, "Harvard Law School," 822–23.

[44] On the early history of American legal education, see Robert Stevens, *Law School: Legal Education from the 1850s to the 1980s* (Chapel Hill, NC: University of North Carolina Press, 1983); William LaPiana, *Logic and Experience. The Origin of Modern American Legal Education* (New York: Oxford University Press, 1994); Steven Sheppard, *The History of Legal Education in the United States* (Pasadena, CA: Salem Press, 1999); W. H. Bryson, *Essays on Legal Education in Nineteenth Century Virginia* (Buffalo, NY: Hein, 1999).

[45] On this theme, see, generally, M. H. Hoeflich, *Gladsome Light*, preface; see also LaPiana, *Logic and Experience*, 29–38. One crucial aspect of the scientific approach to law was the widely held belief that cases were not the law but instead were simply "evidence" of the law; see LaPiana, *Logic and Experience*, 33–34. One ramification of this approach, of course, was the disdain for "case lawyers."

[46] See, for example, the statement of Daniel Mayes about apprenticeships, in his inaugural lecture: "The selection of books is often injudicious, and each book placed in the student's hands is to be read in all its parts, in the same manner. Whether its value be great or small, or whether all its parts are or are not connected with our system of laws is uninformed ...," Mayes, *An Address to the Students of Law*, 157–58. In this statement Mayes makes it clear that a scientific legal education requires both books and the guidance of expert professors who have themselves studied these books; see Haber, *Authority and Honor*, 86.

[47] See John Quincy Adams, *Life in a New England Town: 1787, 1788. Diary of John Quincy Adams while a Student in the Office of Theophilus Parsons at Newburyport* (Boston: Little, Brown, 1903).

[48] Many lawyers spoke quite negatively about the apprenticeship experience; see, for example, the remarks of William Livingston that an apprenticeship was a "servile Drudgery ... fit only for a slave to submit to ..." quoted in Haber, *Authority and Honor*, 73.

key to developing a learned profession was the establishment and spread of university-affiliated law schools that would have standardized courses based on the study and mastery of high-quality law books and supplemented by scheduled lectures by expert jurists.[49] They expressed this ideal by speaking of the need to teach law as a "science" of principles.[50]

This reconceptualization of the law as a science based on principles was not only a jurisprudential advance; it was also a stroke of genius from a marketing standpoint. By insisting that lawyers must learn not from a collection of case reports but rather from principles, they were able to differentiate university-affiliated legal education from all other forms. Further, because scientific legal education was based on printed books, only an institution with a substantial library would be able to provide such an education.[51]

In practice, a scientific legal education required instruction in the law as a set of principles from which particular problems could be solved

[49] It must be said, of course, that not all lawyers agreed with this; see Friedman, *A History*, 318–20. Support for the apprenticeship system remained strong well into the twentieth century, and it took a major effort by university-affiliated law school deans and the formation of the American Bar Association Section on Legal Education to finally kill the apprenticeship system in the United States. (Although it has made a comeback in recent years; Vermont now requires a short apprenticeship after law school.) See M. H. Hoeflich, "The Bloomington Law School," in *Property Law and Legal Education: Essays in Honor of John E. Cribbet*, ed. Peter Hay and M. H. Hoeflich (Urbana, IL: University of Illinois Law School, 1988), 203–16; James White, "Legal Education in an Era of Change: Law School Autonomy," *Duke Law Journal* (1987): 292–305.

[50] See Haber, *Authority and Honor*, 86; Hoeflich, *Gladsome Light*, pref. One of the strongest exponents of the "law as science" movement was Simon Greenleaf at Harvard; see Simon Greenleaf, *A Discourse Pronounced at the Inauguration of the Author as Royall Professor of Law in Harvard University* (Cambridge, MA, 1834). See also LaPiana, *Logic and Experience*, 29–38. One crucial aspect of the scientific approach to law was the widely held belief that cases were not the law but instead were simply "evidence" of the law; see LaPiana, *Logic and Experience*, 33–34. One ramification of this approach, of course, was the disdain for "case lawyers."

[51] Even Benjamin Butler, who advocated a hybrid form of legal education in which students would clerk in offices by day and attend law school lectures at night, recognized the importance of a law school library; see Benjamin F. Butler, *A Plan for the Organization of a Law School in the University of the City of New York* (1835), reported in Hoeflich, *Gladsome Light*, 181: "For the occasional use of both professors and students, and especially with a view to the collection of rare and expensive works, the university should take measures to provide a law library." It is interesting to note that Butler's quote makes it clear that "rare" legal books were already available for purchase in New York City in 1835.

by the application of logical methods.[52] The emphasis of study and instruction in these law schools was not on mastery of individual cases, but rather mastery of the principles that underlay all cases. Simon Greenleaf expressed it this way in his inaugural lecture at Harvard:

> I would not confine the learning of a lawyer to the technical learning of his profession, nor to the code of his particular state. He can with no propriety be considered as sufficiently instructed, whose learning is limited to the remembrance of a few dry maxims, common places, and positive rules; and whose skill consists in the adroit practice of the technicalities of the law. Rules are of little value, without a knowledge of the principles upon which they are constructed.[53]

Daniel Mayes, at Transylvania, agreed:

> If practice be the whole he is taught, practice must also be the whole he will ever know; if he be uninstructed in elements and first principles upon which the rule of practice is founded, the least variation from established precedents will totally distract and bewilder him.[54]

Treatises on the law in general and on specific subjects were at the heart of this instructional method. The curricula of these university-affiliated law schools were explained in terms of the study not of cases or digests, but of specific legal treatises, like those written by Kent and Story. These law schools needed a panoply of such treatises. English treatises would not suffice since Harvard, Transylvania, and other American law schools wanted to teach American law. They needed new American law books by American authors or, at the least, English law treatises that had been "Americanized" by an American jurist.[55]

52 See M.H. Hoeflich, "Law and Geometry: Legal Science from Leibniz to Langdell," *American Journal of Legal History*, 30 (1986): 95–121; Howard Schweber, "The Science of Legal Science: The Model of the Natural Sciences in Nineteenth Century American Legal Education, *Law & History Review*, 17 (1999): 421–66; James R. Hackney, Jr., *Under Cover of Science* (Raleigh-Durham, NC: Duke University Press, 1996), esp. pp. 14–20; Thomas C. Grey, "Langdell's Orthodoxy," *University of Pittsburgh Law Review*, 45 (1983): 1–53.

53 Greenleaf, *A Discourse Pronounced at the Inauguration*, 139.

54 Mayes, *An Address to the Students of Law*, 147.

55 See Chapter 3. It is remarkable how well this movement succeeded. By 1845, C.J. Mittermeier, one of Germany's leading jurists and law professors, could argue that the best juristic work being published in the English language was not coming from England but from the United States; see C.J. Mittermeier, "Uber den Zustand der juristischen Literatur in Nordamerika," *Kritisches Zeitschrift fur Rechstwissenschaft und Gesetzgebung des Auslandes* 17 (1845): 312–32.

Just as books were at the heart of the new university-based scientific legal education, libraries were at the heart of the law schools themselves. When Langdell expressed his belief that the law library was for the lawyer what the laboratory was for the scientist, he was not espousing an original notion; on the contrary, he was describing what had been true of law schools for decades before.[56] Once again, an anecdote about Joseph Story illustrates this point. When Story was first appointed to the faculty at Harvard, the school only had two rooms: a classroom and Story's library, which also served as his study. Almost at once Story realized that this arrangement would give him no peace: Students were constantly coming into his library to borrow books, because the university's law books were few and in the main library a distance from the law school. So many students interrupted his own studies to borrow his books that eventually, he realized that he must sell his books to the law school (at a much discounted price) and acquire for a second time a law library for his personal use.[57]

The need of university-affiliated law schools like Harvard for books for instruction and for their libraries also provided a market for the producers and distributors of such books. As the scientific law schools grew in size and numbers,[58] the number of books needed to satisfy the students in these schools increased apace. Further, students who were trained in such law schools were trained to look to books for their practice needs for the future.[59] Also, as university-affiliated law schools grew in influence and began to compete with apprentice masters for

[56] The text of Langdell's most famous speech from which this is taken is most easily found in Sheppard, *The History of Legal Education*, vol. 1, 514–21.

[57] Story, *Life and Letters*, 39–41.

[58] According to *The American Almanac and Repository of Useful Knowledge for the Year 1839* (Boston: Charles Bowen, 1839), 129, there were eight law schools then in existence in the United States: Harvard, Yale, New York University, Dickinson, William and Mary, University of Virginia, Transylvania, and Cincinnati, with a total student population of 304 (excluding New York University, for which no data are given). According to Henry Chase and C.H. Sanborn, *North and South* (Boston: Jewitt, 1857), 91–92, by 1856 there were eighteen law schools with a total professoriate of thirty-eight and a total student count of 471.

[59] One of the primary activities at antebellum American law schools was digesting and common-placing law texts; see Ann Fidler, "Young Limbs of the Law" (unpublished doctoral dissertation, University of California-Berkeley, 1996); M.H. Hoeflich, "The Lawyer as Pragmatic Reader. The History of Legal Common-Placing," *Arkansas Law Review* 55 (2002–2003): 87–122. By the middle of the nineteenth century, common-placing was even recommended as a technique to be used by schoolchildren who

students, we may suspect that apprentices, too, began to read more law books than previously. These law schools provided not only a larger market for law books, they also, in many cases, provided the authors who would write such books.[60] It is no accident that the centers of university legal education were also, for the most part, the centers of law book publishing and selling.

The transformation of legal education into a scientific, principle-based subject also served another important need of the legal profession. Story, Greenleaf, Mayes, and other members of the founding generation of university-affiliated legal education argued that one of the great advantages of teaching law through general principles rather than through cases was that by so doing they could prepare their students to practice law in any common law jurisdiction, including in the halls of Westminster.[61] Lawyers trained in a law office would only know the law of the jurisdiction in which they studied. Thus, according to the scientific jurists at the universities, they would not be capable of practicing anywhere else. They would know cases, but only those they had studied. Scientifically educated lawyers, in contrast, would know underlying principles, which could then be adapted to any jurisdiction and any newly arising problem. In effect, a case lawyer learned only what the law had been; a scientific lawyer understood what the law could be. Daniel Mayes put it this way:

> The objects of the law department of Transylvania University are not local – confined to the state – they are far more broad and extended. It is not proposed to prepare young men peculiarly for the practice in Kentucky, Tennessee or Ohio; but to supply them with a fund of elementary knowledge equally applicable to the practice in every state in which the common law has been adopted.[62]

aspired to eventual membership in the legal profession; see L. C. Tuthill, *Success in Life . . . The Successful Lawyer* (Cincinnati, OH: Henry Darby, 1854), 173–75. It is not without significance that Darby was one of the leading law book publishers in Cincinnati. It is a mark of the general success of the profession's push for prestige and greater respect that such a children's book was able to be published at all. Earlier children's books tended to be quite critical of the legal profession; see Kimball, *True Professional Ideal*, pp. 111–12; see also M.H. Hoeflich, "Law in the Republican Classroom," *University of Kansas Law Review* 43 (1995): 711–34.

60 Harvard is the best example because of Joseph Story, author of a series of *Commentaries* on subjects such as bailments, agency, conflict of laws, equity, equity pleading, and constitutional law, and Simon Greenleaf, whose *Treatise on Evidence* was the first systematic work on this basic subject in the United States.

61 See Mayes, *An Address to the Students of Law*, 154.

62 Mayes, *An Address to the Students of Law*, 154.

The claim to be able to train lawyers who could practice anywhere was extraordinarily important. It meant, first of all, that university-affiliated law schools could draw their students from across the nation. It also meant, however, that their graduates could practice anywhere. This, of course, was the period of great westward expansion. Law schools like Harvard and Transylvania could claim that their graduates could follow the frontier and apply the principles they had learned to the new problems they would encounter in new territories. From the perspective of the book trade, this meant that their commerce could be truly national and that they could sell their books as easily in Indian Territory as they could in New York and Massachusetts so long as they could find a means to advertise and sell them on such a scale. The statement that the graduate of a university-affiliated law school could as easily practice at Westminster as in Kentucky was also a not-so-subtle arrogation of the prestige enjoyed by barristers in England to the law school–educated American lawyer. The legal profession in England was comprised of three major groups: serjeants, barristers, and solicitors. The smaller and more prestigious groups of barristers and serjeants were centered at the Inns of Court in London and had the exclusive right to practice at Westminster.[63] Solicitors could only do office work or practice in the lowest tribunals. Thus, by claiming that the graduates of university-affiliated law schools could practice at Westminster, men like Story and Mayes were making a statement that these graduates were the "barristers," – that is, the elite – of the American Bar.[64]

Examples of the success of this co-evolution of the law book trade and the rise of a learned American legal elite are frequent in the sources of the period. One finds constant deprecatory references to "case lawyers" and "Blackstone lawyers," lawyers who had little or no formal legal training and had, therefore, read little more than case reports and

[63] On the history of the divided Bar in England, see Wilfrid Prest, *The Inns of Court under Elizabeth I and the Early Stuarts* (Totawa, NJ: Rowman & Littlefield, 1972); David Lemmings, *Gentlemen and Barristers. The Inns of Court and the English Bar, 1680–1730* (Oxford: Clarendon Press, 1990); Raymond Cocks, *Foundations of the Modern Bar* (London: Sweet & Maxwell, 1983). Though more popular in tone, also useful are Michael Birks, *Gentlemen of the Law* (London: Stevens, 1960) and David Pannick, *Advocates* (Oxford: Oxford University Press, 1992).

[64] Interestingly, there were attempts in the American colonies and in the early republic to create a bifurcate Bar and even to model courts after Westminster; see Haber, *Authority and Honor*, 70, and Friedman, *History of American Law*, 315–18.

Blackstone's *Commentaries*.[65] Law professors told their students that they would have far more opportunities than mere "case lawyers." Lawyers would go to extremes to become learned and to advertise that fact, even on the frontier, as Carpenter's willingness to take on a $1,000 debt for his law library shows.[66]

The interconnected and simultaneous growth of the American law book trade, the beginnings of university-affiliated scientific legal education, and the purposive march of the American Bar toward its place as an elite profession during the antebellum period were all part of a greater process by which American lawyers sought to solidify their position among not just the economic but also the cultural elite of the new nation.[67] This process, although partially in response to the growing democratization of American society, was above all a movement to create a legal elite who were learned in not only the law but also other cultural areas such as poetry, history, music, and art. Lawyers who aspired to reach the heights of their profession were told time and time again that they must not only devote themselves to acquiring a deep and wide knowledge of the law itself but also become almost "renaissance men" of broad cultural and even scientific interests and learning. The most acclaimed jurists of the period were those esteemed for not only their legal learning but their accomplishments in other fields as well. Joseph Story frequently counseled young lawyers to read widely

65 See the remarks quoted in Michael H. Harris, "The Frontier Lawyer's Library; Southern Indiana, 1800–1850, as a Test Case," *American Journal of Legal History* 16 (1972): 239–51, esp. 240–41; see also the remarks of James Richardson, the President of the Norfolk, Massachusetts Bar Association, in which he refers to lawyers who are the "scourges of grammar" and the "blunderbusses of the Law"; James Richardson, *An Address Delivered before the Members of the Norfolk Bar* (Boston: Torrey & Blair, 1837), 17.

66 See the beginning of this chapter, p. 4; see also John Livingston's remark, p. 165.

67 On the antebellum Bar's desire for elite professional status, see Bruce A. Kimball, *The "True Professional Ideal" in America: A History* (Oxford: Blackwell, 1994), 106–97; Haber, *Authority and Honor*, esp. 67–90; Maxwell Bloomfield, *American Lawyers in a Changing Society, 1776–1876* (Cambridge, MA: Harvard University Press, 1976), 91–190; see also Stow Persons, *The Decline of American Gentility* (New York: Columbia University Press, 1973). An interesting example of a lawyer's speech in praise of the Bar and in which religious and clerical language is applied to lawyers to show the extent of their goodness and learning is Peter Oxenbridge Thacher, *An Address ... Before the Members of the Bar of the County of Suffolk, Massachusetts* (Boston: Hilliard, Gray, 1831). During the antebellum period literally hundreds of similar talks given at bar association meetings, on national holidays, and at law school and university convocations were printed. These pamphlets deserve further research.

in literature.[68] He himself was a poet and published a volume of poetry in his early adulthood.[69] Justice Theophilus Parsons, Sr., of the Massachusetts Supreme Judicial Court not only contributed a chapter on celestial mechanics to Bowditch's leading treatise on navigation but also invented an improved stove for residential heating.[70] These were men for whom "bookishness" meant more than simply an interest in law books. These were people whose lives revolved around books and learning in multiple areas of knowledge.

As important as the development of the law book trade was to the growth of university-affiliated legal education and its idea of law as a science, in conjunction with the push to give greater prestige to the Bar engineered by its "mandarins" like Story, Kent, and Greenleaf, the development of the trade in law books also played an important role in the propagation of Federalist legal and political ideas of these same elite jurists. It is here that we can see a concrete example of how understanding the history of the production and distribution of law books in antebellum America can fill a gap in the current historiography of American law.

Dan Hulsebosch, in his *Constituting Empire: New York and the Transformation of Constitutionalism in the Atlantic World*, [71] makes the important historical argument that a group of elite Eastern jurists, among whom James Kent and Joseph Story were prominent, developed the notion of the law as a science, consisting of general principles, which they considered to be the true basis for the Common law and which underlay the local variations seen in the case law of the different states, as an essential element for establishing Federalist ideology in the early Republic. Hulsebosch speaks of a "restructuring" of national institutions as the basis for this Federalist program. Among those institutions in need of restructuring were the American legal system and the Bar.[72] According to Hulsebosch:

[68] J. Story, *The Value and Importance of Legal Studies* (1829), reported in W. W. Story, ed., *Miscellaneous Writings of Joseph Story* (Boston: Little, Brown, 1852), 503–48.

[69] On Story's poetical endeavors, see M. H. Hoeflich and Larry Jenab, "Three Lawyer-Poets of the Nineteenth Century," *Green Bag*, 2d ser., 8 (2005): 249–60.

[70] See M. H. Hoeflich, "Theophilus Parsons and the Culture of Practical Virtue in Nineteenth Century New England," in *The History of the Law in Massachusetts: The Supreme Judicial Court*, 1692–1992, ed. R. Osgood (Boston: Supreme Judicial Court Historical Society, 1992), 117–25.

[71] Hulsebosch, *Constituting Empire*. [72] Ibid., 278.

Federalists turned to the nonlegislative dimensions of law and legal training, the areas of legal culture that were beyond the reach of electoral politics. They established new law lectureships and schools to educate aspirants to the bar. They published a new professional literature. They did something else too: they added a new layer of theory to English law.[73]

And:

Federalists and their heirs defined their new law primarily in terms of coherent maxims and principles, *printed it in books*, and fitted it within the newly classified hierarchy of American law.[74]

And:

Soon judges, lawyers, and juries in far-flung outposts pored over these new sources with little regard for the spatial, social, or political distance separating author and reader as Federalist law traveled far beyond its matrix.[75]

Indeed, in speaking of the Federalists' ability to control the law, even when they could not directly control courts and juries, particularly in the West, Hulsebosch states that it was "Eastern law books" that provided the means of doing so.[76]

As brilliant as Hulsebosch's insight into the method by which the Federalists sought to maintain control over the American legal system and, thereby, over American politics, there is one fact missing. How did these "Eastern law books" make it out West? Indeed, how did they get published and distributed in the East? The answer, of course, is that without an active trade in law books, without the complex network of producers and distributors, the Federalists could not have succeeded. And this is precisely the point at which the history of the book can fill the gap.[77]

[73] Ibid.

[74] Ibid., p. 279; emphasis added. One might also supplement Hulsebosch's analysis by recognizing that Story, Kent, and other elite jurists were very familiar with the tradition of European legal treatise writing and owned copies of many of these treatises; see Hoeflich, *Roman and Civil Law*, 9–49. One also should not discount the possible influence the work the English jurist and law professor John Austin had on the notion of scientific legal treatises of which Hulsebosch speaks.

[75] Ibid., pp. 279–80. [76] Ibid., 293.

[77] I am not here suggesting that the members of the law book trade were Federalists who built their industry to further the Federalist cause described by Hulsebosch. Indeed, the evidence on this point is too slim to make such a statement. But, certainly, we can say

Equally important to these various movements in law, politics, and the growth of the law book trade was a growing demand by the American business community for greater consistency and predictability in commercial law. Businesses could not prosper in a legal environment marked by the uncertainty of a judicial system in which decisions were based primarily on a judge's sense of "fairness." The state of the Common law in commercial matters was such that few American judges had deep enough knowledge of the law to render opinions consistent with established precedent when the law was clear, let alone when the precedent itself was conflicting. Merchants wanted "trained judges" judging cases "under standardized procedures, and governed by known principles."[78] The production, distribution, and adoption of the multiple legal treatises written by Story and others on commercial subjects answered this demand. Once again, several different groups with different agendas all came together in promoting the growth of the law book trade during this period.

A book history approach to antebellum American legal history offers another important perspective as well. One of the most fundamental historiographic problems, recognized for millennia, is the issue of periodization. Unless one is, like Bishop Ussher, willing to undertake a history of the world from its beginnings to its end without lacuna, one must impose artificial temporal limits on any historical

that there was a convergence of interests between the law book publishers and the Federalist jurists who used the book trade to propagate their ideology.

[78] Quoted by Kimball, *True Professional Ideal*, 135, citing A. G. Roeber, *Faithful Magistrates and Republican Lawyers: Creators of Virginia Legal Culture 1680–1910* (Chapel Hill, NC: University of North Carolina Press, 1981). One may speculate whether Story, Kent, and other treatise writers in the commercial field may also have been strongly influenced by the example of admiralty law. Story, in particular, was well acquainted with admiralty and wrote several opinions on the subject while serving on the Supreme Court. In his brilliantly argued opinion in *Swift v. Tyson*, 41 U.S. 1 (118), Story stated: "The law respecting negotiable instruments may truly be declared in the language of Cicero adopted by Lord Mansfield in *Luke v. Lyde*, 2 Burr. 883, 887, to be in a great measure, not the law of a single country only, but of the commercial world." Mansfield's decision in *Luke v. Lyde* was an admiralty decision, and Cicero's quote referred to the Law of the Sea (see also the dicta of Justice Harlan in *Railroad Company v. National Bank*, 102 U.S. 14 (1880), 29, interpreting Story's decision in *Swift*). Again, Story and his contemporaries owned multiple treatises on admiralty and would have seen how treatise literature stretching back more than five hundred years had helped to bring consistency to this area of the law, consistency necessary for the well-being of ocean commerce.

study.[79] For the most part, American legal historians have chosen to use conventional historical periods, either based on the calendar (i.e., by years, decades, or centuries) or political events (e.g., the Revolution, the election of Andrew Jackson as President, the Civil War).

When one begins to view the development of the American law book trade as a part of a broader cultural and professional movement, the antebellum period emerges in a different way. If one looks at the history of the American legal profession from a "bookish" perspective and from the related perspective of the cultural development of the American Bar, political moments become a source of more confusion than enlightenment.

From a book historian's perspective, the antebellum period can be viewed quite differently. There is the early period stretching roughly from 1770 until 1820, when book publishing and distribution was an essentially local activity and in which most books published in the United States dealt with local legal concerns. This was also the period when the vast majority of law books – and, indeed, all types of books – was imported from England because of the lack of an adequate publication and distribution network for domestic publications and the lack of both American authors and a national market for their works. It was far easier to ship books directly from London to Boston, New York, or Charleston than it was to ship them by land among these cities.[80] In such a localized industry, investment capital necessary to establish a flourishing industry was unavailable. But this situation began to change in 1770.

[79] Archbishop James Ussher was an Irish protestant cleric and writer who produced a history of the entire world from creation to his own day: James Ussher, *The Annals of the World. Deduced from the Origin of Time, and Continued to the Beginning of the Emperour Vespasians Reign, and the Totall Destruction and Abolition of the Temple and Common-wealth of the Jews* (London: Tyler for J. Crook, 1658). (This is an English translation of the Latin original published in 1650.) Ussher is, perhaps, best known for setting the date for the creation of the world at 22 October 4004 B.C.E. For an excellent discussion of the problem of historical periodization in the European context, see D. Gerhard, "Periodization in European History," *American Historical Review* 61 (1956),900–13; recently, some historians have begun to debate the general question of periodization and "deep history"; see Penelope J. Corfield, *Time and the Shape of History* (New Haven, CT: Yale University Press, 2007).

[80] See James C. Raven, *London Booksellers and American Customers: Transatlantic Literary Community and the Charleston Library Society, 1748–1811* (Columbia, SC: University of South Carolina Press, 2002).

Why do I begin this study with 1770? It was six years before the Declaration of Independence. It was a year of no special legal or political significance to colonial America or to the colonial Bar. But it was, from the perspective of antebellum law book history, a momentous year, for it was the year in which Robert Bell, a Scottish émigré bookseller in Philadelphia, offered to subscribers a complete set of Blackstone's *Commentaries* produced in America.[81] The unexpected and unprecedented success of this offering – more than 1,500 copies were sold – can be marked as the true beginning of the modern law book trade in North America. It signaled to other booksellers and publishers that there was a potential market for law books and that a law bookseller or publisher could actually make a reasonable profit in the business. It was a small beginning, and one that took several decades to grow into an industry – but it was a beginning nonetheless.

The period that begins around 1820 may, from a cultural and book historical perspective, be considered the true founding period of American legal literature.[82] This was the period when the development of a native American literature was deemed a national priority.[83] America needed poets, dramatists, historians, novelists. It was a source of shame to be dependent on the literary culture of England. Patriotic Americans had an obligation to fashion a new literature suitable for a new, republican nation. This was true, as well, for legal literature. It would become a matter of national pride to have homegrown authors of all stripes. Just as Emerson, Hawthorne, Barlow, Thoreau, and Longfellow were lauded for their roles as the founding fathers of American literature, Story, Kent, Du Ponceau, Stearns, Cooper, and other juristic authors were lauded as the founding fathers of American legal literature.[84] But such a national literature could not develop

[81] See Chapter 5.

[82] See Michael T. Gilmore, "The Literature of the Revolutionary and Early National Period," in *The Cambridge History of American Literature*, ed. Sacvan Bercovitch (Cambridge: Cambridge University Press, 1994), 541–694.

[83] See, for example, the remarks of the reviewer of *Selections from the American Poets*, Dublin, 1834 in *The Foreign Quarterly Review* (April 1835): 12–21; see also the remarks of the reviewer of Nathan Dane's *General Abridgement and Digest of American Law* (1823–24) in the *Boston Monthly Magazine* (September 1825): 185–91, in which the reviewer bemoans the lack of an distinctly American legal literature and the proliferation of reprints of English texts in the United States.

[84] See Ferguson, *Law and Letters*.

without a publishing and distribution infrastructure to make it practical. Happily, in the preceding fifty years, that industry had grown out of its infancy and was ready to take a great leap forward.

The development of the American Bar into a learned legal profession, the establishment of university-affiliated scientific law schools, merchants' demands for consistently applied, predictable law, and the spread of Federalist ideas of law throughout the new nation may be characterized, to borrow a term from biology, as a case of co-evolution with the growth of the law book trade. Books provided the authorities that lawyers could cite in their briefs, on which they could model their documents, and with which they could persuade judges and juries. Books provided the authorities and doctrines by which judges, often with little learning of their own, could decide cases in a consistent and fair manner – to the relief of commercial litigants. Books provided the materials for scientific legal instruction at law schools and thereby a way for these law schools to differentiate themselves from the apprenticeship system. Books provided a means by which law professors and jurists could establish their reputations as experts and leaders in their profession and do their patriotic duty to build a new American jurisprudence. The demand created by these things, in turn, provided a growing market for law books and the economic basis on which law booksellers and publishers could expand their businesses and gain economic strength and vitality. As the nation moved westward, ambitious law booksellers, like Little, Brown; Gould, Banks; and John Livingston would establish a national market for their books so that even on the frontier lawyers and judges could leaf through one of their catalogues and order a library.[85] It was a relationship in which the fate of the Bar as a learned elite profession and the development of the law book trade in the United States were inextricably tied to one another.[86]

The second great period in the history of the American law book trade really begins in 1851, when postal regulations were changed

[85] Even before the rise of a national law book trade, frontier lawyers did still acquire libraries, though with greater difficulty, from local booksellers and from auctions; see Michael H. Harris, "A Frontier Lawyer's Library," see note 65, above.

[86] Interestingly, the English experience, in which most legal training was at the Inns of Court, was quite different. Indeed, when the English decided to reform legal education, they used the American model of scientific legal education, especially the Harvard experience, as a model; see, M. H. Hoeflich, "The Americanization of British Legal Education," *Journal of Legal History* (1987), 244–59.

to permit the secure use of the mails to ship books.[87] Before this time, books were not explicitly permitted; it was often left to the postmaster in any place whether to accept books or to ban them from the mail. As a result, the postal service could not be relied upon. When, in the mid-1830s a number of ambitious law booksellers like Little, Brown began to seek a national market for their books, they were forced to rely upon freight companies, intercity coaches, canal boats, and even, at times, the hire of a wagon and taking it to another city by themselves. The lack of a reliable postal service was a limiting factor on the publication and distribution of law books on a national scale. Once the U.S. mails were opened to books, however, this all changed. At the same time, railroad companies began to expand their routes, and by 1870 the entire continent was crisscrossed by rail. The cost of shipping books from one coast to the other became acceptable. It was this continent-wide expansion of transportation, combined with the opening of the mails to books, that permitted John Livingston to build his national legal and publishing empire. Once these changes in transport and shipping took place, the formative period in American law publishing was over; a national industry was established, and the pattern for future development of the industry – and the profession it served – was set.

I have chosen to end this study of the law book trade in 1870, a year that also marked another historical event that justifies its use as the end point of this study. It was in 1870 that Harvard Law School appointed Christopher Columbus Langdell as its dean.[88] That appointment marked not only the beginning of the professional revival of the Harvard Law School and its inexorable march to dominance over legal education in the United States,[89] but also the renewal of American legal education, a renewal that led eventually to the complete destruction of the apprenticeship system and the triumph of university-affiliated

[87] See p. 45.

[88] The literature on Langdell is vast. His most important modern biographer is Bruce Kimball; see, esp., Bruce Kimball, *C. C. Langdell, 1826–1906: The Triumph and the Betrayal of Modern Professional Education* (Chapel Hill, NC: University of North Carolina Press, 2009); Bruce A. Kimball, "Warn Students that I Entertain Heretical Opinions," *Law and History Review*, 17 (1999): 57–140; Bruce A. Kimball, "Langdell on Contracts and Legal Reasoning: Correcting the Holmesian Caricature," *Law and History Review* 25 (2007): 345–99.

[89] See the celebratory work of Charles Warren, *A History of the Harvard Law School and of Early Legal Conditions in America* (Boston: Little, Brown, 1908).

"scientific" legal education. This triumph was encapsulated in Langdell's notion that the lawyer's library was his laboratory, a library which would have been far smaller without a strong law book trade. With the triumph of Langdell's Harvard model of legal education, the various forces that had led to the expansion of the antebellum law book trade such as the drive for professional prestige by the Bar, nationalization of law on the Federalist model, and promotion of scientific legal education had triumphed as well. As a result of his appointment in 1870, Langdell also published the first half of his *Selection of Cases on the Law of Contract* in 1870, a publication that marked the beginning of a whole new type of legal literature, one which would profoundly alter legal education, the legal profession, and the law book trade in the United States.[90] That this transformative work was published by Little, Brown, one of the oldest of the national law book publishers and booksellers in the United States is itself quite significant, for, had the law book trade not grown and developed as it had in the preceding century, Langdell's work would never have been able to change the American legal scene as it did. It would not have had so powerful a publishing and distribution network pushing it into thousands of law students' hands across the United States.

[90] Christopher Columbus Langdell, *A Selection of Cases on the Law of Contracts* (Boston: Little, Brown, 1871). And see Kimball, "Langdell on Contracts," 347–52.

Chapter 2
Birth of the Law Book Trade

GENERAL BOOKSELLERS

From early in the colonial period, there were both lawyers and law books in North America. By the eighteenth century, the average American bookseller almost always carried among its general stock some law books. Of course, these were mainly books on English common law. We know from both catalogues of lawyers' libraries and booksellers' advertisements that it was far from impossible for an eighteenth-century lawyer to amass a good working law library in the major urban centers. Thomas Jefferson's library was one such in Virginia.[1] Edwin Wolf, in his *The Book Culture of a Colonial American City*, has shown that eighteenth-century Philadelphia had an active, if somewhat small, law book trade.[2]

For the most part, our information about the size and scope of the law book trade in the period before the Revolution comes from newspaper advertisements and, in some cases, separately printed catalogues. These reveal that as the eighteenth century progressed, the number of law books being sold became significant. James White, who carried on a printing and bookselling business in Boston from 1778 until 1801, published a listing of law books he had for sale in the *Independent*

[1] Millicant E. Sowerby, *Catalogue of the Library of Thomas Jefferson* (Washington, D.C.; The Library of Congress, 1952–1959).

[2] Edwin Wolf II, *The Book Culture of a Colonial American City: Philadelphia Books, Bookmen, and Booksellers* (Oxford: Clarendon Press, 1988), 131–63.

Chronicle and Advertiser of 11 July 1799, a newspaper he published in 1799 and 1800.[3] He listed eighty-two titles for sale. The vast majority of these were English reports and treatises, including two editions of Blackstone's *Commentaries*. He also offered for sale a *Law Grammar*, a set of the *Laws of the United States*, and a two-volume set of Jacob's *Law Dictionary*.

The books that White put up for sale were almost all technical law volumes, intended for practicing lawyers. In fact, next to one set of English reports, those of Durnford and East, in seven volumes, White advertised that the "last volume [was] printed this year."[4] Such a focus on currency was clearly aimed at practicing lawyers desirous of having the most recent precedents.

The sale of law books by generalist booksellers continued into and throughout the early national period. In Philadelphia, Robert Campbell issued a series of catalogues during the 1790s in which he offered for sale a substantial number of law books.[5] In 1794, he issued a catalogue with 1,200 titles, a large proportion of which were law books.[6] In 1796, Campbell's catalogue listed 200 law books out of a total of 2,100 titles offered for sale.[7] In his 1797 catalogue, he offered 195 law books out of a total of 2,605 titles.[8] Thomas Stephens, another Philadelphia bookseller, offered a total of 1,098 titles for sale

[3] "Law Books for Sale by James White." *The Independent Chronicle and the Universal Advertiser*. 11 July 1799: 4.

[4] "Law Books for Sale."

[5] Robert Campbell, *A Catalogue of Books, Sold by Robert Campbell, at His New Book and Stationery Store, on the West Side of Second Street, Below the Market and Five Doors Above Chestnut Street* (Philadelphia: published by Robert Campbell, 1790).

[6] Robert Campbell, *Robert Campbell's Catalogue of Books Now Selling on the Lowest Terms, at number 54 South Second Street, Second door Below the Corner of Chestnut Street, on the West Side* (Philadelphia: published by Robert Campbell, 1796).

[7] Robert Campbell, *Robert Campbell's Catalogue for 1796 Containing a Very Extensive and Valuable Collection of Books in the Different Departments of Literature and Science; Now Selling at Very Reduced Prices at No. 40, South Second Street: Where Country Storekeepers, Public and Private Libraries, Are Supplied on Very Low Terms: N.B.A. Liberal Price Will Be Given for Libraries or Parcels of Books* (Philadelphia: published by Robert Campbell, 1796).

[8] Robert Campbell, *Robert Campbell and Co.'s Catalogue for 1797 Containing a Very Extensive and Valuable Collection of Books in the Departments of Literature and Science; Now Selling at Very Reduced Prices, at No. 40, South Second Street: Where Country Storekeepers, Public and Private Libraries, Are Supplied on Very Low Terms: N.B.A. Liberal Price Will Be Given for Libraries or Parcels of Books* (Philadelphia: published by Robert Campbell, 1797).

in 1795.[9] Of these, forty-two were law books, all of which were, according to a catalogue notation, "second hand."[10]

A few major booksellers in large colonial American cities became known for dealing in law books. One such was David Hall of Philadelphia.[11] Hall started as Benjamin Franklin's partner in bookselling. According to Edwin Wolf, when Hall took over the bookselling business from Franklin in 1748, "he offered a fair selection of legal texts."[12] Robert Bell, a Glaswegian transplanted to Philadelphia, was another bookseller who stocked what law books he could obtain and sell.[13] In addition, Bell became one of the first American booksellers to publish a law treatise on American soil when he published his edition of Blackstone's *Commentaries*.[14]

Law books continued to be available from generalist booksellers throughout the antebellum period and today as well. Of course, most generalist booksellers had neither the market nor the expertise to provide all of the professional books a practicing lawyer or judge would have wanted. But even booksellers in smaller cities would have had some law offerings. In 1832, Hoyt, Porter & Co. Booksellers in Rochester, New York, advertised that they had "on hand the most complete stock of theological, law, classical, medical, miscellaneous and school books to be found in Western New York."[15] Among the law books they advertised to back up this statement were thirty-two

[9] Thomas Stephens, *Stephen's Catalogue of Books, &c. for 1795 the Whole Contained in the List Will be Sold on the Most Reasonable Terms, at Thomas Stephen's Book and Stationary Store, No. 57, South Second Street; Where Every Encouragement Is Offered to Wholesale Purchasers, and the Highest Value Immediately Given for Libraries or Parcels of Books* (Philadelphia: No. 57 South Second Street, 1795).

[10] Ibid. [11] Wolf, *The Book Culture of a Colonial American City*, 136–43.

[12] Ibid., 136.

[13] "Books of various kinds, containing sentimental food of all sorts, among which are included ..." *The Pennsylvania Packet*, 4 October 1779, 4; on Bell, see Chapter 5; see also James N. Green, "English Books and Printing in the Age of Franklin," in *The Colonial Book in the Atlantic World, Vol. 1: The History of the Book in America*, ed. Hugh Amory and David D. Hall (New York: Cambridge University Press, 2000), 284–87.

[14] William Blackstone, *Commentaries on the Laws of England. By William Blackstone, Esq. Vinerian Professor Law and Solicitor General to Her Majesty. In four volumes.: Reprinted from the London Copy, page for page with the last edition.* (Philadelphia: Printed by Robert Bell for the subscribers, 1771).

[15] "Bookstore, Printing Office & Bindery." *The Rochester Daily Advertiser*, 25 December 1832, 1.

titles, of which twelve were case reports, one was a set of Blackstone, another a set of Kent, and another a set of the court rules for the New York Chancery and Supreme Courts. At the end of their listing, they stated that they also had "many others not named, necessary to complete a Law Library."

SPECIALTY BOOKSELLERS

Although law books constituted a part of the stock of many generalist booksellers in colonial and early national America, even as late as the period immediately preceding the Revolution, the number of American lawyers and the number of law books they required for the practice of their profession was not sufficient, in the early years, to support the development of many specialist law booksellers. The number of lawyers in even the most populous and commercially sophisticated states was just too small. For example, Massachusetts had only 15 lawyers in 1740 out of a total population of approximately 150,000.[16] By 1790, the number of Massachusetts lawyers had climbed to 112, and by 1800, the number had risen to 200.[17] Even if all of these had built substantial libraries, it would not have provided enough business to support a bookseller who sold only law books. In fact, only a few lawyers amassed large law book collections in eighteenth-century America. John Dickinson of Philadelphia and Thomas Jefferson of Virginia were two members of this small elite.[18] Dickinson had a library of 187 legal volumes at the time of his death.[19] Jefferson had substantially more. But these men were in a very small minority. Most lawyers of the time possessed only a few volumes. Even if there had been more lawyers like Dickinson and Jefferson in the American colonies, who had what were considered large law libraries, it would not have created enough demand to support specialist bookshops. There was, in fact, not a sufficient market for law books in the colonies at the time of the

[16] Lawrence M. Friedman. *A History of American Law* (2nd ed., New York: Simon and Schuster, 1985), 304.

[17] Ibid. and note 5.

[18] Wolf, *The Book Culture of a Colonial American City*, 146–49 on Dickinson's law library.

[19] Ibid., 146.

Revolution to support specialist law booksellers, even in the nation's largest cities.

The late eighteenth century was the beginning of a period of rapid growth in law book production, from authorship to publication, but in the 1770s and 1780s, this rapid growth was still several decades away. There were very few law books published in the colonies and the English publishers and booksellers were unwilling to ship a wide variety of law books to the colonies, for fear that they would not sell. Thus, American lawyers in the last half of the eighteenth century were limited both in the law books they could purchase and where they could purchase them.

Indeed, we have evidence of the number and distribution of booksellers who, if not dealing exclusively in law books, at least were known to sell a wide range of legal texts. This is the *Annual Law Register* published by William Griffith in two volumes during 1822 and 1823.[20]

Griffith was a lawyer with literary and bibliographical leanings. He decided to publish a legal annual that would provide information on critical facts about the law and the legal profession in the United States. He sent surveys to leading practitioners in each of the states and solicited all significant information about their state's laws and lawyers. He then compiled these data and included them in his *Annual Law Register*. One of the questions Griffith asked of his correspondents was this: "Who is the principal bookseller of the seat of government?" Although he did not ask who was the principal *law* bookseller, a question that would probably have elicited few, if any, responses, we may assume with some certainty on the basis of the responders and the context in which the question was asked that the booksellers listed were in the business of selling law books as well as other texts. The responses themselves give a fascinating picture of the early legal book trade in the United States.

Two correspondents, those from Illinois and Delaware, answered that there were no major booksellers in their capital cities.[21] The correspondent from Ohio also stated that there was no "principal bookseller" in his capital, but that one "John Kilbourn has a small one."[22] Both the Alabama and Georgia correspondents named Ginn & Curtis

[20] William Griffith, *Annual Law Register of the United States* (Burlington, NJ: David Allinson) 1821–22, (Reprinted New York: Arno, 1972).

[21] Ibid., 413, 1033. [22] Ibid., 391.

as the major bookseller in their capitals.[23] The correspondent from Mississippi stated that there were none in the capital, but that Snodgrass & Whitney of Natchez was noteworthy.[24] Maryland had George Shaw, South Carolina had Tillinghast & Arthur, and Vermont had a Mr. Goss.[25] New Jersey had three booksellers of note, according to its correspondent: Joseph Justice, E. Littell, and John Dannson.[26] Louisiana's correspondent listed four: Benjamin Levy, Rochefueres, A. Croft, and Jourdain. Massachusetts listed two: Wells & Lilly and Cummings & Hilliard, and the Virginia correspondent replied that "there are some three or four booksellers here; I am unable to say which is the principal."[27]

If booksellers specializing in law books were still relatively scarce at the time of Griffith's survey, things had changed within a decade. First, the production of law books and the demand for law books was on the rise. The number of lawyers in the United States was increasing decade by decade in the first part of the nineteenth century. Law practice was also becoming more complex as American and foreign commerce and industry grew. Unlike their English brethren or colonial predecessors, American lawyers of the antebellum period needed a substantial number of books to carry on their practice. They needed books on their respective states' law; English law, which was still used extensively in the courts; federal law; and the law of other states in which they might practice.[28] Indeed, by the late 1820s, American legal periodicals began a chorus of complaints, which was to remain strong throughout the century: The American lawyer needed to master too many legal texts. By 1832, an anonymous reviewer in the *American Jurist* bemoaned the growing habit of multiple citations to various authorities in law books and law cases.[29] But to read and cite these authorities, lawyers needed to have the books available. American law libraries were not common except in the largest cities, and even then, membership was not inexpensive. Lawyers who wished to be known as learned had no choice but to begin buying books. Indeed, by 1855, John Livingston, a bookseller

[23] Ibid., 569, 432. [24] Ibid., 658. [25] Ibid., 906, 831, and 6.
[26] Ibid., 1199. [27] Ibid., 677, 495, and 323.
[28] Erwin C. Surrency, *A History of American Law Publishing* (New York: Oceana, 1990).
[29] Anonymous, "The Citing of Authorities." *The American Jurist and Law Magazine*, 8 (1832): 111–17.

in New York, observed that a lawyer desirous of having even a barely adequate library needed to spend at least $1,000 to acquire it. As demand grew, booksellers came to fill it.[30] Thus, the period from 1800 until 1865 was one that saw a substantial increase in the number of law books available for sale and the number of booksellers entering into the trade.

One aspect of the growing trade in law books that did not change during the period under study was the importance of location. Towns with small numbers of lawyers could not support law bookstores. Thus, one finds that the majority of important law booksellers established themselves in the legal centers of the nation: New York, Philadelphia, Albany, Boston, and Baltimore. These major urban centers offered several advantages to the law bookseller. The first, of course, was a large number of lawyers. Second, these cities were all port cities and tended to be transportation hubs so that, in the period before 1851, when books could not be sent by mail, there were sufficient freight companies and major roads available for fulfilling catalogue orders.

One of the first American retail booksellers to specialize in law books was Stephen Gould.[31] We know little about Stephen Gould personally but, fortunately, we do know a reasonable amount about his bookshop. Gould opened a retail shop at the corner of Wall and Broad Streets in the financial district of New York City sometime before 1800.[32] An engraving of his shop is contained in I. P. Stokes's *Iconography of Manhattan Island*.[33] According to this engraving, Gould's shop was in a three-story building, in the basement of which was a shoe store. The ground floor of the bookshop had a door and a large front window, presumably for the display of new works. Above the first floor hung a sign: "Stephen Gould. Law Book and Stationery Store." In the center of

[30] On Livingston, see Chapter 6.

[31] Surrency. *A History of American Legal Publishing*, 7. [32] Ibid.

[33] I. N. Phelps Stokes, *The Iconography of Manhattan Island 1498–1909: Compiled from Original Sources and Illustrated by Photo-Intaglio Reproductions of Important Maps, Plans, Views, and Documents in Public and Private Collections* (New York: Robert H. Dodd, 1915–28). In 1820, Oliver Halsted established his bookstore on this site; see Baker and Voorhies, *One Hundred Years in Business* (1920), 9. A reproduction of an engraving of the store in 1820 is found on p. 2. This engraving does not reveal what the interior of the shop looked like, but we may gain some insight into this by a ca.1796 engraving of the interior of Ebenezer Larkin's bookshop reproduced in Amory and Hall, *The Colonial Book in America*, 47.

the sign was a bust portrait of Lord Edward Coke. In at least two books which Gould printed, he identified his store as "at the sign of Lord Coke."[34] In choosing an image of the great lawyer Edward Coke as his trade sign, Gould followed a bookselling tradition of adopting images that represented the shop's specialty.[35] For example, one of Gould's bookselling contemporaries in New York, Naphtali Judah, who specialized in revolutionary political works, chose the head of Thomas Paine as his insignia.[36] Further, Gould must have remained at this location for quite some time. He used the Lord Coke imprint in a volume published in 1808 and another in one published in 1820, indicating a long tenure at this address.[37] Gould also appears to have been one of the pioneer booksellers of this location. John Tebbel notes that by 1817, all but seven New York booksellers were located in the region south of Maiden Lane and east of Broadway.[38]

Like virtually all of the law booksellers of the first few decades of the nineteenth century, Stephen Gould was not simply a bookseller but a printer and publisher as well. His store also sold stationery and may well have sold some non-law books at least. Indeed, the fact that his shop appears to have been a good size may also indicate that it served as a meeting place for members of the Bar, another common use of early American bookstores.

Much of this information may be gleaned from the imprint information contained on the title pages of books printed or published by Gould. During the period from 1800 until 1828, Gould printed or had printed for him at least thirty-five volumes. Of these, the majority were law books. He listed himself on the title page of twenty of these as

[34] Surrency. *A History of American Law Publishing*, 7. [35] Ibid.

[36] George McKay, *A Register of Artists, Engravers, Booksellers, Bookbinders, Printers and Publishers in New York City, 1633–1820* (New York: The New York Public Library, 1942); George G. Raddin, *Hocquet Caritat and the Early New York Literary Scene* (Dover, NJ: Advance Press, 1953), 29.

[37] G. Booth, *The Nature and Practice of Real Actions, in Their Writs and Process Both Original and Judicial*, ed. J. Anthon (New York: Printed as Published, at the Sign of Lord Coke, opposite the City-Hall, 1808); Isaac Espinasse, *A Digest of the Law of Actions and Trials at Nisi Prius* (New York: Published by Stephen Gould, sign of Lord Coke . . .,).

[38] John Tebbel, *A History of Book Publishing in the United States* (New York: R. R. Bowker Co., 1972–81), 263.; see the 1853 map of New York reproduced at www.antebellumlegalpublishing.org.

simply "printer."[39] Of these, all but one were printed in 1810 or earlier.[40] On one volume, a Spanish text, listed as "published and sold by Ezra Sargeant," a bookseller with a shop at 39 Wall Street, there is on page four a note that "S. Gould" was the printer.[41] In two volumes of 1807 and 1808, Gould also listed himself as both the printer and the publisher.[42] In one volume of 1806, he listed himself solely as publisher.[43] After 1810, Gould listed himself solely as publisher in thirteen volumes. It is difficult to determine what significance these different imprint usages have, but it seems reasonable to assume that in cases in which Gould listed himself as publisher, he was printing books for himself or having books printed for sale at his own financial risk, as opposed to being simply a printer on commission. There may well have been other distinctions involved.

Gould's title pages also indicate that he did not undertake the printing and publishing of all of these volumes on his own. In one case he is listed as co-publishing a volume with Treadway.[44] In those 1824 volumes, he lists his business as "S. Gould & Son."[45] One of these volumes also lists a Joseph P. Gould in Utica, New York, in the imprint.[46] The title page of an 1828 volume states that it was printed by "A. Gould &

[39] Generally, the use of the term "printer" in such a context at this early date without any further information as to "publisher" or "sold by" would suggest that Gould was functioning in multiple roles, i.e., as printer, publisher, and bookseller.

[40] The exception was not a law book; it was David Young, *A Lecture on the Laws of Motion* ... (Caldwell, NJ: Printed by Stephen Gould, 1825).

[41] Pedros Cevallos, *Expocision de los Hechos y Maquinaciones que han Preparado la Usurpacion de la Corona de Espana* ... (New York: E. Sargeant ..., 1808).

[42] *Rules of the Supreme Court of the State of New-York*, (New York: Printed as Published by S. Gould, 1807); Louisa Williams, *Ebenezer's Dream, as It Appeared at the Trial of Mrs. Louisa Williams on a Indictment for an Assault and Battery* ... (New York: Printed as Published by S. Gould, 1808).

[43] *Rules of the Court for the Trial of Impeachments and the Correction of Errors* ... (New York: Published by S. Gould, opposite the City-Hall, 1806).

[44] Isaac Espinasse et al., *A Digest of the Laws of Actions and Trials at Nisi Prius* (New York: Published by Stephen Gould, sign of Lord Coke ... and by Gould and Treadway, Charleston, S.C., E. & E. Hosford, printers, Albany, 1812, 14).

[45] *Tariffs or Rates of Duty, After the Thirtieth Day of June, 1824* .... (New York: Printed & Published by Stephen Gould & Son ..., Opposite the Custom House, 1824); Thomas Charlton, *Reports of Cases Argued and Determined in the Supreme Courts of the New Eastern District of the State of Georgia* (New York: Stephen Gould & Son); R. S. Roper, *A Treatise on the Law of Property Arising from the Relation Between Husband and Wife* (New York: Published by Stephen Gould and Son; Utica, NY: Joseph P. Gould, 1824).

[46] Ibid.

L. Jacobus, Essex-Street, for Stephen Gould," a further indication that Stephen may have been slowly withdrawing from active business, although perhaps still financing the printing of new books.[47] Gould also co-published law books with William Gould of Albany, thought to be his relative.[48] One of the most interesting of these joint imprints is a two-volume set of Henry Maddock, *A Treatise on the Principles and Practice of the High Court of Chancery*, published in 1817.[49] The title page of these volumes states that they were printed by Clayton and Kingsland of No. 15 Cedar Street in New York City for "Gould, Banks, and Gould, Law Booksellers, Sign of Lord Coke, Corner of Wall and Broad Streets, and William Gould and Co., State Street, Albany." A later volume, Amos and Ferard's *Treatise on the Law of Fixtures* carries a publication date of 1830 and the imprint of "Gould & Banks, Law Booksellers, Corner of Nassau and Spruce Streets, Opposite City-Hall and W. Gould & Co., State Street, Albany."[50] The Banks in question was an in-law of the Albany Goulds.[51] It would seem that Stephen Gould operated his business, from a relatively early date – Tebbel pinpoints it as 1804 – in coordination and, at times, in loose partnership, with other Goulds and Banks, presumably members of his extended family.[52] These various partnerships and co-publishing ventures eventually became one of the longest-lived law book publishing and selling businesses in the United States: Banks & Gould.

Another volume sold by Stephen Gould further indicates that he commissioned other printers to produce law books for him. The title page of D. T. Blake's *Historical Treatise on the Practice of the Court of Chancery of the State of New-York*, published in 1818, states that the book was

[47] John A. Graham, *Memoirs of John Horne Tooke* ... (New York: Printed by A. Gould & L. Jacobus, Essex-Street, for Stephen Gould ... and sold by all the principal booksellers, 1838).

[48] Surrency, *A History of American Law Publishing*, 215.

[49] Henry Maddock, *A Treatise on the Principles and Practice of the High Court of Chancery* (New York: Printed by Clayton and Kingsland for Gould, Banks, and Gould; Albany: W. Gould, 1817).

[50] Andrew Amos and Joseph Ferard, *A Treatise on the Law of Fixtures, and Other Property, Partaking Both of a Real and Personal Nature, Comprising the Law Relative to Annexations to the Freehold in General, and also Emblements, Charters, Heir-looms, etc., With an Appendix Containing Practical Rules and Directions Respecting the Removal, Purchase, Valuation, etc. of Fixtures Between Landlord and Tenant, and Outgoing and Incoming Tenants* (New York: Gould and Banks, 1830).

[51] Ibid. [52] Tebbel, *A History of Book Publishing in the United States*, 457.

"printed by J. T. Murden, no. 110 Pearl Street, for Stephen Gould."[53] An 1820 volume, a reprint of Isaac Espinasse's *Digest of the Laws of Actions and Trials at Nisi Prius*, is even more interesting in that it is listed as published by Stephen Gould in New York and "Gould & Treadway, Charleston, S[outh] C[arolina]" and "E. Hosford, printers, Albany."[54]

What one can learn about Stephen Gould's bookselling business from this study of his imprints is that Gould used several different business models to provide books to sell. Some he printed for others, some he printed for himself alone, and some he had printed for him to sell with others. Although his primary business was based for a long period in his shop at Wall and Broad Streets, he was also willing to extend his business activities beyond the boundaries of New York City to upstate New York and Charleston, South Carolina.

In terms of the types of books he printed, published, or sold at his shop, he was also somewhat diversified. He printed and sold official legal publications such as the *Rules of the Supreme Court of the State of New-York*, published in 1812, in which he listed himself as the "copyright holder."[55] Such a text would have been a necessity for every New York lawyer. He also printed and sold the *Reports* of the Maryland Courts from 1700 to the Revolution.[56] One might ask why a New York bookseller would interest himself in the reports of cases from another state. The answer would be that in 1806, when this volume was printed, there were still so few published colonial decisions from any American state that they would have been useful even to New York lawyers. Gould also interested himself in reprints of English law books, which

[53] D. T. Blake, *An Historical Treatise on the Practice of the Court of Chancery of the State of New-York Containing all the Proceedings of a Suit, as well in the Court of Chancery, as in the Court for the Trial of Impeachments and the Corrections of Errors* (New York: Printed by J. T. Murden for David Banks, New York, and William Gould, Albany, 1818).

[54] Isaac Espinasse et al., *A Digest of the Laws and Actions at Trials of Nisi Prius* (New York: Published by Stephen Gould, sign of Lord Coke, Corner of Wall and Broad Streets, Opposite the Custom House, and by Gould and Treadway, Charleston, S.C. E & E Hosford, Printers, Albany, 1820).

[55] *Rules of the Supreme Court of the State of New-York, with Short Notes of Cases in Relation to the Rules, to Which are Added, Decisions of the Supreme Court Relating to Affidavits, Notices, and Service, Together with Copies of Bills of Costs to Serve as Precedents* ... (New York: Gould, Banks, and Gould, 1812).

[56] Stephen Gould, *A New Bibliotheca Legum Americana, or, American Law Catalogue: Together with the English Works, Reprinted or Imported for Use Here* (New York: W. Gratton, 1821), 13.

were of great importance to American lawyers throughout the antebellum period. Of course, Gould was interested in homegrown works as well, but these were few and far between.

The fact that Gould's store sign listed himself not only as a law bookseller but also as a stationer illustrates the economic reality that law booksellers, like booksellers in general during the colonial and early national periods, simply could not make a viable living by selling only books. Lawyers, especially, were major consumers of stationery goods (e.g., paper, pens). They also were willing buyers of legal forms. In Gould's first substantial separately printed catalogue of 1821, the *New Bibliotheca Legum Americana*, pages 49–54 list a large variety of legal forms available to Gould's customers.[57]

The image of Stephen Gould's law bookselling business of the early nineteenth century that emerges from these sources is one of entrepreneurship and financial flexibility. No doubt Gould chose Wall and Broad Streets as the location for his business because of its proximity to government offices, the courts, the financial district, and lawyers' offices.[58] He frequently mentioned on his title pages that he was located across from City Hall or the Custom House in New York.[59] Such a location would have guaranteed that potential customers would often pass his premises and, he hoped, stop in to make a purchase. His goal was to sell these customers, mainly lawyers, all of the books and paper goods they might need to practice their profession. If he could obtain these from others, that was fine. If not, he was willing to take the risk of printing or publishing what his customers needed. The fact that he was able to remain in business for nearly three decades, surviving financial panics and growing competition, demonstrates his success in achieving his goals. As will become obvious, Gould's methods of business were, to a large extent, much the same as those of his competitors and of those who followed him later in the period before the Civil War.

ACQUIRING STOCK

No merchant can succeed without stock. The stock in trade of antebellum law booksellers was law books of all varieties and, in many

[57] Note 60, below. [58] Gould, *A New Bibliotheca Legum Americana* (1821).
[59] Tebbel, *A History of Book Publishing in the United States.*

cases, other supplies useful to lawyers. The law booksellers of this period needed to stock a variety of law books for their customers. First, they needed to stock law reports, from the various states of the Union, the various federal courts, as well as England. Second, they needed to stock legislative volumes containing the growing number of statutes being passed by the national Congress and state legislatures. They needed to stock other relevant official legal texts, such as municipal codes or court rules. They needed to stock treatises, those written by both American lawyers and English authors, often with American notes appended. Those booksellers in major urban centers or those wishing to have a more comprehensive collection would also stock foreign legal materials. If the local bar had organized and published fee schedules or association rules, these, too, would need to be stocked. And, of course, lawyers and, eventually, institutional law libraries might consider purchasing older volumes, perhaps even a black letter English report or treatise. These might well find their way onto the bookseller's shelves. How, then, did the antebellum American law bookseller acquire his stock?

There were, in fact, many ways in which a law bookseller could obtain stock. First, as was done by Stephen Gould, the bookseller could print books, either alone or jointly with other booksellers. One could do this with one's own press or by subcontracting the work to another printer. Gould could also obtain books from other publishers and booksellers, either by purchase or by trade arrangements. The bookseller could obtain used books through purchase by private treaty and at auctions. Booksellers could also, and needed to, supplement the stock of domestic texts by importing books from abroad. This often required buying trips across the Atlantic or the establishment of relationships with foreign booksellers and publishers to ensure a steady supply of goods. To run a successful law book shop like Gould's, it was necessary for the proprietor to use all of these methods.

PRINTING AND PUBLISHING

In the early nineteenth-century United States, printing, publishing, and bookselling had not yet developed into separate trades. Often, booksellers began their careers as printers and then became booksellers and publishers who commissioned other printers to produce books. Most of the major law booksellers of this period, including Stephen Gould, Isaac Riley, Matthew Carey, William Gould, the Banks, and Little, Brown all fit into this model. There were substantial reasons for this adoption of multiple roles.

During the early years of the nineteenth century, the primary source of law books for the American market was England and, in particular, the English publishers and booksellers. As is discussed subsequently, the importation of English books was difficult and expensive. It was necessary to establish a relationship with an English supplier, first of all. Second, transportation charges for the trans-Atlantic crossing were high and the risk of loss not insubstantial. Third, the American customer was always at the mercy of the English supplier. Often the London booksellers would not supply the books requested but, rather, send those volumes that were not selling well in England because of age or inadequacy.[60] Fourth, English books written for English lawyers were often not optimal for American lawyers to use in American courts, a problem not encountered with novels, poetry, or school books.

As a result of these problems with importation, many American law booksellers recognized that there could be a strong market for books published in the United States. These could be straight reprints of English texts. They could be "Americanized" English texts – that is, texts that had been specially edited for the American market or those that had American notes added to be of use to American lawyers. Of course, there was also a growing market for law books written by American lawyers for American lawyers and published in America. These could be books that dealt solely with American topics, about which no English lawyer would write, such as those on local procedure, or they could be books focused on American practice and developments in the Anglo-American common law, about which English lawyers

[60] See S. Botein, "The Anglo-American Book Trade Before 1776: Personnel and Strategies," in *Printing and Society in Early America*, ed. William Joyce et al. (Worcester, MA.: AAS, 1983), 48–82; see also J. Raven, *London Booksellers and American Customers* (Columbia: University of South Carolina Press, 2002), 11–13. Although Professor Botein's study deals with all imported books to American shores, law books sent over the U.S. seem to have followed a similar pattern in many cases. Occasionally, English booksellers would assist their American counterparts if an imported text failed to sell. William Strahan agreed to share the losses with David Hall on the sales – or lack thereof – on one volume; see Wolf, *The Book Culture of a Colonial American City* , 140.

would have been ignorant. Finally, as American courts and legislatures began to produce more and more decisions and statutes, these, too, needed to be published and disseminated.

All of these factors contributed to a steady growth in American law publishing in the antebellum period, a growth that paralleled and fed the rise of the American legal profession. Although official statistics of this growth are not available, there is a contemporary source for these. Samuel Griswold Goodrich, born in Connecticut in 1793, became a prominent publisher, author (under the pseudonym "Peter Parley"), and periodicals editor before his death in 1860.[61] In 1857, he published his memoirs, *Recollections of a Lifetime*, which are a treasure trove of information about the antebellum book trades.[62] In the course of his discussion of the growth of book publishing in the United States, he provides rough statistical estimates of the development of American law book publishing. According to Goodrich, in 1820 approximately $200,000 worth of law books were published in the United States.[63] If one assumes, based on priced booksellers' catalogues of the period, that the average law book cost between one and two dollars per volume, this means that somewhere between 100,000 and 200,000 books were produced in this year. At this time only school books and classical books published had a greater total value than the law books.[64]

By 1830, Goodrich estimated that approximately $300,000 worth of law books were published.[65] Assuming a modest increase in the price of books, this indicates a quite substantial increase in production. One may attribute this to the increase in both the numbers of American lawyers as well as court reports, legislative publications, and other materials. For 1840, Goodrich estimated an increase in the value of law books published to $400,000.[66] He expressly notes that this increase was due, in part, to the increase in treatise literature produced by American authors, particularly Kent, Wheaton, Story, Duer, and Cowen.[67] Interesting, also, is that Goodrich estimates that not only school books and classical works outnumbered legal books, so also did theological tracts.[68] In addition, whereas total law book publication

[61] Samuel G. Goodrich, *Recollections of a Lifetime, or Men and Things I Have Seen: In a Series of Familiar Letters to a Friend, Historical, Biographical, Anecdotical, and Descriptive*, 2 vols. (New York: Auburn, Miller, Orton, and Mulligan, 1857).

[62] Ibid. [63] Ibid., 380. [64] Ibid., 380. [65] Ibid., 380. [66] Ibid., 382.

[67] Ibid., 381. [68] Ibid., 382.

values had doubled in twenty years, school book publication value had increased by 267 percent.[69] By 1850, the last year for which Goodrich presents statistics, law book values had increased to $700,000, an increase of 75 percent in just a single decade.[70] Again, Goodrich attributes this increase to the rise in the number of popular treatises by such authors as Greenleaf, Curtis, W. W. Story, and others.[71]

What Goodrich's statistics mean for the analysis of legal publishing and book selling in the United States is that over the course of the period from 1820 until 1860, there was a major increase in the volume and value of law books published by Americans, which contributed significantly to the growth of both the law book publishing and law bookselling sectors. The law book trade in antebellum America was a "growth" industry.

Several factors, however, inhibited law book publishing by individual booksellers and encouraged various forms of joint publishing arrangements in the first decades of the antebellum period. First, until 1851, books could not be sent through the U.S. Postal Service.[72] Some publishers, particularly those who reprinted English texts, avoided this problem by publishing their works in parts and mailing them as periodicals.[73]

[69] Ibid., 382–83. [70] Ibid., 385. [71] Ibid., 384.

[72] *Laws and Regulations for the Government of the Post Office Department* (Washington D. C.: C. Alexander, 1852), Sec. 15, p. 74. Note: "Bound books, as parcels of printed matter, not weighing over thirty-two ounces, made mailable by the 2d section of the act of 3d March, 1851." Richard R. John, *Spreading the News. The American Postal System from Franklin to Morse* (Cambridge, MA: Harvard University Press, 1995), 39 and note 57; Richard B. Kielbowicz, "Mere Merchandise or Vessels of Culture? Books in the Mail, 1792–1942," *Papers of the Bibliographical Society of America*, 82 (1988): 169–200; see also Richard B. Kielbowicz, *Books in the Mail* (New York: Greenwood Press, 1989); David M. Henkin, *The Postal Age* (Chicago: University of Chicago Press, 2006); Michael Hackenberg, "The Subscription Publishing Network in Nineteenth Century America," in *Getting the Books Out: Papers of the Chicago Conference on the Book in 19th-Century America*, ed. M. Hackenberg (Washington, D.C.: Center for the Book, Library of Congress, 1987). For a comprehensive discussion of the antebellum postal system in the United States, see Twenty-Third Congress, Second Session, House of Representatives Report No. 103: "Examination of the Post Office Department" (Washington, D.C.: Government Printing Office, February 13, 1835).

[73] Ibid., 39. These works in parts would be sent as "magazines" and were thus not prohibited from the mails. However, the Post Office was not required to carry them if such carriage proved "burdensome."

But, for the most part, when a law book was published, it either had to be sold in its own hometown, sold at steep discounts to "jobbers" who would then distribute it, or shipped by private freight companies or by other methods more expensive than the mail, to individual or country booksellers. This factor alone tended to make law book publishing an industry centered in the larger cities like New York, Philadelphia, Boston, and, eventually, Cincinnati. Second, it was the big cities of the Northeast that served as the entry ports for transatlantic trade, including shipments from London booksellers. Third, it was in the big cities that one found the ancillary industries necessary to publishing and bookselling, such as papermaking, printing, and bookbinding. Although during the earliest part of the nineteenth century, one finds law books published in such places as Northampton, Massachusetts, these small-town law publishers tended to disappear by the end of the first quarter of the century. By the 1830s, the principal suppliers of law books published in the United States were the large law publisher–bookseller houses of the major northeastern urban centers and, eventually, Cincinnati for the western part of the country.

Second, law book publishing, like virtually all publishing, was risky. The publisher took on the full cost of the production of the book. If the book did not sell, which could be true even of law books, then the publisher could lose a substantial amount of money. The risk was even greater with books written by American authors, because American publishers generally had to pay these authors, something they did not always do for English authors.

These two factors – the difficulty of distribution and the financial risk of production – contributed to the differentiation of law booksellers from law book publishers later in the antebellum period. In the big cities, the great law book publishing and law bookselling companies flourished. Houses like Little, Brown in Boston; T. & J. W. Johnson in Philadelphia; John S. Voorhies of New York City; Gould, Banks of New York City and Albany; and J. C. Derby and Robert Clarke & Co. in Cincinnati came to dominate the law publishing market.[74]

[74] In New York, among the major law booksellers, especially important was Isaac Riley, of Hocquet Caritat, on whom, see pp. 57–58. In Philadelphia, Matthew Cary of Carey & Lea, as well as John Campbell, T. & J. W. Johnson, and Stephen Gould and family were dominant; on Carey and Lea, see David Kaser, *Messers. Carey & Lea of Philadelphia*

In smaller cities, law booksellers continued to operate, but solely as retail sellers and rarely as primary publishers. It was the great urban houses that supplied not only themselves with law books published in America, but also their smaller country cousins.

In the first part of the century, the safest way for a bookseller to publish a book was to find other booksellers, both in the same city and in different cities, to share the risks of production and the burden of distribution.[75] This is precisely the pattern we have seen in several of the publications of Stephen Gould. Gould's earliest publications tended to be short, usually official or quasi-official texts such as court rules or reports, and printed by Gould alone. One may assume that the printing costs of such pieces were relatively low, because no author or editor had to be paid and the actual texts were brief. In 1810, we begin to see co-publishing or co-selling arrangements for law books. In this year, Gould published *A General Course of Preparatory Study for the Duties of the Bar by a Counsellor of the City of New-York*.[76] The imprint on this volume of thirty-five pages reads: "S. Gould, 1810: Gould & Van Winkle." It would seem that Gould shared the printing but not the publishing of this educational text with one other: Mr. Van Winkle. This gentleman was probably C. S. Van Winkle, a printer and partner in the firm of Van Winkle and Wiley, which, according to Henry Wolcott Boynton, operated a business at Wall and New Streets in New York, and who, on his own, later became the printer–publisher of several of Washington Irving's novels.[77] One may surmise that Gould brought

(1957); R. Kenneth Bussy, *Two Hundred Years of Publishing* (Philadelphia: Lea & Febiger, 1985); Lea & Febiger, *One Hundred and Fifty Years of Publishing, 1785–1935* (Philadelphia: Lea & Febiger, 1935). On Campbell, see W. Brotherhead, *Forty Years Among the Old Booksellers of Philadelphia* (1891, rpt. 1972), pp. 36–41. On Philadelphia printing of this period, generally, see R. Remer, *Printers and Men of Capital* (1996). In Boston, of course, the great law booksellers of the period were Hilliard and Little and Brown. On Derby and Clarke, see W. Sutton, *The Western Book Trade.* Cincinnati as a Nineteenth-Century Publishing and Book-Trade Center (Columbus: Ohio State University Press, 1961); and J. C. Derby, *Fifty Years Among Authors, Books, and Publishers* (New York: Carleton, 1884).

75 Remer, *Printers and Men of Capital*, 87–91; on the English antecedents to such risk limitation techniques, see James Raven, *The Business of Books* (New Haven, CT: Yale University Press, 2007), 315–17.

76 John Anthon, *A General Course of Preparatory Study for the Duties of the Bar by a Counsellor of the City of New-York* (New York: S. Gould, Gould and Van Winkle, 1810).

77 Henry W. Boynton, *Annals of American Bookselling 1638–1850* (New York: J. Wiley and Sons, 1932), 157–58.

Van Winkle into the publication for any number of reasons, including, perhaps, that of sharing the financial risk.

In 1829, Gould listed himself and his New York business as a co-publisher of Isaac Espinasse's *A Digest of the Law of Actions and Trials at Nisi Prius*, along with "Gould & Treadway, Charleston, South Carolina."[78] With this volume, there can be no doubt that Gould shared the publication with Treadway and may well have done so to both share risk and also provide a better entrée into the Southern law book trade. A nonlegal volume published in 1828 indicates another arrangement. In this year Gould published the *Memoirs of John Horne Tooke*, the supposed author of the *Letters of Junius*, a popular book of the period.[79] The imprint of this volume states that it was "printed by A. Gould & L. Jacobus, Essex Street, for Stephen Gould, 39, Nassau Street." It also reveals that the volume would be "Sold by all the principal booksellers." This latter phrase may indicate simply Gould's hopes for the book, but it seems more likely that it involves, at the very least, some pre-publication arrangement for the sale of these volumes by multiple booksellers in New York.

Law booksellers had good models for such arrangements in the publication partnerships common in the production and distribution of many non-law standard works. William Charvat has described one type of these arrangements:

> a loose inner-city structure of tie-ins between particular booksellers. A large publisher had agreements with one or more firms in every other large city. These firms were "correspondents" and acted as bankers, post office, retailers, co-publishers, and sometimes jobbers[80]

In some cases, even though the title page of a volume might not indicate that the risk of publication was being shared among several booksellers, we have external evidence to show that this was the case. During this period, a number of law books were sold by subscription, either because no bookseller could be found to act as publisher or because

[78] Espinasse, *A Digest of the Law of Actions and Trials at Nisi Prius*.

[79] John A. Graham, *Memoirs of John Horne Tooke, Together with His Valuable Speeches and Writings: Also, Containing Proofs Identifying Him as the Author of the Celebrated Letters of Junius* (New York: Printed by A. Gould and L. Jacobus, for S. Gould, 1828).

[80] William Charvat, *Literary Publishing in America, 1790–1850* (Philadelphia: University of Pennsylvania Press, 1959); Remer, *Printers and Men of Capital*.

the author simply preferred to distribute the book independently.[81] Such subscription arrangements could be used by booksellers to ensure that they had a quantity of the books to sell and, in so doing, guaranteed the author that books would be sold at retail after the publication.

Two volumes can illustrate this arrangement. In 1789, Matthew Carey commissioned William Cobbett, an Englishman then residing in Philadelphia, to translate Georg von Martens' *Summary of the Law of Nations*.[82] Because of the perceived risk in publishing a new translation of a relatively unknown continental law text, Carey decided to sell the book by subscription. The majority of the subscribers were individuals, but the two largest, in terms of quantity, were booksellers. One, James Rivington of New York, was the leading bookseller in colonial and early republican New York.[83] He subscribed for one hundred copies of the work. George Keatinge, a Baltimore bookseller, took twelve copies.[84] Although such a subscription arrangement did not generally provide the publisher with advanced funds in the way a co-publishing agreement might, it did, at the least, promise early and substantial sales upon publication.

As discussed previously, as the market for law books grew in the United States, the law publishing industry grew, centered in the big cities, as well. The need for risk sharing and co-publishing arrangements grew less common as larger publisher–booksellers could undertake to publish and distribute works entirely on their own. These could afford to take the financial risks of being sole publisher of not only individual volumes but even series of law books. They could also sell the books through retail sales in their urban shops, through catalogue sales, and by sales to country booksellers and jobbers at a discount. Further, by the third decade of the century, several authors could virtually guarantee that a book would become a legal "bestseller." For instance, Little, Brown served as the sole American publisher for the works of Justice Joseph Story.[85] One may presume that Little, Brown calculated that

[81] Ibid.

[82] George Von Martens (William Cobbett trans), *Summary of the Law of Nations, Founded on the Treatise and Customs of the Nations of Europe: With a List of the Principle Treaties Concluded since that Year 1748 etc.* (Philadelphia: 1795).

[83] Boynton, *Annals of American Bookselling*, 11–112. [84] Ibid.

[85] *One Hundred and Fifty Years of Publishing, 1837–1987*, (1987); *One Hundred Years of Publishing* (1937), 16.

there was little risk of these works not selling. Further, as catalogue sales came to be increasingly important after 1830, precisely the time when Story was most productive as an author, interstate distribution, even without mail service, became much more feasible. Larger cities like New York, Boston, and Philadelphia were by then well served by private freight companies. For example, in 1835, the *National Gazette and Literary Register* carried advertisements that promised Philadelphians that they could travel to distant towns easily.[86] By this date, express companies, specializing in the transport of large parcels were springing up.[87] Merchants chose from a number of freight companies going to different locations for their shipments. They could send parcels to Wilmington, Delaware, by steamboat; to Pittsburgh and various towns en route by stage; to Wheeling, West Virginia, and towns en route by stage and railroad; as well as to Pittsburgh by canal boat. This meant, in practice, that the Philadelphia law booksellers had as potential customers not only the Philadelphia bar, but lawyers throughout the region served by these freight companies. And, of course, after 1851, when postal regulations finally allowed the mailing of books, every post office in the United States, of which there were many, became a potential book distribution site.[88]

One gains a more focused idea of the extent of the importance of American law book publishing as a source of law books by examining a few representative booksellers' catalogues spread over the era. In the earliest period, the vast majority of law books available for sale in the United States were printed abroad. As the antebellum decades passed, this became much less the case.

In the Lucas law book catalogue published in Baltimore in approximately 1810, United States imprints accounted for roughly 25 percent of the books offered.[89] Of these, more than half consisted of state legislation and reports of state and federal court cases. Only a very small number of the treatises on offer were written by Americans and published in the United States. Several of the American imprints were American reprints of British books, some with annotations by Americans. If one, therefore, were to rank the various books in terms

[86] *National Gazette and Literary Register*. April 13, 1835, 4. [87] Ibid.

[88] Hackenberg, "The Subscription Publishing Network in Nineteenth Century America," 48.

[89] Fielding Lucas, *Lucas' Law Catalogue* (Baltimore, MD: printed by J. D. Toy, 1810).

of imprint and authorship, three-quarters were texts published by foreign (mostly English) authors. One-quarter were published in America, but most of these were "official" or "quasi-official" texts. Only a very small number were actually American printed texts by American jurists.

By 1821, when Stephen Gould published his first major catalogue, the *Nova Bibliotheca Legum Americana*, this proportion had changed.[90] In his preface to the catalogue, Gould revealed that he had originally intended to divide the volume into three sections: the first consisting of books by American authors printed in the United States; the second written by foreign (mainly English) authors but printed in the United States; and the third consisting of works written by English authors and printed in England.[91] He abandoned this plan, presumably because there were simply not enough works in the first two catalogues to constitute sections on their own. The first section, books printed in the United States, regardless of the national origin of the author, consisted of 222 titles (including two from an addendum), and the second section, consisting of books printed abroad, numbered 207 titles (including two from an addendum). By 1821, the split had become virtually fifty-fifty between American printed law books and those printed in Great Britain.

This situation was further changed by the time John S. Voorhies published his *Catalogue of Law Books* in New York in 1849.[92] In this catalogue, only about 20 percent of the approximately 750 titles on offer were published abroad, about half in London and half in Dublin. Of the remaining 80 percent published in the United States, far fewer than half were reprints of English or foreign texts, and most of these contained notes by American jurists specially for the American audience. Further, although case reports and legislative compilations continued to be numerous among the American imprints, the majority of the American texts were treatises and related works. Within forty years, American law publishers had taken over as a primary source of law books to be sold by American booksellers.

The geographical distribution of the American imprints listed in Voorhies's catalogue also demonstrates the growing importance of

[90] Gould, *A New Bibliotheca Legum Americana* (1821). [91] Ibid.

[92] John S. Voorhies, *A General Catalogue of the Best Editions of English and American Law Books* (New York: Printed by William Osborn, 1849); on this firm see generally, Baker and Voorhies, *One Hundred Years in Business, 1820–1920* (1920).

just a few major cities as the homes for most American law book publishing in the antebellum period. By far, the American cities that most often appear as the place of publication in the entries in this catalogue are Boston, New York, Albany, and Philadelphia. If one leaves aside state reports and legislative documents, which were often published in the state capital by "official" state printers, only a few other American cities appear as places of publication for law books. Cincinnati, the home of W. C. Derby Co., which was succeeded by Robert Clarke, appears as well, representing the beginnings of this law publisher's activities. Springfield, Massachusetts, appears a number of times. The reason for this was that Springfield was the home of G. & C. Merriam, a bookseller and publisher best known today for publication of *Webster's Dictionary* but then equally well known as the principal American publisher of the works of Joseph Chitty. Baltimore appears occasionally, for Baltimore was an outpost of the Philadelphia publisher–bookseller P. H. Nicklin, who published a number of law books using the Baltimore imprint. Finally, Harrisburg, Pennsylvania appears several times. Harrisburg was the home of M'Kinley & Lescure, a printer–publisher that began in the 1840s to produce a series of reprints of English law texts under the series title of *The Library of Law & Equity*, obviously inspired by Nicklin's *Law Library* series published in Philadelphia.

There is one glaring geographical absence in the list of cities where law book publishing developed: the American South. This is not overly surprising when viewed in light of the fact that there was very little book publishing at all in the antebellum South. Thomas Nelson Page, a Virginia lawyer and prominent author during the latter part of the nineteenth century, observed from his own personal experience: There was genius enough to have founded a literature, but there were no publishers generally, and there was never any public.[93]

There was one small exception to this. Benjamin Levy, a Jewish printer and book binder born in New York City and apprenticed there, moved to New Orleans in 1811 and established there a bookbinding

[93] Thomas Nelson Page, *The Old South* (New York: Scribner, 1892), 74; cited in Paul Starr, *The Creation of the Media. Political Origins of Modern Communications* (New York: Basic Books, 2004), 139. It is beyond the scope of this book to speculate why the antebellum South never developed its own publishing industry, but we might suggest that the close ties with England, combined with the lack of much industry, contributed to this failure.

business, which he soon expanded into bookselling and publishing.[94] During a career of more than three decades he was the principal legal book publisher and seller in New Orleans and Louisiana as a whole. In 1842, as a result of stock and real estate investments that had turned sour, he was forced to declare bankruptcy.[95] During the period 1811–1842, Levy published 109 books, of which 55 were legal texts of some sort.[96] Many of these texts were not treatises but rather were printed briefs for submission to court and other legal documents. But he also published Livingston's *Commercial Code*, several volumes of Moreau-Lislet's *Louisiana Term Reports*, and Moreau-Lislet's *General Digest of the Acts of the Legislature of Louisiana*.[97] He also printed several versions of Livingston's *Penal Code*.[98]

Levy did publish one book that is often cited as a treatise: Jacob Wheeler's *A Practical Treatise on the Law of Slavery*.[99] In fact, this volume was neither a treatise nor actually published by Levy. Rather than a treatise on the scientific lines of those by the Northeastern jurists, Wheeler's book is more of a case digest of the more traditional type. Further, although the title page lists both Pollock and Levy as publishers, contemporary announcements of the book state that it was published by Pollock alone and printed by Craighead & Allen in New York City.[100] It seems most likely that Pollock and Levy entered into a co-financing arrangement for the book and that Pollock handled the actual publication and sent a certain number of volumes (most likely in sheets since Levy was a binder) down to New Orleans to be sold by Levy. According to Korn, Levy's modern biographer, he also operated a popular retail bookstore where he maintained a "stock of law books and got along well with attorneys."[101]

One question remains to be answered directly. What did law booksellers gain from also serving as publishers of law books? Of course, the first answer is stock for their own shops. Second, there was profit to be

[94] The only source for Levy's life and career is Bertram Wallace Korn, *Benjamin Levy: New Orleans Printer and Publisher* (Portland, ME: Anthoensen Pr., 1961).
[95] Korn, *Levy*, 32–35. [96] Ibid., 27.
[97] Ibid., 43–69, which contain a full list of Levy's general imprints. [98] Ibid., 65–69.
[99] Jacob D. Wheeler, *A Practical Treatise on the Law of Slavery* ... (New York: Allan Pollock & New Orleans: Benjamin Levy, 1837).
[100] Ibid., preliminary material, no page number [second leaf recto] reprints announcements from the *New York Mercantile Advertiser* and *The New York Star*.
[101] Korn, *Levy*, 28. Unfortunately, Korn does not provide his source for this statement.

made, if books sold well, not only from the sale of their own stock in their shops and through their catalogues, but also to other booksellers at a profit. There was also a third important benefit: One of the most common methods by which antebellum American booksellers generally – not just law booksellers – acquired stock for their shops was through the use of what became known as the exchange system.[102] The exchange system was a variant of the co-publishing and co-selling ventures discussed previously. Many booksellers, chronically short of cash, engaged in bartering with other booksellers. If one bookseller published a popular school book and a second bookseller published a well-known songster, they could make exchange of books, and no cash need pass between them until the end of the year, when there might be a cash settling of accounts. In theory, the exchange cost each bookseller less than having to pay cash, because cash payments often involved outside financiers, interest, and, perhaps, lower discounts. Also, at various times and places in antebellum America, it was difficult to acquire currency negotiable throughout the nation. Often, booksellers in the West simply couldn't find enough currency acceptable to eastern booksellers and publishers.[103] The exchange system, by eliminating the need for cash, avoided this difficulty as well. By becoming a law book publisher, booksellers could not only use their publishing arm to supply the books they published for their own stock-in-trade, but also gain an inexpensive, cash-free means of obtaining books from other publisher–booksellers.

IMPORTED AND REPRINTED FOREIGN WORKS

Although acting as printers–publishers was a common means by which antebellum law booksellers acquired new books with which to stock their shops, it was by no means the only method. Very few law antebellum American publisher–booksellers ever produced more than a few dozen American law books in any one year. The vast majority of books that they needed had to come from other sources. Indeed, during much of the antebellum period, the largest part of American law

[102] Hackenberg, *Getting the Books Out*, 29, 36.

[103] See, Daniel Hulsebosch, "An Empire of Law: Chancellor Kent and the Revolution in Books in the Early Republic," *Alabama Law Review*, 60 (2009), 377–424.

booksellers' stock consisted of books published abroad, particularly in England and Ireland, or foreign books reprinted in the United States.[104] As discussed previously, during the early decades of the nineteenth century, as much as three-quarters of American law booksellers' stock came from abroad, particularly London and Dublin. By the close of the 1850s, this proportion had declined to closer to 25 percent, but even this percentage was quite significant. No law bookseller during this period could operate without using imported law texts.

Although every law bookseller through the young nation wanted to stock foreign law books, not everyone could, in fact, act as an importer. By and large, the biggest booksellers in the eastern cities dominated this section of the trade, just as they did law printing. In addition to easy access to transatlantic shipping as well as internal express routes, an eastern location had the advantage of access to international finance brokers in the Northeast.

Michael Winship has observed that:

> in order to participate in the transatlantic trade in books and texts, a firm needed to be linked to three separate communication networks, designed for the transfer of information, merchandise, and credit[105]

Although Winship was speaking of antebellum general purpose booksellers, his statement is also applicable to law booksellers, albeit with some qualifications. The same ships that carried the novels that stocked the shelves of such booksellers as Ticknor & Fields (the focus of much of Winship's work) could also transport the volumes ordered by the law booksellers. But one must also remember that the quantities of many law texts that were imported to the New World were far smaller than that of popular British novelists or divines. The works of only a very few jurists, like those of Joseph Chitty, could sell in large quantities, and even his works could hardly compare with Scott's *Waverly Novels* or Dickens' tales of the English underclass. This smaller quantity could be an advantage (e.g., in some cases, a passenger could simply bring texts as luggage) or a disadvantage if space were at a premium.

104 The cash situation in the United States during this period, see, N. Angell, *The Story of Money*, (Garden City: Garden City Publishing Company, 1929) 275–312.

105 Winship, Michael, *American Literary Publishing in the Mid-Nineteenth Century: The Business of Ticknor & Fields* (Cambridge; New York: Cambridge University Press, 1995).

In terms of financing the importation of texts, the law booksellers may well have been at an advantage because they were purchasing smaller quantities of books. However, there was great risk with law books because they could become obsolete very quickly, whereas novels rarely suffered this fate. Many antebellum law book advertisements for imported works stressed that they were of the most current editions then available in London.[106] The risk of obsolescence, therefore, was also a risk for the financier.

The third network that Winship describes, an information network is, in many respects, the most interesting. To purchase the latest law books from Great Britain and Europe, an American bookseller had to know that they were in process of publication or recently published. There were several ways this could be accomplished. First, an American bookseller could establish a relationship with one or more British booksellers. During the antebellum period, there were eight major English law booksellers and publishers.[107] Of these, six, led by Stevens & Son, early formed what they called the "The Associated Law Booksellers," which served as a publishing consortium.[108] The two booksellers who refused to join this group were the two Butterworths, Henry and George, who cooperated with each other but not the other six.[109] All eight were based in London. These London booksellers also served as importers for continental law books and could supply notice of these, as well as the books themselves, to their American customers.

American law booksellers also could keep up with the newest of the foreign law texts by reading foreign legal journals such as the *London Law Magazine* from London, the *Themis* from Paris, and

[106] See, for example, the advertisement in *The American Citizen* (New York: Cheetham, Oct. 22, 1807), p. 3. The passion for the most recent English goods, of course, was not limited to books; see, for example, "English Drugs, &c.... for sale by Charles Ellis & Co," *The National Gazette* (Philadelphia: W. Fry, July 3, 1837), 1.

[107] M. W. Maxwell, "The Development of Law Publishing," in *Sweet & Maxwell, Then and Now: 1799–1974* (London: Sweet & Maxwell, 1974), 121–36; Surrency, *A History of American Law Publishing*. See also Tariq Baloch, "Law Booksellers and Printers as Agents of Unchange," *Cambridge Law Journal* 66 (2007): 385–421 on the development of this oligopolistic structure.

[108] Maxwell, "The Development of Law Publishing," 122–23.

[109] On the Butterworth company and its practices in this period, see H. Kay Jones, *History of a Publishing House* (London: Butterworths, 1980), 7–17.

several law journals from Italy and Germany.[110] For example, *The American Law Magazine and Review*, published during much of the antebellum period by a consortium of Boston and Philadelphia law booksellers, included in most issues both a section on "Legal Intelligence" and one on the latest law publications in the United States and abroad.[111] The editors of both of these sections took much information directly from foreign legal periodicals. Indeed, this journal and other antebellum law journals often published reviews of foreign law texts.[112]

Without question, the best way for an American bookseller to establish an import line was to send a representative to Britain and the continent to set up lines of communication and trade. One of the best examples of a law bookseller who did this is Hocquet Caritat, who operated a law book business in New York City at the beginning of the nineteenth century, both on his own and in partnership with Isaac Riley.[113]

Louis Alexis Hocquet de Caritat was born in province of Champagne in France in January 1752, the son of a minor aristocrat. During the French Revolution, he supported the new regime and in 1792, he traveled to the United States in the hope of establishing a Franco-American trading company. Domestic problems in Paris led Caritat to extend his stay in New York for nearly a decade. Relatively early in his New York residence, Caritat decided to devote his energies to the book business. Until 1797, he presided over a bookstore, a circulating library, and a "literary salon." In 1797, he joined forces with Isaac Riley, a rather unscrupulous book dealer and merchant.[114] Together the two carried on one of the largest book businesses in the United States.

110 Even if the booksellers did not read the foreign legal and literary journals themselves, they could read lists of new books and book reviews extracted from these journals, translated, and reprinted in a number of American periodicals sold to *The American Jurist* and *North American Review*, which routinely included such material.

111 Maxwell, "The Development of Law Publishing." See, for example, *American Law Magazine* (Phila.: Johnson, 1846), v. 46.

112 Ibid.

113 George G. Raddin, Jr., *The New York of Hocquet Caritat and His Associates 1797–1817* (Dover, NJ: Dover Advance Press, 1953) and George G. Raddin, Jr., *Hocquet Caritat and the New York Literary Scene* (Dover, NJ: Dover Advance Press, 1953). Biographical details on Caritat are found in *Literary Scene*, 11–23. On Caritat and Riley, see *Associates*, 122–45.

114 Raddin, *Literary Scene*, 78, 89.

Caritat and eventually Caritat and Riley soon specialized in importing foreign works, especially law books. To achieve this, Caritat traveled to England and the continent several times. In London he established an affiliation with Henry and George Butterworth.[115] This guaranteed that Caritat's shop in New York would have a steady supply of imported law books and law journals for sale. Eventually, this alliance also made it possible for Isaac Riley to begin reprinting English law books in the United States. To finance this import trade, Riley, the financial half of the partnership, arranged for credit arrangements with the London merchant bankers Bird, Savage, and Bird.[116] Riley was also able, through family connections, to provide Caritat with an entrée to the American minister in London, in case he encountered any problems.[117]

Although importation of law books from abroad was absolutely necessary to the American law book trade in the first half of the nineteenth century, it was not easy. Establishing and maintaining the type of networks described here was both time-consuming and expensive. Men like Hocquet Caritat, forced to spend months and years abroad in the pursuit of stock, were often left at the mercies of partners and employees. In the case of Caritat, his partner Riley used this time to defraud and eventually ruin Caritat. What led ultimately to the decline of the dominance of imported law books in the American market was economics.

Importation of law books was not only inconvenient and risky, it was also expensive. In addition to the cost of transportation across the Atlantic, law booksellers that imported foreign books had to contend with protectionist federal trade laws. Although the Copyright Act of 1790 left foreign authors without copyright protection in the young nation, a fact exploited by American reprinters of foreign books, the tariff laws made the importation of foreign books exceptionally expensive.[118] Under the tariff laws enacted after Independence, books were considered just another item of merchandise subject to duties.[119] Until

[115] Ibid., 77. [116] Ibid., 77; Raddin, *Associates*, 123.

[117] Raddin, *Literary Scene*, 77. [118] Copyright Act of 1790, § 5.

[119] For an excellent discussion of the antebellum tariff system as applied to books, see Michael Winship, "The International Trade in Books," in *The History of the Book, Volume 3: The Industrial Book*, ed. Scott E. Casper, Jeffrey D. Groves, Stephen W. Nissenbaum, Michael Winship (Chapel Hill: University of North Carolina Press), 148–57, from which my account is drawn. On the early American tariff system,

1846, the amount of duty owed was scheduled and often a crippling amount.[120] From 1846 until 1857, a flat 10 percent was charged as duty on foreign books, with the exception that those being reprinted in the United States would be liable for twice that amount.[121] In 1857, these duties were lowered to 8 and 15 percent.[122] This downward trend was reversed in 1862, when the duty was set at 20 percent, and in 1864, when it was raised to 25 percent, presumably to help raise funds needed by the Union then engaged in the Civil War.[123]

In the case of imported law texts, the practical result of the expenses of transportation, finance, and duty was, in many cases, to double the cost of law books imported from abroad rather than printed in the United States. Just a short glance at antebellum catalogues bears this out. For example, John S. Voorhies of New York City had three copies of Sir James Burrows's *Reports of Cases in King's Bench, 30 Geo. II to East. 12 Geo. 1772*.[124] The first set he offered had been printed in London in 1790, as a fourth edition in five volumes and was available at twelve dollars.[125] The second set was published in Dublin in 1794 in five volumes, available at ten dollars.[126] The third set, however, was a condensed version, published in New York in 1833 and available for only five dollars.[127] The condensed version was one without the materials solely of interest to British lawyers and thus just as useful to American lawyers as the London and Dublin editions. Budget-conscious Americans would certainly have opted for the native printing whenever it was available. The often large price advantage in purchasing an American reprint of a British text resulted in a steady decline in the stocking of imported English and Irish legal texts by American law booksellers and an increase in both the production and sale of American reprints.

One of the English law texts most frequently reprinted in the early Republic was Sir William Jones's *Essay on the Law of Bailments*. It was

see R. W. Thompson, *The History of Protective Tariff Laws* (3rd ed., Chicago: Peale, 1888); Edward Stanwood, *American Tariff Controversies in the Nineteenth Century*, 2 vols. (Boston/New York: Houghton, Mifflin, 1903); William H. Futrell, *The History of American Customs Jurisprudence* (New York: privately printed, 1941, esp. 1–38.

120 For more detail, see Winship, "The International Trade in Books," 149.

121 "Walker Tariff Act of 1846," [9 Stat. 42 (1846)].

122 "Tariff Act of 1857," [11 Stat. 192 (1857)].

123 "Tariff Act of 1864," [13 Stat. 202 (1864)]

124 J. Voorhies, *A General Catalogue*, 39. 125 Ibid. 126 Ibid. 127 Ibid.

reprinted multiple times between 1796 and 1828 in several American cities (viz. Boston, Philadelphia, Albany, New York, and Brattleboro, Vermont).[128] The earliest reprints were exact reprints of London editions, either with Jones's text alone, or with notes by John Balmanno, a barrister of Lincoln's Inn. In these editions, there are to be found no copyright pages, because the works of foreign authors were not copyrightable under the 1790 Act. Later American editions were also adorned with American notes. O. Halstead, a leading New York law bookseller of the 1820s and 1830s, published an edition of Jones's work in 1828.[129] Taken from the third London edition, it contained notes by William Nichols, a Lincoln's Inn barrister, as well as "additional notes and references to American decisions" by William Halstead. This edition carries in it a separate copyright notice in conformity with the 1790 Act and that states that the edition had been registered and deposited with the Clerk of the Federal Court for the Southern District of New York to gain copyright protection for Halstead.

The addition of American notes by an American citizen to the reprinted English text created advantages for both the publisher–bookseller as well as for the purchaser of the book. For the publisher, the addition of the notes rendered the work subject to copyright protection in the United States, a competitive advantage.[130] To the purchaser, the notes made the work far more useful, because although most American courts permitted English law to be cited, they did not consider it authoritative as American case law would be.

Although many law booksellers and publishers in the United States reproduced one or more English legal texts for the American market, a few actually specialized in the genre. Leading among these were two: G. & C. Merriam of Springfield, Massachusetts, and John S. Littel, succeeded by T. & J. W. Johnson, of Philadelphia.

[128] William Jones, *An Essay on the Law of Bailments* (Boston: from the press of S. Etheridge for J. West, 1796).

[129] William Jones, *An Essay on the Law of Bailments* (New York: O. Halstead, 1828).

[130] Another method of controlling the competitive reprinting of foreign works by multiple American publishers was through the informal "courtesy of the trade system"; for a discussion, see Jeffrey D. Groves, "Courtesy of the Trade," in *The Industrial Book*, ed. Casper, et al., 139–48. I have not found evidence of extensive use of this system among the specialized law publishers and booksellers.

G. & C. Merriam became the largest American reprinter of the works of the great English treatise writer Joseph Chitty.[131] Chitty, born in 1776, was a successful barrister until 1816, when illness forced him to retire. From this date until his death thirty years later, he produced a series of treatises on English law matched only by his American counterpart, Joseph Story. Joseph's son, also Joseph, born in 1800 and dead at the age of thirty-eight, assisted his father in creating a Chitty dynasty and also produced a number of legal treatises as well. The reputation of these two men was widespread, and the books were immensely popular in both Britain and the United States. The Merriam company, which later gained international fame as the publisher of Webster's dictionary, specialized in the publication of Chitty's work in America, including the works on pleading, bills of exchange, criminal law, contracts, and precedents. Many of these texts were accompanied by American notes, commissioned by the Merriams. The popularity of these books is illustrated by an advertisement by G. & C. Merriam of 1844.[132] This advertisement states that the various Chitty volumes were for sale, not only by the Merriams themselves in Springfield, but also by Gould, Banks, and Voorhies in New York City, T. & J. W. Johnson, Grigg & Elliot, and Thomas, Cowperthwait in Philadelphia, C. C. Little in Boston, "and the principal law booksellers throughout the United States."

John S. Littel and T. & J. W. Johnson were law booksellers and publishers based in Philadelphia.[133] They pioneered a series of reprints from English law texts known collectively as *The Law Library*, a series that continued to expand from 1833 until 1860 and eventually numbered 104 volumes, many of which contained multiple titles.[134] The series was issued in monthly parts, and purchasers were asked to subscribe for a full year. In 1846, such a subscription cost ten dollars from the publisher. *The Law Library* was notable on several accounts.[135] First, it reprinted the English texts without American notes, which led to a competing series titled "The Library of Law and Equity" to be issued by publishers in Harrisburg, Pennsylvania, beginning in 1845.[136] Second, it was done by subscription in parts,

[131] On Chitty, see H. C. G. Matthew and B. Hanson, ed. *Oxford Dictionary of National Biography* (Oxford: Oxford University Press, 2004), *s.v.* "Chitty."
[132] See www.antebellumlegalpublishing.org.
[133] Surrency, *A History of American Law Publishing*, 167.
[134] Ibid. [135] See Chapter 3. [136] Ibid.

not only to guarantee Littel and then Johnson with a set number of advanced sales but also to permit the monthly parts to be shipped as periodicals through the United States mails. Third, the series reprinted both well-known as well as obscure English texts, which guaranteed that these texts likely would penetrate far into the New World.[137]

PURCHASING NEW AND USED LAW BOOKS

What antebellum law booksellers could not print, reprint, or import, they had to purchase. There were any number of ways this could be done.[138] As mentioned previously, a bookseller could subscribe to a set number of copies of books announced but not yet published. This had the advantage to purchasers of leaving them with the option to refuse to take the finished books or a lesser quantity if desirable at the time of publication. They could also purchase new books from printers and publishers. Advertisements of the period make it clear that all law booksellers and publishers offered substantial discounts for quantity purchases, often as much as 20 percent or more off the listed retail price. This option was especially important for law book dealers in smaller towns and rural areas who would have to look to their larger urban counterparts for much of their stock. It was, in effect, relatively easy to purchase law books for resale although the discount limited the profit potential for these resellers to some degree. Indeed, catalogues of various dealers reflect some variation in price for the same new books, and this may well represent differences in the booksellers' costs of acquisition.

In addition to buying direct from larger or more urban law booksellers or publishers, booksellers wishing to purchase law books for their stock could also purchase quantities at trade sales. Trade sales in antebellum America were auction sales held periodically in larger cities and restricted to members of the book trade.[139] Generally, publishers would consign

[137] Ibid.

[138] For a general discussion of this subject, see Michael Winship, "The National Book Trade System. Distribution and Trade," in *The Industrial Book, 1840–1880*, 117–29.

[139] On the history of trade sales, see C. Blagden, "Booksellers' Trade Sales 1718–1768," *The Library*, 5th serv., 5 (1951): 243–57; Terry Bellinger, "A Booksellers' Trade Sales 1718–1768," *The Library*, 5th ser., 30 (1975): 281–302; Tebbel, *A History of Book Publishing in the U.S.*, 230–38; Baloch, "Law Booksellers and Printers as Agents of

quantities of overstocked texts to such sales for quick disposal. Such sales began in the United States in 1802 in New York, after the failure of attempts to establish "literary fairs," where books might be displayed and sold by publishers.[140] Later, trade sales were held in Philadelphia, Boston, and Cincinnati. A typical trade sale was held by Bangs, Brother & Company during March 1855 in New York.[141]

The March 1855 New York trade sale, like others in different cities and during different years, was not devoted exclusively to any one type of book. Instead, books on all subjects were welcome to be sold. In addition, stationery, stereotype plates, and other typical bookstore stock were offered. Purchasers of at least one thousand dollars of merchandise at the sale were offered credit for up to six months; those who purchased between one hundred and one thousand dollars worth of goods were given four months to pay, and those who bought less than one hundred dollars worth of goods were required to pay cash.[142] The sale lasted ten full days spread over two weeks.

Although the majority of the books sold at this sale were not law books, those in attendance who wanted to purchase law books would not have been disappointed. A number of booksellers and publishers offered law texts in quantity. Chief among these were Lippincott, Grambo & Co. and Kay & Brother, both of Philadelphia, and Masters, Smith & Co. of Hallowell, Maine.[143] Lippincott, Grambo offered six law titles, including Blackstone's *Commentaries* in two volumes with American cases noted and Smith's *Elements of the Law*.[144] There were ten copies of each for sale. The Blackstone had an asking price of four dollars for cash and the Smith of one dollar cash. We do not know the hammer prices received, though we may assume that they were less than the cash price because a two-volume set of the Blackstone published in 1855 was available from Little, Brown the next

Unchange," 394; C. Blagdon, "Booksellers' Trade Sales, 1718–1768," *The Library*, 5 (1950–51): 243ff.; Michael Winship, "Getting the Books Out; Trade Sales, Parcel Sales, and Book Fairs in the Nineteenth-Century United States," in *Getting the Books Out*, 4–25.

140 Tebbel, *A History of Book Publishing in the U.S.*, 230.

141 *Catalogue of the Sixty-First New York Trade Sale Books, Stereotype Plates, Stationery, &c, by Bangs, Brother & Co., Trade Sale Rooms, No. 13 Park Row, New York, Commencing on Tuesday, March 13, 1855, And to be Continued Daily in the Order Stated in the Catalogue. Sales to Commence Each Day at 8 o'clock, a.m.* (New York: Bangs, Brother & Co., 1855).

142 Ibid. 143 *Catalogue of the Sixty-First New York Trade Sale Books.* 144 Ibid.

year for four dollars retail.[145] Because individual publishers and booksellers often extended both credit and a quantity or trade discount of 10–20 percent, there would have been no inducement to trade purchasers to buy at the cash price unless the works were otherwise unavailable.

Kay & Brother offered five copies each of seventeen different legal works plus one set of the second series of the Harrisburg *Library of Law and Equity*, fourteen volumes in twelve.[146] The cash prices listed for most of these texts were the same as those listed the next year in Little, Brown's retail catalogue, but not for all. An 1848 edition of Wharton's *Law Dictionary* was for sale from Little, Brown in 1856 for $5.50.[147] The copy available at the 1855 trade sale (not necessarily the 1848 London edition) was listed at only three dollars cash price.[148] Kay & Brother also listed for sale five copies of Wharton & Stille's *American Medical Jurisprudence*, with the caveat that it would be available for sale only "if ready" at the time of the auction.

The 1855 catalogue does not always list the binding of the books for sale. In fact, there is no information as to binding for most of the law offerings. Where binding is listed, it usually is listed as "law sheep."[149] In one case of a law book, however, purchasers were given a choice of bindings. Lea & Blanchard of Philadelphia had on offer ten each of John Lord Campbell's *Lives of the Chief Justices* and *Lives of the Lord Chancellors*.[150] Of these five each were bound in cloth; two were bound in half leather and boards, and three were bound in sheep "library style." The cash prices were set accordingly: $3.00 per copy in cloth; $4.70 in half leather; $4.20 in sheep.

Although no bookseller wishing to specialize in law books could depend solely upon trade sales like the one of March 1855 for purchasing all or even most of its stock, these sales did provide an opportunity to buy small quantities of a number of significant titles presumably at a discount.

Virtually every law bookseller's catalogue from the antebellum period also contains used books, both foreign and domestic. Law

[145] *A General Catalogue of Law Books: Including all the Reports, Both English and American, From the Earliest Period* (Boston: Little, Brown, & Co., 1856), 15.
[146] *Catalogue of the Sixty-First New York Trade Sale of Books*, 224–225.
[147] *A General Catalogue of Law Books*, 134.
[148] *Catalogue of the Sixty-First New York Trade Sale*, 224.
[149] Ibid. [150] Ibid.

books had been imported into the United States since the very earliest period of colonization.[151] By the Revolution, a substantial number of such books were to be found in American libraries. The vast majority of such libraries were private. There were very few institutional law libraries at the beginning of the nineteenth century. This is important because whereas institutional libraries tended to hold onto their books, private libraries were far more commonly dispersed upon the death of the owner.[152] Thus, a bookseller could supplement his stock of new books by acquiring used books at estate auctions and by private treaty with heirs. In addition, many lawyers of the period, like lawyers today, held no great affection for their private libraries. When they retired from practice, it was tempting to sell off their books and take the cash. This type of sale, too, must have been useful for law booksellers of the period.

We can get a fairly good idea of the importance of used law books to booksellers by examining some typical catalogues of the period. For example, the Lucas catalogue of 1819 offered a number of used texts for sale. Many of the English law books offered were far from new. Lucas offered numerous volumes of eighteenth-century British reports and even some from the seventeenth century – for example, the London 1783 edition of Cunningham's *Law Dictionary*.[153] He offered several sets of Coke's works, including a 1670 edition of the *Institutes* as well as a 1669 edition of William Sheppard's *Common Assurances*.[154] The prices put on these volumes are also instructive: There seems to have been no discount placed on those used volumes for which there were not newer, better editions, such as many of the English case reports. In contrast, when there were newer editions, particularly those with American notes, the older texts without notes were priced at a lower level.

Another interesting example of how the age of a law book affected price can be seen in the history of David Hoffman's *Course of Legal*

[151] See Wolf, *Book Culture*; Mary S. Bilder, *The Transatlantic Constitution* (Cambridge, MA: Harvard University Press, 2004), 15–30; Mary S. Bilder, "The Lost Lawyers: Early American Legal Literates and Transatlantic Legal Culture," *Yale Journal of Law & the Humanities*, 11 (1999): 47–117; see also Robert D. Harlan, "David Hall's Bookshop and its British Sources of Supply," in *Books in America's Past: Essays Honoring Rudolph H. Gjelsness* ed. David Kaser (Charlottesville, VA: University of Virginia Press, 1966), 2–23 [discussing mainly nonlaw book importation].

[152] J. Lyons, *Recollections of an Old Cartman* (Newark, NJ: Daily Journal Office, 1872; reported in New York Bound Bookshop, 1984), esp. 101–14.

[153] Lucas, *Lucas' Law Catalogue*, 6. [154] Ibid., 8, 19.

Study. David Hoffman was a Baltimore lawyer who began the first, albeit short-lived, law school in Maryland. More successful was his massive introductory teaching book, *A Course of Legal Study*. The first edition of this book was published at Baltimore in 1817.[155] An expanded version was published in two volumes in 1836.[156] The book was widely praised by such luminaries as Harvard's Joseph Story. It appears for sale in law booksellers' catalogues even after the Civil War. Hoffman's rules for a lawyer's deportment, appended to the second edition of the work, are generally recognized as the first major American work on legal ethics and were influential in the drafting of the first ethics code by the American Bar Association in 1908.[157]

Stephen Gould, in his 1821 *New Bibliotheca Legum Americana*, offered a first edition of Hoffman's book for $4.50 bound in sheep.[158] Of course, only four years after its publication it would have been considered a new book, and Gould may well have purchased his copy from the Baltimore publisher Coale. By the 1840s, copies of the first edition disappeared, and one finds the second, revised and enlarged, edition in most law booksellers' catalogues. In 1849, John S. Voorhies of New York offered a copy of the set for sale for six dollars.[159] Little, Brown in Boston offered a set for sale in their 1844 catalogue for the same price.[160] But, by 1852, the price had dropped. In that year Banks, Gould in New York and Gould, Banks in Albany offered a set in their joint catalogue at five dollars.[161] In the Little, Brown catalogue for 1856 the set appeared at this same, reduced price.[162] Banks, Gould in an 1856 short catalogue again offered the Hoffman volumes at five dollars.[163]

155 David Hoffman, *A Course of Legal Study Respectfully Addressed to the Students of Law in the United States*. (Baltimore: Coale and Maxwell, 1817).

156 David Hoffman, *A Course of Legal Study, Addressed to Students and the Profession Generally* (2nd. ed., Baltimore: J. Neal, 1836).

157 Hoffman, *A Course of Legal Study*, (1836).

158 Stephen Gould, *New Bibliotheca Legum Americana* (1821), 13.

159 *A General Catalogue of the Best Editions of English and American Law Books; Intended as a Guide to Purchasers* (New York: printed by William Osborn for John Voorhies, 1849), 58.

160 *A Catalogue of Law Books Published and For Sale by Charles C. Little and James Brown* (Boston: printed by Thurston, Torry and Co., 1844), 39.

161 *A General Catalogue of Modern Law Books: Including the Old Reports* (New York: Banks, Gould & Co., 1852), 55.

162 *A General Catalogue of Law Books: Including all the Reports, both English and American, from the earliest period* (Boston: Little, Brown & Company, 1856), 69.

163 *Catalogue of Law Books* (New York: Banks, Gould & Co., 1856), 7.

Even distance didn't make a difference in price. Robert Clarke & Co.'s Western Law Book House catalogue for 1860 also offered the work at the discounted price of five dollars.[164]

One can put several different interpretations on these price differences over time. Although Hoffman's book was not necessarily only of value for a short period, it did become dated and lost popularity as new works, particularly the English lawyer and novelist Samuel Warren's *A Popular and Practical Introduction to Law Studies*, gained a wider audience in the United States in the 1840s.[165] Certainly, the virtual disappearance of the 1817 edition of Hoffman's work after the appearance of the second edition of 1836 testifies to the selectivity in purchase exercised by lawyers in their choice of books and their desire to have the most recent editions they could find. That the second edition declined in price from the 1840s to the 1850s may well represent a need to discount older, less popular books, particularly those experiencing competition from other texts. Also, if in fact the booksellers were offering the same copy of Hoffman's work over a long period of years, they may well have been willing to offer it more cheaply just to get it off their shelves. As it is today, shelf space is always at a premium in bookshops.

One other point about the pricing of Hoffman's work is worth note. The fact that the price of the work was the same in different catalogues of booksellers from different cities is significant. One would expect a rather close range, if not the same price, to be set for new books by various booksellers, because most would have paid the same for them and hesitated to price above the market. That older volumes, like the Hoffman, not only declined in price but declined in price in all booksellers' catalogues suggests that when one bookseller decided to lower the price, all did, regardless of actual cost. It also hints strongly at the development of a national market and national uniformity of pricing, caused by the competing catalogue booksellers.

Law books are and were fundamentally different from most novels or other creative works. Most novels, except the select few that are

164 *General Law Catalogue of Robert Clarke & Co.* (Cincinnati: Robert Clarke & Co., 1860), 63.

165 Samuel Warren and Thomas Clerke, *A Popular and Practical Introduction to Law Studies and to Every Department of the Legal Profession, Civil, Criminal, and Ecclesiastical: With an Account of the State of Law in Ireland and Scotland, and occasional Illustrations for American Law* (New York: D. Appleton, 1846).

"canonized" by a particular group or age, have ephemeral popularity. Although the works of Scott or Dickens may well have continued to sell throughout most of the nineteenth century, works by most others fell by the wayside after only a short period of popularity, if any. Law books, especially statute books and case reports, retained value to lawyers and thus economic value in the marketplace for far longer periods of time. Even treatises and teaching texts retained some value until replaced by more current works and, sometimes, even after. Thus, used law books had and have always occupied a place on law bookshops' shelves.

OTHER STOCK

Although law books were, by definition, the primary merchandise for sale by antebellum law booksellers, as already noted, most also carried stationery, forms, and even nonlegal books. Stephen Gould in New York and Little, Brown in Boston both listed stationery for sale on their stores' trade signs. Gould, in his 1821 catalogue, also devoted six pages to law blanks and stationery items.[166] There were several reasons law booksellers sold these items. First, of course, most shops wanted to be able to supply the members of the legal profession with all of their professional needs. Second, many of the booksellers who also acted as printers did not utilize their presses fully in printing law texts. They needed to keep the presses going, and stationary and forms provided a ready use for otherwise idle machinery. Third, the actual cost of printing these forms was low, and so profit potential in such business was high.

Gould offered an impressive variety of blanks.[167] He offered deeds, mortgages, bonds, bills of exchange, bail bonds, trial notice forms, summons, various documents for process, as well as notarial certificates. He also offered a range of documents for Chancery practice as well as for practice in Magistrate's Courts and before Justices of the Peace. He even offered military blanks for discharge and warrants. Gould made sure that his customers understood that these blank forms were good under New York law.[168] They had been drafted by two attorneys, Winter and Bolton, and had "been examined" by one of

[166] Gould, *New Bibliotheca Legum Americana* (1821), 49–54.
[167] Gould, *New Bibliotheca Legum Americana* (1821). [168] Ibid.

three prominent New York lawyers – Thomas Addis Emmet, Samuel Jones, and David Jones. Indeed, Gould points out that "the more important blanks" had been examined by all three.

A little more than fifty years later, Pease & Prentice, law booksellers and stationers in Albany, New York, issued a separate catalogue of their law blanks.[169] Again, they offered an impressive array of law blanks taking up seven octavo catalogue pages and covering as wide a spectrum of activities as those offered by Gould earlier. Interestingly, there is no mention of who drafted the documents or whether they had been examined for errors, but we may surmise that by the Civil War period, the use of law blanks had become more common than in 1821. What is significant about the Pease & Prentice offering is that there is a catalogue specifically devoted to law blanks and that "special rates" were available for quantities.[170] Also of interest, from an historical perspective, is that Pease & Prentice's law blanks were numbered and purchasers were asked to order by name and number, a system still in use today.

The production and availability of law blanks in the antebellum period is important in the history of the business of law. Form books had been available for most jurisdictions for centuries. But a law office that used a form book was saved only the necessity of creating the document from nothing. The form still had to be copied out laboriously by a law clerk or scrivener, a time-consuming and expensive process. Further, form books could go out of date every time a reform of procedure or substance was adopted by the courts or legislature. It was financially impossible to reprint these books every time a new law was adopted or case decided. Law blanks, in contrast, simply required the lawyer or law clerk to fill in the blanks with the specific names and facts of his transaction. No copying was necessary. Further, blanks could be quickly and cheaply updated and reprinted in accordance with the latest laws. As a result, these blanks helped to revolutionize the practice of antebellum law offices.

In addition to his extensive collection of law blanks, Stephen Gould, like other antebellum law booksellers, sold other items of use to his lawyer clients. He advertised that he had:

[169] Pease & Prentice, *Catalogue of Law and Pension Blanks* (Albany, NY: 1868).
[170] Ibid.

on hand, an extensive and select variety of stationery of all description, some of which is here mentioned: royal writing, medium, folio post, foolscap, quarto post, bath, and every other description of paper, quills, red tape, [p]aste, red and black ink, ink stands, pencils, rulers, wafers, sealing wax, wafer-seals, portable pens, penknives, pocket-books, playing and visiting cards, &c. Law registers, cost books, feint lined, and on excellent paper.[171]

In short, Gould's customers could find at his shop virtually everything other than office furniture necessary to the practice of law and even beyond, assuming that the playing cards were not strictly used for professional purposes!

SERVICES

Law booksellers also provided several services to their customers. No bookseller, not even the largest of urban companies, could keep every law book in stock. This was especially true for foreign law books, for which there was no ready market. Thus, in addition to selling existing stock on their shelves or in the warehouses, most law booksellers also were willing to serve as purchasing agents for clients with special orders. Indeed, in the hinterlands, particularly the southern and western United States, law booksellers often would special order books not only from abroad but also from northeastern booksellers.

Interestingly, it would seem from catalogues that some booksellers would list volumes in their catalogues although they might not actually have them in stock. This occurred primarily in two cases. The first case involved books in print in Europe that might be hard to obtain. John Livingston, a prominent New York bookseller beginning in the late 1840s, seems to have done this with several German law books.[172] The second case involved books that were promised by publishers but not yet in print. Presumably, in both cases, the law bookseller would take an order and fill it as the book became available.

A second service that law booksellers, and other general booksellers, performed regularly for clients was binding.[173] In the antebellum period, many books would be sold to booksellers in sheets (i.e. unbound). In

[171] Gould, *New Bibliotheca Legum Americana* (1821), 49. [172] See Chapter 6.
[173] David Kaser, *A Book for a Sixpence: The Circulating Library in America.* (Pittsburgh: Beta Phi Mu, 1980).

addition, legal periodicals were generally issued unbound, unless bought after the year in which published. Throughout the antebellum period, a large number of shorter works, such as bar rules, rules of courts, eulogies, sermons, and so on, which were of interest to and purchased by lawyers, were also sold unbound.[174] Thus, lawyers would often have found themselves in need of binding services.

Some law booksellers may well have owned or been financially affiliated with binderies, as they were with printers. Others may have subcontracted binding work out.

Whichever was the case, it would appear that lawyers purchasing law books had several options as to how they could purchase their law books. First, of course, they could purchase them unbound and folded. In this form they would get the book in uncut sheets but folded into quires ready for binding. Or, if they so chose, they could purchase the book bound in sheep, the common binding for law books. They could also purchase the volume bound in boards, which usually meant that the book was bound in cardboard covered by paper or cloth of some type. If the purchasers were willing to pay the expense, they could also have their books bound in leather: half leather (i.e., with a leather spine and corners), quarter leather (i.e., with a leather spine only and cloth or paper covered boards), or full leather. And, of course, they could ask for further embellishments, including spine labels, tooled covers, and so on. Often, one will find in antebellum law books a bookseller's sticker on the inside front or rear cover and, in some cases, a binder's ticket bound in as well. Such remnants of the manufacture and sale of the book can be of great use in determining details of the local trade.

A third service a few booksellers provided to lawyers was the rental of law books. According to David Kaser, twenty-six booksellers in the United States were in the business of renting law books to customers in antebellum America.[175] These circulating libraries were found in most major American cities including Boston; New York City; Salem,

174 See the Thomas Catalogue of the Carey & Riley Law Book Auction of September 13, 1830, discussed, pp. 121–22.

175 Kaser, *A Book for a Sixpence*, 173–75; see also James Green, "Subscription Libraries and Commercial Circulating Libraries in Colonial Philadelphia and New York," in *Institutions of Reading: The Social Life of Libraries in the United States*, ed. T. Augst and K. Carpenter (Amherst: University of Massachusetts Press, 2007), 53–71, esp. 70.

Massachusetts; Hagerstown and Baltimore, Maryland; and Washington, D. C. They seem to have been most active in the period before 1830.[176] For the most part, the law collections available for rental were relatively small parts of general circulating libraries, most often under a hundred books, but there were some exceptions.

The most important of the circulating law libraries was that operated by Hocquet Caritat in New York City in the early years of the nineteenth century.[177] Caritat founded his circulating library in 1799 and carried it on for a number of years into the nineteenth century. He apparently maintained a special collection of circulating law books for lawyers as well as a collection for sale known as his "London Law Book-store."[178] In 1804 he seems to have decided to announce to the public that the law books for sale were also for rent, although he may well have made these available earlier on request.[179] Caritat made a large selection of the most important American and English treatises, law reports, and statute books available to his lawyer borrowers. In exchange for the privilege of borrowing, the lawyers generally were required to subscribe to an annual fee.

None of the commercial circulating law book collections remained in business very long. In the absence of records, we may speculate that they could not survive financially because of theft, damage to frequently used books, or the increasing number of public and institutional libraries, such as the Harvard Law Library or the Social Law Library in Boston. Whatever the reason, these were never, so far as we can know, a major commercial activity for the law book trade. Certainly, where they existed, they would have been a great service to those lawyers who could not afford to purchase their own law books or gain access to a large enough library either through purchase or affiliation to serve their needs.

A final service which many law booksellers provided to their customers gratis was to serve as a place in which members of the Bar might meet casually. J. C. Derby, the Cincinnati law bookseller and publisher reminisced in his memoirs about the New York store of Baker & Voorhies:

[176] Ibid. [177] Raddin, *Literary Scene*, 22–35; see pp. 57–58.
[178] Ibid., 47–48, 61. [179] Ibid., 33–34.

I frequently had dealings with Mr. Voorhies, during that period. He had the confidence and patronage of the leading lawyers of that time, his store being the favorite resort of such eminent men as Chancellor Kent, George Wood, Hugh Maxwell . . .[180]

One can easily imagine the leaders of the New York Bar browsing and chatting among the shelves of law books in Voorhies's shop, acquainting themselves with the newest titles and the most recent court gossip.

The antebellum publishers and retail sellers of law books could not depend simply on word of mouth and attractive premises to attract customers. They, like other antebellum merchants, needed to develop a communications network to advertise their wares. This network was built on the large number of newspapers and magazines published and the growing ability to send these newspapers and other printed advertisements to every corner of the nation through the postal system.[181] This is the subject of the Chapter 3.

[180] Derby, *Fifty Years Among Authors, Books and Publishers* 655; see also Ruth Wallach, "The Publication of Legal Treatises in America from 1800–1830," *Law Library Journal*, 45 (1952): 140.

[181] See Paul Starr, *The Creation of the Media. Political Origins of Modern Communications* (New York: Basic Books, 2004), 47–146. In 1834, the United States had 1265 newspapers, of which 90 were dailies; ibid., 86.

Chapter 3

Spreading the Word: Catalogues and Cultivation

EARLY CATALOGUES

In 1859 Daniel Mulford Valentine, a twenty-nine-year-old resident of Fontanelle, Iowa, decided to study law.[1] He thought about going to Cincinnati to study at the law college there, but this was impractical given his wife and new child. Eventually, he moved to Kansas and prospered, becoming a justice of the Supreme Court in 1869. But in this pivotal year of his life, he was just beginning the systematic study of law. Unfortunately, for him, Fontanelle was a small farming community, and there were no bookstores from which to purchase the basic texts he needed to study law. Fortunately for him, however, by 1859 the largest law booksellers and publishers across the eastern United States had already been in the business of selling every text a young lawyer might need by mail. In his diary for 1859, Valentine recorded his utter delight at receiving a number of booksellers' catalogues for free and his concomitant ability to purchase law texts through the mail. He dealt with booksellers in Chicago, New York, and Boston, including Banks & Co.[2] From them, he purchased all the law texts he would eventually study and master.

The sale of law books through printed catalogues dates back in the English-speaking world at least to the early part of the seventeenth

[1] M. H. Hoeflich, and Virgil W. Dean, eds., "'Went at Night to Hear Hon. Abe Lincoln Make a Speech': Daniel Mulford Valentine's 1859 Diary." *Kansas History*. 29 (Summer 2006): 100–115, available at http://www.kshs.org/publicat/history/2006summer_hoeflich_dean.pdf.

[2] Ibid.

century.[3] Catalogues served several purposes. They were a form of advertising that let potential customers browse their stock without actually coming to the store. They also permitted the bookseller to tout new texts, often newly published or newly arrived from foreign shores. They were also a means of selling books to those who were not able to purchase them at the store. Armed with a catalogue, lawyers and law students could either purchase books by mail or have local acquaintances purchase books for them. Eventually, as catalogues became longer and more sophisticated, the catalogue could also serve as a bibliographical guide for the lawyer who possessed it, making it a valuable text in itself.

The earliest forms of law book catalogues published in the United States took the form of single-page broadsides separately printed and distributed or placed as newspaper advertisements. This practice dates to the colonial period and continued throughout the antebellum era. An early example of such a catalogue is related to the one discussed previously printed in the *Independent Chronicle and the Universal Advertiser* published in Boston by Ebenezer Rhoades on August 26, 1799. In this issue, James White, of Court Street, advertised seventy-eight law books for sale.[4] The vast majority of these were reports and collections of laws, interspersed with a few treatises. Each of the titles is listed briefly with no additional information as to publisher or date or place of publication, though a price is given. The most expensive item listed was the set of seven volumes of Durnford's *Reports*, at thirty-five dollars. The least expensive was an item listed only as "commercial reports," at eighty-eight cents. After the list, White noted that he would offer a discount of 10 percent on all purchases totaling fifty dollars or more. He also noted that all of the books for sale were available "well bound in calf." Finally, he advertised that he also had books in other fields available at his store as well as "writing-paper and quills" and a "large assortment of stationery, wholesale and retail."

[3] See, generally, on the sale of books by catalogue, Archer Taylor, *Book Catalogues: Their Varieties and Uses* (Chicago: Newberry Library, 1957); Graham Pollard and Albert Ehrman, *The Distribution of Books by Catalogue from the Invention of Printing to A.D. 1800* (Cambridge: Cambridge University Press, 1965). James Raven, in his *The Business of Books* (New Haven, CT: Yale University Press, 2007), 283, places the beginning of English law book sales catalogues in the 1740s.

[4] "Law Books for Sale, by James White," *The Independent Chronicle and Universal Advertiser* (August 26, 1799), 4.

There are several points to note about White's newspaper catalogue. First, we may presume that his intended audience was the legal profession in Boston and nearby areas, for this would have been the likely geographic area in which the paper circulated. There is no mention of mail order sales, not surprising given the early date of the advertisement and the lack of adequate postal service at that time. Second, the absence of much in the way of bibliographical details is significant. The clientele to whom this catalogue was targeted would have known what texts were for sale even by the very brief entries in the catalogue. In a few listings, there is a note as to the particular edition of the text for sale, information that would have been important for a potential buyer; most would be concerned with purchasing the most recent and best edition.[5] Third, it is interesting that all of the books for sale were already bound in calf, a more expensive way of selling than had they been unbound in sheets. There may be several reasons for this. First, the majority of these texts were most likely imported, and imports generally came bound. Second, White was not a printer or publisher and, therefore, was buying his texts from others; he may well have preferred to sell only bound copies rather than have to deal with sending books out for special-order binding.

The final point to notice in the White newspaper catalogue is, perhaps, the most interesting. White emphasizes that the prices listed for the books as bound are "at the retail price" but then goes on to promise a 10 percent discount for quantity orders. At the discounted price, according to White, the books were "presumed to bring them as low as they can be procured in America." The availability of the 10 percent quantity discount not only reveals a common practice of the law book trade in the antebellum era but also evidences the existence of competition, for there would be no reason to offer discounts except for competitive advantage.

Isaac Riley, Hocquet Caritat's partner in his bookselling ventures in turn-of-the- century New York, made extensive use of local newspapers for advertising and printing catalogues.[6] Because of Riley and Caritat's financial difficulties, Riley did business under the firm name of Alsop,

[5] Ibid.

[6] George G. Raddin, *Hocquet Caritat and The Early New York Literary Scene.* (Dover, NJ: Dover Advance Press, 1953).

Brannan, and Alsop; he placed numerous newspaper advertisements under this name.[7] In 1806 and 1807, they made extensive use of *The American Citizen*, a New York City newspaper that was published between 1800 and 1810. In 1808 they also began to publish their advertisements and catalogues in *The Public Advertiser*.

Riley's published catalogues differed from White's in a number of ways. First, they were longer listings of between one hundred and two hundred titles. Second, Riley and his partners specialized in imported law texts, and his catalogues emphasized this fact. The catalogue printed in the October 22, 1807, issue of *The American Citizen* begins as follows:

> Alsop, Brannan, and Alsop have just received by the ship Enterprise and Gold Hunter, from London, 22 trunks of Law Books, comprising the latest and most valuable publications in that line . . .[8]

The list itself is, again, sparse on bibliographical detail, although the size and number of the volumes for sale is given for each listing. It is interesting to note that there is no information regarding either type of binding or price. Presumably, if would-be purchasers wanted to comparison shop, they would need to go to the store to find out prices and format.

Although the catalogue published on October 22, 1807, did not list prices or terms available, a later catalogue published on December 2, 1807, gives more information. The individual titles remain unpriced in the catalogue, but there is a note at the end of the listing that sets forth discount terms:

> Booksellers, country storekeepers, and attornies in any part of the U. States will be supplied on the most favorable terms – Large discounts to those who purchase quantities.[9]

Here, again, we see evidence of a quantity discount. But we also see something new and of great importance. The target audience for this catalogue is not simply local New York lawyers but, instead, booksellers and store owners in more rural areas as well as lawyers from other parts of the country. This is a very early instance of an

[7] Ibid. [8] *The American Citizen* (New York: Cheetham), October 22, 1807, 3.
[9] *The American Citizen* (New York: Cheetham), December 2, 1807, 3.

American law bookseller aiming for a national marketplace. How successful Riley and his partners were in reaching this marketplace is unclear, because the problems of mail-order sales were great at this time. Certainly, however, such sales were very much in Riley's mind at the time he placed this advertisement.

Riley and his colleagues were not the only law booksellers to make extensive use of newspaper catalogues. Bernard Dornin operated a bookshop at three separate locations on Pearl Street in New York City between 1804 and 1808.[10] He specialized in not only law books but also books designed for the Irish-Catholic market. He was also a publisher on a small scale, again, primarily of Catholic interest books, although he did publish the occasional legal text.[11] On September 27, 1806, he published an extensive catalogue of law books available at his shop in the *American Citizen*, one of the New York City newspapers also used by Riley.[12]

Dornin's list in the *Citizen* was quite ambitious, numbering more than 200 items and filling more than a full column of the third page of the paper. His claim was even greater. According to the preface to the list, the list was but an "abstract" of what was available in his shop at 136 Pearl Street. And his collection of law books there was "in variety ... inferior to none on this continent."

The list is, like Riley's first list, rather sparse in bibliographical details. A typical entry is "Abbot on Shipping" or "Croke's Reports, 3v." But, again, the lawyers who were his customers would have needed little other information to whet their acquisitive appetites.[13] In terms of origin, the books were divided between English and American texts, with the majority being English, reflecting the few American texts available at this early date in the nation's history.

[10] George McKay, *A Register of Artists, Engravers, Booksellers, Bookbinders, Printers, & Publishers in New York City, 1633–1820* (New York: New York Public Library, 1942), 24.

[11] See David Kaser, "Bernard Dornin, America's First Catholic Bookseller," in *Books in America's Past*, ed. David Kaser (Charlottesville, VA: University of Virginia Press, 1966), 106–28, esp. 113–14 on his law book publishing; see also "Short Biography of Bernard Dornin," *New Advent Catholic Encyclopedia*, accessed at http://www.newadvent.org/cathen/05135c.htm.

[12] *The American Citizen* (New York: Cheetham), September 27, 1806, 3.

[13] Ibid., for titles of nonlaw books, as well.

At the end of the list, Dornin advertised a new law book that he was publishing, *Remington on Ejectments*. He also announced that he was opening a new bookstore in Edenton, North Carolina:

> [H]aving opened a bookstore in Edenton, North Carolina, Gentlemen professing the Law, from that part of the union, are informed that all of the above books may be had in Edenton, with an extensive assortment of books in Miscellaneous literature, and every new publication.[14]

This notice is particularly interesting, for it not only evidences a very early example of an American law bookseller attempting to operate in multiple locations in different states but also indicates an implicit assumption that the advertisement in a New York City newspaper would reach lawyers in North Carolina.

It was precisely the issue of geographical range that was the greatest inherent limitation of newspaper advertising in the early years of the nineteenth century in the United States. Although Dornin seemed to have hoped to reach some Southern readers with his advertisement in the *American Citizen*, one must recognize that such newspapers were, for the most part, limited in their circulation to a local or, at best, regional market. Thus, newspaper catalogues of the type used by Riley and Dornin could only have been of limited effectiveness in reaching a national audience. Reaching such an audience, however, was significant to the development of national law booksellers. Individual publishers could reach a national market by entering into cooperative publishing or marketing agreements with booksellers in other cities and states. But to reach a national market as a bookseller, one required only a different form of advertising. Thus it was that law booksellers relatively early began to publish separately printed catalogues, usually in pamphlet form, that could be sent through the mail to lawyers throughout the new nation.

Here again, Isaac Riley was an early pioneer of this method of selling law books. In 1806, he published his *Priced Catalogue of Law-Books to be Had at the Law-Repository of I. Riley, and Co ... Comprising Besides all the Most Common and Useful Works, A Selection from the English Law-Catalogue, of Many Old Reporters, Now Become*

[14] Ibid.

Extremely Scarce in London.[15] The catalogue that follows is thirteen pages long, alphabetically arranged, and lists more than 450 titles. It is a fascinating document, bibliographically, and reveals much about the law bookselling business of the time.

One of the first things that is noticeable about Riley's catalogue is the large number of titles on offer, many of which were either antiquarian or printed in Europe. But it is also interesting that a large number of these titles do not carry a price, as do most of the titles listed in the catalogue. This may indicate Riley's unwillingness to set a definite price on scarce items or that Riley didn't actually have these items in stock, but rather included them in the belief that he could obtain them if they were ordered by a customer. Indeed, many of the unpriced items also lack bibliographical details included with other items, such as the listing for a copy of the "Corpus Iuris Civilis." This description would apply to more than a dozen different editions of this book then available. Certainly, Riley would have had little trouble acquiring this book either in London or Paris through the efforts of his partner, Hocquet Caritat, or another agent. But he is unlikely to have had great demand for this or other European titles in New York in 1806. By listing them he could make it known that he would sell copies of the work, but by not stocking them at his store, he could save precious capital, albeit at the cost of potential delays of shipping. Several of the titles listed in the catalogue carry special notes as to availability or special pricing. One of the commonest notes is to the effect that a particular title "will be sold to the trade at a very liberal discount." For example, this phrase is appended to the listing of both the London and American editions of Marshall's treatise on insurance.[16] One may suppose that Riley had multiple copies of these titles and was, in effect, wholesaling them to other booksellers. Riley also appended comments to books of which he was the publisher. For example, the listing for Buller's work on the law of Nisi Prius is noted as follows:

[15] Isaac Riley, *A Priced Catalogue of Law-Books, to Be Had at the Law-Repository of I. Riley, and Co. ... Comprising, Besides All the Most Common & Useful Works, a Selection from the English Law-Catalogue, of Many of the Old Reporters, now Becoming Extremely Scarce in London* (New York: I. Riley & Co., 1806).

[16] Ibid., Samuel Marshall, *A Treatise on the Law of Insurance in Four Books* (Boston: Printed by Manning & Loring for Daniel Johnson of Portland, 1805).

This very important work which is universally acknowledged one of the first in point of sound law and weighty authority, has just been republished by I. Riley & Co. And the edition printed page for page from the last London copy, and carefully corrected by a gentleman of the bar.[17]

Another note, to Caine's New York *Reports* states:

Subscriptions ... are received, and the books delivered ONLY by the publishers in New York, and by Whiting, Backus, and Whiting in Albany.[18]

Riley also used this catalogue to announce new books in press and available for subscription purchase. For example, he announced the coming availability of the Massachusetts *Reports* which were "in press."[19]

The prices listed in the catalogue are also quite revealing, particularly in those cases in which a text had been printed in more than one location or edition. For instance, Customers were offered both the London and the American editions of Marshall's treatise on insurance. The London edition, in two octavo volumes, cost eight dollars and fifty cents, a substantial sum. The American edition was available for only six dollars.[20] They could also choose between two editions of Evan's treatise on bills and notes. The London edition, in octavo, was available at three dollars, whereas the edition printed in Newbern, North Carolina, could be had for just two dollars.[21] In the case of Park's treatise on insurance, Riley's customers had three choices of edition: They could purchase the London edition, in octavo, for five dollars; the Dublin edition, also in octavo, for three dollars; and the Boston edition at four dollars.[22] Invariably the London editions were

[17] Isaac Riley & Co., *A Catalogue of Approved Books, in English, French, Italian, Spanish, German, Greek, Latin, &c. & in all Arts and Sciences; Forming a Most Extensive and Universal Assortment, Inferior to None in the United States* (New York: I. Riley & Co., 1806); Francis Buller, *An Introduction to the Law Relative to Trials at Nisi Prius, Pertaining to the Present Time* (New York: I. Riley & Co., 1806).

[18] Ibid. George Caines, *New York Term Reports of Cases Argued and Determined in the Supreme Court of that State* (New York: I. Riley, 1813–1814).

[19] Riley, *A Priced Catalogue*, 6; Ephraim Williams, *Reports of Cases Argued and Determined in the Supreme Judicial Court of the State of Massachusetts, from September 1804 to June 1805, Both Inclusive* (Boston: Tileston & Weld, 1816).

[20] Ibid.; Marshall, *A Treatise on the Law of Insurance.*

[21] Riley, *A Catalogue of Approved Books*, 6.

[22] Riley, *Priced Catalogue*, 4. James A. Park, *A System of the Law of Marine Insurances: with Three Chapters on Bottomry, on Insurances on Lives, and on Insurance against Fire.* (Dublin: Printed J. Moore, 1792).

priced higher than the Dublin editions. In part, this is because the vast majority of Dublin editions were pirated, meaning that no royalties were paid to the copyright holder. Also, these editions were often more cheaply produced, often on rather bad paper, than the London editions. The American editions were almost always, at this period, less expensive than the London editions, but not always cheaper than the Dublin editions in spite of tariffs. It is unlikely that in cases in which the American edition was less expensive, the difference was attributable to the quality of the production rather than royalty costs; American printers rarely, if ever, paid royalties to British authors because copyright protection was not available to British authors under the Copyright Act of 1790.[23]

Although the pamphlet form permitted catalogues like Riley's to be sent through the U.S. mail at a time when books could not be so sent, there was another common method for distributing these catalogues. Many of these early pamphlet catalogues were stitched into bound volumes, at times in the front of the law book and, more commonly, at the end of the book, after the index and any other final matter. An example of a law book catalogue distributed in such a manner is that printed by Barnard B. Macanulty, who maintained a bookselling and publishing business at the sign of "Franklin's Head," on Essex Street in Salem, Massachusetts.[24] Macanulty was one of the prominent booksellers in Salem during the early years of the nineteenth century. Macanulty, an Irish immigrant, first landed at Philadelphia but quickly moved to Salem, where he set himself up in the book business in 1794. He was a bookish jack-of-all-trades, offering binding services, publishing the occasional text, and selling books and stationery. He also apparently had an interest in science. He sold patent medicines along with his books and claimed to have invented a new, superior binding method that allowed account books to lie flat when opened.[25]

In 1805, Macanulty moved into his new shop on Essex Street and published, in that January, Joseph Story's first major law work, his

[23] *Copyright Act of 1790*, § 5; see p. 58.

[24] Harriet S. Tapley, *Salem Imprints 1768–1825: A History of the First 50 years of Printing in Salem, Massachusetts. With Some Account of the Bookshops, Booksellers, Bookbinders and the Private Libraries* (Salem, MA: The Essex Institute, 1927).

[25] Ibid.

Selection of Pleadings in Civil Actions.[26] Macanulty and the young Story were friends; Macanulty published not only Story's first legal work but also his first poetical work, *The Power of Solitude*.[27] Macanulty took the opportunity, when publishing Story's work on pleading, to bind into the volume a six-page catalogue of books for sale at his shop. The catalogue is alphabetically arranged but only lists fifty titles. For each title, there is a full bibliographical description but no price. Ten of the fifty titles offered are American works. The remainder are British. Several of the British works are offered either in an American edition or with American notes. The American titles tend to be focused on Massachusetts law. There are standard British law reports and treatises, several form books, and both federal and Massachusetts statutes. The list would have provided the lawyers of Salem and surrounding Massachusetts towns with the necessary texts for building a working Massachusetts law library. The catalogue lacks the scope and extensive offerings of Riley's catalogue, which may well reflect both the smaller stock and capital investment made by Macanulty and the more restricted market for which he had printed his catalogue. The fact that none of the entries are priced most probably indicates Macanulty's expectation that his customers were located close enough to actually come into his shop.

About five years later, a Baltimore bookseller, Lucas, published another catalogue of law books for sale in pamphlet form.[28] It is today impossible to know with certainty whether this was distributed through the mail or bound into law books, although the lack of a title page, the minimal information given about the bookseller, and the fact that the volume starts with page three suggests that it was intended to be bound into another book, as was Macanulty's. The Lucas catalogue is much more cheaply produced than either Macanulty's or Riley's, but it is rich in listings: It has 271 titles listed, some of which are different editions of the same work. This catalogue shows the same diversity of offerings as does the Riley catalogue. There are a substantial number

[26] Joseph Story, *A Selection of Pleadings in Civil Actions Subsequent to the Declaration with Occasional Annotations on the Law of Pleading* (Salem, MA: Barnard B. Macanaulty, 1805).

[27] Joseph Story, *The Power of Solitude. A Poem. In Two Parts* (Salem, MA: Macanaulty, 1804). The contract between Macanulty and Story for publishing this work is now owned by the Peabody-Essex Museum in Salem.

[28] Lucas, *Law Catalogue* (Baltimore, 1810).

of foreign and antiquarian books, again, perhaps, evidence of the sophisticated nature of the Baltimore Bar. In general, the bibliographical content of listings is scanty; often only the size of the text and the number of volumes are listed. All of the items are priced. In addition to Maryland and federal law, texts offered include those representing New York, New Jersey, Pennsylvania, and English law. There are several volumes on ecclesiastical law listed. In several cases, listings include both the original English edition of a text as well as the pirated Dublin edition at a substantially lower price. Lucas sometimes offered more than one edition of the same text; for example, the catalogue lists a copy of Lilly's 1771 London edition of *Modern Entries* at seven dollars and fifty cents.[29] The 1791 London edition of the same title is listed at ten dollars.[30] This is clear evidence of the value lawyers of the day placed on the most current and recent authorities and the rapid decrease in value of older editions. Several entries also point out the existence of American notes appended to British texts, again indicating the demand for the most relevant authorities for the American practitioner.

Stephen Gould's first catalogue in pamphlet form marks a significant advance in law book catalogues in the United States. That Gould had great aspirations for his catalogue is made plain by the title he chose for it: *A New Bibliotheca Legum Americana or American Law Catalogue*, a deliberate play on John Worral's great eighteenth-century *Bibliotheca Legum Anglicana*, still in use in Gould's day as a bibliographical reference work.[31] This work was published in December 1821.

[29] Lucas, *Law Catalogue*, 14. John Lilly, *A Collection of Modern Entries, or Select Pleadings in the Courts of King's Bench, Common Pleas, and Exchecquer, viz. Declarations, Pleas in Abatement and in Bar, Replications, Rejoinders, &c ... Many of Them Drawn or Purused by Mr. Broderick, Carthew, Comyns, Darnel ... and Other Learned Counsel. As Also Special Assignments of Errors, and Writs and Proceedings Thereupon, both in the Said Courts and in Parliament. With the Method of Suing to the Reversing Outlawries by Writ of Errors or Otherwise. To Which Is Added a Collection of Writs in Most Cases now in Practice. With Two Tables, One of the Names of the Cases, and the Other of the Pleadings and Writs* (London: Printed by Strahan and Woodfall. For J. Worrall and B. Touey, &c, 1771).

[30] Lucas, *Law Catalogue*, 14. Lilly, *A Collection of Modern Entries, or, Select Pleading in the Courts of Kings Bench, Common Pleas, and Exchecquer ...: to which Is Added a Collection of Writs in Most Cases now in Practice: with Two Tables, ...*. (London: Printed by A. Strahan & W. Woodfall ... for J. Rivington and Sons, 1791).

[31] Stephen Gould, *A New Bibliotheca Legum Americana* (New York: W. Grattan, 1821).

The arrangement of the catalogue is innovative. There are actually two catalogues: The first is an alphabetical list of books either on American law or British works, which had been republished in the United States, often with American annotations; and the second list consists of British works published abroad. It seems that the rationale behind this split was (1) that the American books and books republished in the United States with American notes would be of greater general interest to the Bar than purely foreign works, and (2) as Gould noted in his preface, he was unable to stock all of the purely foreign works he listed at all times.[32] Moreover, the prices of such foreign works, which he might have to obtain through agents abroad, were variable. Thus, he warned his customers that the prices given for these works were, to a degree, "arbitrary" and an "average," although he reassured those who might want to purchase these that the catalogue prices would not be more than 10 percent off the true price.[33] There was also the question of availability. American works, which he generally had in stock, could be made available immediately. British works, which had to be procured elsewhere and, possibly, abroad, might take "a few weeks."[34] There are no listings of European printed books and, therefore, very little on foreign law.

The two lists are, like earlier catalogue lists, arranged alphabetically by author. Each entry lists author, title, date of publication, and price, but no place of publication. Several entries contain cataloguer's notes. For the most part, these give the reader the information on continuations and new editions. A few give notice of upcoming editions in press, and a small number give details about the author or content. In total there are 429 titles listed, split roughly between American and British titles.

One piece of information provided for some of the titles that is not found in the earlier catalogues discussed is information about bindings. Many entries list the binding of the work for sale as sheep, calf, or boards. Books bound in boards are, not surprisingly, the least expensive of the bound volumes identified. Among the works listed in the list of English printed books, several also are identified as to their size ("folio" or "quarto") and several more are identified as "old." One would assume that by "old," Gould was not simply pointing out books that

[32] Ibid. [33] Ibid. [34] Ibid.

were used, because several volumes of some antiquity were not so identified, but rather that books so marked were what we would today label "antiquarian" or "rare." Among those volumes was a copy of the 1673 edition of Aston's *Book of Entries*.[35] It would seem likely that the foreign printed titles marked "old" were probably ones that Gould actually had in stock, because it would not have been possible to easily procure these volumes on the open market on demand.[36]

At the end of the law books catalogue, Gould included a short list of forty-three "classical and miscellaneous books." The inclusion of this list is quite interesting because Gould was one of the first booksellers to identify himself as having "experience exclusively in law bookselling." Why, then, did Gould stock and list these forty-three titles in his first major catalogue? The answer lies in the culture of the legal profession in the antebellum period. Lawyers were practical men, *hommes d'affaires*, as the French say, but many lawyers also had literary aspirations. Joseph Story was not the only lawyer–poet of his generation. The literary titles Gould listed in the catalogue tend to be classic works of Latin and English prose: Shakespeare, Gibbon, Locke, and translations from the Greek and Roman canon. There are a few of what would have passed as "popular" works; instead, authors such as Fielding, Milton's works in prose and poetry, and Pope's were represented. There were also for sale sets of the *Spectator* for those who wished to be au courant with the London literary scene as well as such standards as Adam Smith's *Wealth of Nations*. Most of the nonlegal works for sale were multivolume sets, and whereas several were bound in boards, others were more expensive deluxe editions bound in calf with gilt decoration. Most were quite expensive. One can easily imagine up-and-coming

[35] Richard Aston, *Placita Latiné Rediviva: A Book of Entries: Containing Perfect and Approved Precedents of Counts, Declarations, Barrs, Avowries, Replications, Please in Abatement, Issues, Judgments, as well as in Actions Real as Personal, and Sundry Other Entries; Useful for all Clerks, Attorneys, and Practisers in the Courts at Westminster, and Inferious courts: not Heretofore Published in Print: Collected in the Times, and out of Some of the Manuscripts, of Those Famous and Learned Protonotaries, Richard Brownlow, John Gulston, Robert Moyl, and Thomas Cory. Digested into an Exact Method, with a Table* (London: Printed for H. Twyford, T. Dring, and John Place, 1673).

[36] Gould might well have searched in other booksellers' catalogues for a rare volume, but with no certainty of success.

lawyers purchasing a set or two to display to friends and clients as testimony of their learning, wealth, and culture. Whether they read them, of course, is an entirely different question.

CATALOGUES AND THE RISE OF THE NATIONAL LAW BOOKSELLERS

By the 1830s, the use of catalogues in pamphlet form had become common for the sale of law books. It was in this period that catalogues began to become far more extensive and in which these catalogue sales fueled the rise of an elite group of regional and national law booksellers. Several factors contributed to the extraordinary rise in the importance of what became a group of national law booksellers that sold through widely distributed catalogues. First, by 1830, the transportation infrastructure in the new nation was finally coming of age. The Erie Canal was finished in 1825 and, when used in conjunction with the steamboats that plied the Hudson River, provided the merchants of New York City with rapid and inexpensive access to the West. Other canals in Pennsylvania assisted Philadelphia merchants in similar ways. Boston, a thriving port, became a major hub for the new railroads, and Boston merchants soon dominated the New England area.

A second factor that contributed to the growth of a select group of urban booksellers was the rise in the number of lawyers practicing in the United States and the subsequent remarkable increase in the number of law books being produced to satisfy the demands of those lawyers. By the 1830s, the United States had found its Blackstone in Chancellor James Kent, whose *Commentaries* were a perennial bestseller, and Joseph Story had begun his career as a treatise writer with an unprecedented outpouring of books every lawyer would need. The courts and the legislatures of each state, as well of the federal government, were hard at work making and interpreting new laws, and their large output created an ever-increasing number of reports and statute books that the booksellers needed to stock. Important, also, was the growing interstate commerce that followed the improvements in transportation. As commerce across state lines increased, so did legal business. As lawyers began to do more work involving multistate transactions, they began to need legal books from more than one state. This meant that they would not only purchase more law books but also seek out booksellers who could supply all their needs at once.

In New York, Boston, Philadelphia, and, to a lesser extent, Baltimore and Cincinnati, the great law bookselling houses began their rise to prominence during the 1830s. Their catalogues both aided this rise and reflected it. In 1833, P. H. Nicklin and T. Johnson, with a store at 175 Chestnut Street in the heart of Philadelphia's business district, issued a major law catalogue.[37] Their national aspirations come clear in the statement "to members of the Bar," which opens the pamphlet:

> The Subscribers beg leave to call the attention of legal gentlemen *throughout the United States*, to their American editions of Reports in the English *Common Law and Ecclesiastical Courts*.[38]

This introductory advertisement is then followed by two pages of lists. The first gives a full index to the Common Law Reports published by the booksellers. The second lists the parts of the Ecclesiastical Reports and a list of selected titles, by subject, contained in those reports. The following two pages of the catalogue are more interesting because they list works not published by Nicklin and Johnson. On these two pages are found a listing of the published reports of the United States Supreme Court and Circuit Courts, and lists of all the state reports. These lists, which give much information about the reports, including the names of the reporters, would have served as not only a list of available books but also a reference work for lawyers. These lists were designed to give added value to the catalogue, to make it into a work to be saved by those who received it and, therefore, a valuable book in its own right.

Included on the third page is a list of agents around the United States who carried Nicklin and Johnson's law publications. They had agents in Maine, New Hampshire, Vermont, Massachusetts, Connecticut, New York, Virginia, Pennsylvania, the District of Columbia, North Carolina, South Carolina, Georgia, Tennessee, Mississippi, and Louisiana, as well as in Montreal and Kingston in Canada. A number of their agents for their own publications were also prominent booksellers and publishers in their own right, such as John Voorhies and Banks, Gould in New York

[37] P.H. Nicklin and T. Johnson, *Catalogue of Law Books for Sale by P.H. Nicklin & T. Johnson* (Philadelphia: 1833).
[38] Ibid., preface, emphasis added.

City, and J. S. Littell in Baltimore. The existence of this large network of affiliated law booksellers helped to establish a national market for their publications, which could also increasingly be purchased through their catalogues and shipped if one of the agents was not within convenient distance.

In fact, although travel and transportation (but not mail) was improving by 1833 (when this catalogue was issued), going directly to a bookshop, if possible, was the preferable means of purchase. This was precisely why booksellers like Nicklin and Johnson set up a network of agents to sell their own publications. Thus, the catalogue served two related purposes. For those who were within easy traveling distance of a law bookseller, the catalogue served as an advertisement and a list of what was available at the shop. For those who were not within traveling distance, the catalogue was the point of sale itself.

One intermediate method of purchasing books using a catalogue is illustrated by a correspondence between two young lawyers. Amos Dean wrote to his friend Daniel Hawks in response to a request Hawks had sent him. Hawks lived in Cortland Village, New York, a small hamlet not within easy reach of a major law bookseller. Dean lived and practiced in Albany. Hawks wrote to Dean, asking him to visit the shop of Banks, Gould to inquire after a number of books he was interested in purchasing. Dean obliged his friend by visiting the shop, discovering the cost of the volumes and also ascertaining that the shop was willing to sell the books on credit for a year, so long as Hawks would pay interest on the amount owed.

To return to Nicklin and Johnson's catalogue, after the preliminary matter discussed previously, they listed a catalogue of forty-two titles they had published or had in press. The entries for these titles are very full and often include comments in praise of the works by noted lawyers and judges, such as Chancellor Kent. After this catalogue of publications, there is a short list of "odd volumes" available from Nicklin and Johnson, presumably to help purchasers finish incomplete sets they might own.

The remainder of the catalogue consists of four double-column pages in small print that list a selection of the books available from Nicklin and Johnson's store. The titles are divided into two categories: American and English books. Very little detail is given about the more than 400 volumes listed. Often there is not even a full title and author's name but simply an abbreviated approximation. No prices are given. Here, again, this would seem to be evidence of the transitional nature of the catalogue. It provided enough information so that someone unable to come into the shop would be sufficiently informed to make further inquiries, but the assumption seems to have been that most users of the catalogue would be coming in themselves to purchase. Indeed, the catalogue states:

> Legal gentlemen will save themselves much trouble and expense by calling at this establishment, where they will be able to fill their orders on the best terms.[39]

By the 1840s, catalogue sales of law books had advanced even more as the Bar grew and transportation and travel became easier. Also, law publishers had found a way of circumventing the prohibition of shipping books through the mails. Although the use of the postal system was prohibited for books, publishers and booksellers were permitted to send periodicals through the U.S. mail. The definition of *periodical* was sufficiently broad as to permit short texts in unbound pamphlet format to be sent through the postal service. Several legal publishers began to exploit this loophole, including the publisher of the major reprint series of English legal texts, the *Law Library*.[40]

One of the greatest of all law publishers and booksellers of the nineteenth century, Little, Brown of Boston, began to exploit the catalogue format in the 1830s. The company was innovative from the start. Its 1837 catalogue, for example, boasted an illustration on the title page of a lawyer reading, something no other catalogue had yet done.[41] By 1844, the Little, Brown law catalogues had taken on a characteristic form, one that remained standard for decades. The 1844 catalogue of law books for sale is typical of these productions.

The 1844 Little, Brown catalogue is a small octavo comprising eighty-eight numbered pages listing books for sale and sixty pages of

[39] *Supra* note 40. Collins, Keene & Co. of No. 254 Pearl St. in New York stated, in a short catalogue bound into a copy of Thomas Starkie, *A Treatise on the Law of Slander, Libel, Scandals and False Rumors* (1832), that it had "constantly on hand all the standard English Reports, Digests, and Treatises on Statutes, together with the various State Reports and Digests, and a general assortment of Law Books of every description" in order to bring customers to its store.

[40] *The Law Library* (Philadelphia: J.S. Littel, 1833–1860).

[41] Charles C. Little and James Brown, *A Catalogue of Law Books Published and for Sale by Charles C. Little and James Brown (*Boston: Little & Brown, 1837).

preliminary matter. It is stitched and bound in covers made of a light card stock. The title page is reprinted on the front cover and the obverse of the rear cover carries advertisements for newly published, nonlegal texts. There is a short preface occupying the first two pages of the preliminary material. In the preface, the booksellers informed their potential customers of the changes to the catalogue and to their stock. First, this catalogue contains listings for a large number of foreign books on the civil law, perhaps reflecting the increasing interest of the elite Bar and the judiciary in these sources.[42] The booksellers also note the inclusion of the latest editions of English works. More importantly, they note the contents of the catalogue that are not designed directly to sell books. This catalogue's preliminary material includes lists and indices of all of the American, both state and federal, reports, as well as lists and indices of both the English and Irish reports. Included in these lists, which the booksellers are proud to point out were current as of the date of the composition of the catalogue, are notes of the abbreviations used for all of these reports as well as the names of the reporters. This material is followed by a text that became standard in all Little, Brown catalogues thereafter and was also used by other booksellers, such as John Livingston. This was the "Catalogue of a Select Law Library," put together by Simon Greenleaf, then the Royal Professor of Law at Harvard. The purpose of this catalogue was to provide a recommended library and reading list for lawyers and law libraries.

The preliminary material in the Little, Brown catalogue of 1844 (and subsequent issues) accounts for nearly half the pages in the pamphlet and would have added significantly to both the printing and mailing costs. Further, Little, Brown did not charge for their catalogues; they were sent free of charge on request. Why, then, did they take on the added cost of the inclusion of this nonsales material? The reason is relatively clear: They wanted to make the catalogue into a reference work for all lawyers. By so doing, they hoped to ensure that lawyers who received the catalogue would keep it on their shelves and use it for not only reference purposes but also ordering needed books. Greenleaf's

[42] Charles C. Little and James Brown, *A Catalogue of Law Books Published and for Sale by Charles C. Little and James Brown* (Boston: printed by Thurston, Torry & Co., 1844).

catalogue within the larger catalogue also served as an inducement for ambitious lawyers to follow the great professor's advice and purchase texts they might otherwise not have known about. The publishers of the catalogue put it simply when they said only that they hoped that their catalogue would "be thought worthy of a place on the young Attorney's table."[43]

Eighty-eight pages of books for sale is quite impressive. All of the works are priced, although the preface notes that the prices given are for single copies and that purchases of a whole library or in quantity would be given a discount.[44] Full bibliographical details are given for each title, including full name of author, exact title, number of volumes, place of publication, and date of publication. Several entries also have annotations. Some of these notes are drawn from reviews by journals such as the *American Jurist*.[45] Others seem to have been produced by the booksellers themselves. For example, a note is appended to the listing for George Minot's *Digest of Massachusetts Reports*:

> The publishers are very happy to announce to the profession, that this Digest, so long delayed by the scrupulous exactness of the author, who has given it more than two years' unremitted labor, is now in the hands of the printer, and will be offered for sale in the course of the coming winter.[46]

In this note one can hear the frustration of the bookseller waiting patiently for the slow scholar to finally produce his work.

What is most notable about this 1844 catalogue is the number and diversity of the books offered for sale. Twenty years before, a list of 300 titles would have been considered immense. By the time this catalogue was printed, Little, Brown could offer more than 1,000. They could boast of their "regular" correspondence with their "experienced agents in England, France, and Belgium," and their use of transatlantic steamers to ensure that their "returns are satisfactory and prompt."[47] Lawyers in possession of this catalogue had before them a world of legal learning undreamt of by their predecessors of a generation before.

[43] Ibid., preface. [44] Ibid., preface.

[45] *American Jurist* (Boston: Freeman and Bolles, 1829–1843).

[46] George Minot, *Digest of the Decisions of the Supreme Judicial Court of Massachusetts, Reported in the Seventeen Volumes of Massachusetts Reports, the Twenty-Four Volumes of Pickening's Reports, and the First Four Volumes of Metcalf's Reports (1804–1842)* (Boston: C.C. Little & J. Brown, 1844).

[47] See note 43, Collins, Keene & Co. catalogue. Also see preface.

They could order all of the new law books published in the United States, England, and Europe. Little, Brown also gave them choices as to editions and format. For example, if readers of this catalogue wanted a set of Burrows' *Reports*, a set of great importance in many fields of the law including copyright, they had a choice of a five-volume set in octavo, published in New York in 1833, priced at twelve dollars; a 1768 London quarto edition, published in three volumes, priced at seven dollars and fifty cents; a 1794 Dublin edition in octavo in five volumes, priced at fifteen dollars; or a 1786 London folio edition in one volume, priced at six dollars. And, if buyers did not believe they needed the whole set but could make do with a condensed version, they could have this in two volumes published in New York in 1833 at seven dollars.[48]

Lawyers interested in English legal history could satisfy their wants with such titles as the 1663 edition of John Selden's *Mare Clausum* published in folio in London and priced at four dollars, and fifty cents or they could purchase a 1693 folio edition of Richard Brownlow's *Book of Entries* printed in London and priced at only three dollars and fifty cents.[49] If they were inclined to study Roman law, they could purchase a two-folio volume set of Gothofredus's edition of the *Corpus Iuris Civilis* published at Vitray in 1728.[50] This noble work was priced at thirteen dollars and fifty cents, not a bargain price, but the cataloguer noted that it was bound in "neat half calf." This variety of foreign and antiquarian works is fascinating. In some cases, we may speculate that they did not sell quickly because the same title often appears for years in successive catalogues. The fact that Little, Brown stocked them at all is evidence of

[48] Ibid.

[49] John Seldon, *Mare Clausum the Right and Dominion of the Sea in Two Books: In the First the Sea is Proved by the Law of Nature and Notions not to Be Common to All Men, but to Be Susceptible of Private Dominion and Propriety as well as the Land: In the Second It Is Asserted that the Most Serene King of Great Britain is the Lord and Proprietor of the Circumfluent and Surrounding Sea as an Inseparable and Perpetual Appendix of the British Empire* (London: Printed for Andrew Kembe and Edward Thomas, 1663); Richard Brownlow, *Brownlow Latine Redivivus: A Book of Entries, of Such Declarations, Informations, Pleas in Barr and Abatement, Replications, Rejoynders, Issues, Verdicts, Bills of Exception to Verdicts, Judgments, Demurrers, and Other Parts of Pleadings, (Now in Use) in Personal and Mixt Actions; Contained in the First and Second Parts of the Declarations and Pleadings* (London: Printed by the assigns of R. And E. Atkyns; and are to be sold by S. Heynick in Holborn, 1693).

[50] Gothofredus, *Corpus Iuris Civilis* (Vitray: Gothofredus, 1728).

both the profession's elite members' growing desire to transform the law into a "learned" profession as well as, perhaps, the booksellers' desire to add to their respectability and standing in the community by carrying such books. Also, by the date of this catalogue, the number of university-affiliated law schools in the United States was growing, and Little, Brown may well have hoped to sell some of their more esoteric stock to their libraries.[51]

Five years after Little, Brown published their catalogue, John S. Voorhies, located at 20 Nassau Street, published his second major catalogue (his first was published in 1844).[52] Voorhies began his law bookselling career as first an associate and then a partner of Oliver Halsted; on Halsted's death in 1842, Voorhies set up in business on his own.[53] By the time he published his catalogue in 1849, he had become a major force in New York law publishing and bookselling circles, and had gained the coveted exclusive right to publish the 1848 New York *Code*. Thus, his position in New York City closely approximated that of Little, Brown in Boston. This 1849 catalogue, in octavo format, consists of ninety-one numbered pages. The catalogue begins with a priced list of American state reports, collections of statutes and digests on pages 3–9. Beginning on page 10 is a reprint of Professor Greenleaf's "Select Library of Law Books." This is followed on pages 16–29 by an annotated and priced list of Voorhies's law publications. This list is followed by the list of law books for sale, which takes up the remaining sixty-one pages of the catalogue.

Voorhies's terms of sale were similar to those of Little, Brown. He solicited orders by letter from lawyers and their local merchants throughout the United States and promised that his terms would be as favorable "as any other establishment in the United States." He also promised that his mail-order prices would be "as low as if they were on the spot."[54] Finally, he advertised that he was always willing to purchase or exchange used law books. In terms of pricing in the main

[51] M.H. Hoeflich, *The Gladsome Light of Jurisprudence: Learning the Law in England and the United States in the 18th and 19th Centuries* (New York: Greenwood Press, 1988).

[52] John S. Voorhies, *Catalogue of Law Books for Sale by John S. Voorhies* (Law Bookseller & Publisher, sign of Lord Eldon, No. 20 Nassau, Near Cedar-Street, New York. New York, 1847).

[53] Ibid. [54] Ibid.

portion of the catalogue, Voorhies noted that some titles lacked a price. He explained that they were so listed because they are "scarce or of uncertain value," an indication that he, too, may have been listing titles that he did not always have in stock. And Voorhies, like his competitors, promised quantity discounts for large orders.[55]

The nature of the stock revealed by Voorhies's catalogue is not quite the same as that offered by Little, Brown. Voorhies offered most of the same then-current American and English titles as did Little, Brown. And like Little, Brown he included annotations, often extracts from reviews, of several of these titles. Unlike Little, Brown, however, Voorhies had few European books and very few books published before the Revolution. There may be several explanations for this difference. First, Voorhies may have judged that his customers had little use for civil law books, although Chancellor Kent certainly liked to cite selected civilian titles in his decisions and texts.[56] Another possibility is that Little, Brown's stocks reflected the greater availability and marketability of such texts because of the presence of Harvard, an institution whose faculty and students were quite interested in foreign law in the antebellum period.

Although the growth of railroads, canals, and the shipping companies that used them in the 1830s and 1840s helped to build the market for catalogue sales of law books, it was the change in postal regulations of 1851 to permit the shipping of books through the mails that gave the greatest advantage to the catalogue sales movement. At last, orders could be sent by mail to even distant parts of the Union. This change was reflected in both the size of catalogues and the entry into this market of new dealers who aspired to become national in their reach.

The Little, Brown catalogue of 1856 reflects the maturing of the catalogue sales market for law books.[57] This catalogue consists of 142 numbered pages and 72 pages of prefatory material. On offer are nearly 2,000 titles, of which more than 120 were published by Little, Brown.

[55] Ibid.

[56] William Kent, *Memoirs and Letters of James Kent, LLD* (Boston: Little, Brown, 1898), 117. See also Alan Watson, "Chancellor Kent's Use of Foreign Law," in *The Reception of Continental Ideas in the Common Law World, 1820–1920*, ed. Mathias Reimann (Berlin: Duncker & Humboldt, 1993).

[57] Charles C. Little and James P. Brown, *A General Catalogue of Law Books; Including all the Reports, Both English and American, from the Earliest Period* (Boston: Little, Brown & Co., 1856).

The proprietors make a point of the size and diversity of their offerings in their preface:

> Our long experience in the law-book selling business; the extent and variety of our assortment, comprising works in every department and branch of the law; the frequent visits of one of our firm to Europe for the purchase of making new purchases; together with the numerous and valuable and important issues of our own press, embracing the productions of many of the first law-writers of the age, – all enable us to offer inducements to those afforded by any other establishment.[58]

In this statement we see a reflection of a mature, successful business with a stable of established authors for the publishing arm and a reliable stream of foreign as well as domestic books for the selling arm. In fact, the opening of the U.S. mail to books removed one of the great advantages firms like Little, Brown and Voorhies enjoyed – namely, proximity to major shipping lines and transportation networks. After 1851, anyone near a post office, even in the remote West, could ship and receive books. One advantage East Coast firms like Little, Brown continued to enjoy, which they were quick to point out, was their proximity to transatlantic shipping, thus making their access to foreign, including English books, greater than those of their inland and rural competitors.

Like its predecessors, the 1856 Little, Brown catalogue includes in its prefatory material not only a list of Little, Brown's own law publications but also lists and indices of English and American reporters, clearly intended not only to sell these volumes but also to serve as a reference for lawyers using the catalogue. Something contained in this catalogue, not present in the catalogues from the 1840s and before, is a subject index at the back of the catalogue. Subject headings in this index include "English Law," "Bailments," and so on. This would have been a very useful tool for beginning lawyers both in terms of building their libraries and as a reference to works on a particular area of the law; therefore, this index would have served as a replacement for Greenleaf's list, which, by 1856, was growing outdated.[59]

[58] Ibid.

[59] John G. Marvin, *Legal Bibliography, as a Thesaurus of American, English, Irish, and Scotch Law Books; Together with Some Continental Treatises. Interspersed with*

Banks, Gould, and Company, the venerable New York law publishers and booksellers, also saw a rapid increase in their catalogue's size and offerings in the 1850s. Their 1852 catalogue, in octavo, contains 143 pages of prefatory material, 134 pages of books for sale, and a final subject index. In their preface, they too boasted of the quantity and diversity of their stock:

> We believe that we have on hand the largest and most complete assortment of Law Books ever offered for sale in the United States ... The increasing disposition to study the Civil Law has induced us to turn our attention also in that direction, and we are prepared to execute any order for Foreign or Continental Law Books with great promptness.[60]

In addition to the growth of the great northeastern law book companies, the 1850s also saw the rise of Cincinnati as a hub of printing and publishing for the western United States.[61] H.W. Derby & Company was one of the first and most successful of the Cincinnati law book publishers and retail booksellers.[62] Derby was bought out by Robert Clarke & Company, which published a catalogue of its stock in 1860.[63] This catalogue was published in quarto with paper covers and consists of four pages of unnumbered preliminary matter and eighty-five numbered pages.[64]

Like its eastern counterparts, the Clarke catalogue is designed to not only showcase the books for sale but also have value as a reference guide for those lawyers lucky enough to possess a copy. It provides a list of Clarke's own legal publications as well as more than 450 other titles for sale, and includes an alphabetical index to American state and federal reports, a list of the American editions of English reports, and

Critical Observations upon their Various Editions and Authority. To which is Prefixed a Copious List of Abbreviations (Philadelphia: T. & J.W. Johnson, 1847); on Marvin, see M.H. Hoeflich, "Annals of Legal Bibliography," *Law Library Journal*, 96 (2004): 333–43.

60 Banks, Gould, & Co., *A General Catalogue of Modern Law Books: Including the Old Reports* (New York: Banks, Gould, 1852).

61 W. Sutton, *The Western Book-Trade* (Columbus: Ohio State University Press, 1961); Gerald S. Greenberg, "Isaac N. Whiting: Pioneer Bookseller and Publisher of Columbus, Ohio," *Publishing History*, 28 (1990): 57–77.

62 Ibid., 134–49.

63 Erwin C. Surrency, *A History of American Law Publishing* (New York: Oceana, 1990), 229–30.

64 Robert Clarke & Co., *General Law Catalogue of Robert Clarke & Co., Successor to H W. Derby & Co., Publishers and Importers* (Cincinnati, OH: Robert Clarke, 1860).

a chronological list of British reports and reporters. After the list of treatises for sale (the reports and other official publications are priced separately), there is a useful subject index.

As is true in other catalogues discussed here, the preface is the place for puffery. The Clarke catalogue states:

> Our stock embraces a large and general assortment of Law Books, both ancient and modern – the most complete in the Western States. New Books and new Federal and State Reports received as soon as issued ... We would call especial attention to the Importing Branch of our business. Orders for Foreign Books, Law and Miscellaneous, old and new, are forwarded weekly.[65]

It is clear from these statements that Clarke was prepared to go head-to-head with his eastern competitors, not just with his American and English books but with foreign texts as well. Clarke also offered a service not offered, or at least not publicized, by the eastern law booksellers. He stated:

> Our business connection in London affords great facilities for the collection of OLD, RARE WORKS, and such modern Books as are "OUT OF PRINT." LOVERS OF OLD BOOKS can consult at our store priced catalogues of old booksellers' stocks in London, Edinburgh, Dublin, and other cities of Great Britain and Ireland, which are regularly received, and from which we import selections made ... Copies [of the catalogues] sent by mail to persons at a distance, on application.[66]

In this statement we learn not only that Clarke hoped to conduct a business in rare and used law books and that he had arranged to receive catalogues from law booksellers throughout England, Scotland, and Ireland, but also that he was even prepared to send copies of these to customers who could not visit his Cincinnati shop. Thus, by 1860, even those lawyers, like Daniel Mulford Valentine, who were located far from the major eastern centers of trade and learning, could purchase by mail a complete law library, including works on foreign law as well as antiquarian and out-of-print texts, should they so desire.

Clarke's pricing policies were similar to those of the larger eastern houses. The prices recorded in the catalogue were retail prices at "the regular publisher's rates." He was more than willing, however, to give a discount for quantity orders and for "particular books purchased."[67]

[65] Ibid. [66] Ibid. [67] Ibid.

Interestingly, Clarke also stated that these were cash prices or prices for those who were "punctual customers." We may assume that for others, interest would be charged for credit extended. The insistence on cash may well have been particularly necessary in the West, where trustworthy specie was often scarce or unavailable.[68] A letter from the "Western Law Book House" of D. B. Cooke & Company, based in Chicago, dated 1858 and sent to a would-be customer in Iowa, illustrates this problem:

> Yours ... received, we do not wish to trade books for land for the reasons that we cannot trade land for books to the publishers, and we do not wish to go into outside operations. Should you make a selection from the inclosed catalogue we will make you a liberal discount for cash money.[69]

One might suggest that so eccentric a proposed transaction from a frontier lawyer in 1858 shows how widespread was the sale and distribution of law books by catalogue by the advent of the Civil War. The American law book trade had most certainly grown up.

BOOK ADVERTISEMENTS

Although catalogues were by far the most widespread and effective means of selling law books in antebellum America, a number of law publishers and booksellers did not stop at this technique. Indeed, several houses developed extensive advertising programs using various printed materials. This is not at all surprising because the large bookselling houses were also usually printers and publishers and often had close connections with periodicals, including newspapers.

The format taken by the various types of advertisements used by law booksellers (and general booksellers, as well) was dictated, in part, by costs of both production and distribution. The most inexpensive way to distribute an advertisement for a bookseller's products was by binding a short catalogue or advertisement into a law book. This was done frequently throughout the antebellum period. Several factors affected the use of this technique, however. First, this could only be effective

[68] On the collapse of the currency after the Jacksonian victory over the Bank of the United States in 1836, see H.W. Brands, *The Money Men: Capitalism, Democracy, and the Hundred Years War over the American Dollar* (New York: Norton, 2006), 57–95.

[69] See www.antebellumlegalpublishing.org.

when the book was sold bound or to be bound by the bookseller or its affiliated binder. During the earlier part of the century, when many law books were sold unbound, this was less feasible. But by the mid-1830s, the catalogues reveal that increasing numbers of law books were sold bound, in boards, sheep, or calf. Thus, as the antebellum period progressed, the use of bound-in advertisements became more feasible, and the evidence of extant books from this period is that it came to be used quite often.

A second means of distributing law book advertisements was through the mails. The most inexpensive means of achieving this after 1845 was to send such advertisements as letters.[70] These advertisements took the general format of a single folded sheet, usually to form a quarto, printed on several sides with one side left blank to serve as the outer portion of the letter-advertisement on which the address could be written and the postage stamped. An example of such an advertisement is that sent by Robert H. Small, a law bookseller and publisher based in Philadelphia.[71] This advertisement was printed and mailed in September 1852. It is a single folio sheet that has been folded to form a quarto four page pamphlet. Three sides are printed on and carry details of books available. The fourth page was left blank. When mailed, the pamphlet was folded in half horizontally and then in thirds vertically in order to approximate a normal-sized letter. On this final version, the address of the recipient was written by hand along with the annotation "circular" for the post office. The example examined carries a one-cent postal marking from the Philadelphia Post Office. This was the normal postal rate for a standard-weight domestic letter.

The content of this advertisement is what one would expect. The advertisement is titled "Valuable Law Books." The advertisement states that "ready money" will bring a 20 percent discount from the listed prices. There then follows a listing of eighteen law books, newly published, for sale by Small. Several are annotated extensively with extracts drawn from legal periodicals such as the *Boston Law Reporter* and *The Jurist*.[72]

[70] The cost of such a letter before 1845 was prohibitive, beginning at twenty-five cents. After 1845, the cost dropped to five cents for the first half-ounce.

[71] See www.antebellumlegalpublishing.org.

[72] Small also utilized the inside covers of law books he published for advertising; see, for example, R.S.D. Roper and H.H. White, *A Treatise on the Law of Legacies* (Philadelphia: R.H. Small, 1848), 2 vols. In both volumes the inside covers contain a

Advertisements such as Robert Small's served several important purposes. First, they sold books. But they also served a valuable function for the lawyers who received them: These were notices that the books that they had been using were now either outdated or supplemented by later editions. Further, because the production of new legal treatises was increasing substantially after the mid-1820s, these advertisements also notified the practicing Bar of texts on legal subjects heretofore not yet announced otherwise.[73] We can only imagine the positive reaction of practicing lawyers when notified by such advertisements of a new treatise by Justice Story or Mr. Chitty.

The didactic function of law booksellers' advertisements reached its high point in the 1840s and 1850s, when several law booksellers actually began to publish legal periodicals that combined advertising with helpful articles. This was a large step beyond simply adding annotations to book listings. In 1845, Lea & Blanchard of Philadelphia published Volume 1, Number 1 of the *Literary News and Law Intelligencer*.[74] In format, it is a quarto pamphlet of thirty-two pages. Therefore, it would have been sent as a periodical, as the name indicates, at the reduced rate for such mail. It is an elaborate production, with pictorial illustrations and a large variety of type fonts designed to make the text striking.

The content of the pamphlet is not solely devoted to the law books and the law. There are advertisements and notices about other books, including several on Western exploration, history, geography, cooking, gardening, and medicine. The final few pages advertise school books. Although the pamphlet has the physical appearance and title of a periodical, only the first two pages of the thirty-two are not advertisements. These two pages are a melange of literary and legal gossip along with notices of new law books to be published.[75] Especially interesting are the notices of three recent English cases.[76] Further, there is also a

list of books published and for sale by Small. This is especially interesting in that it indicates that Small sold these volumes already bound; note that the advertisements are on the inside covers rather than on separate sheets, as is usually the case during the period.

[73] Although legal periodicals like *The American Jurist* and general literary journals like *The North American Review* and *Southern Literary Messenger* did make lists of recently published books, by no means were all new books listed.

[74] *Literary News and Law Intelligencer*, 1 (1) (Philadelphia, Lea & Blanchard, 1845).

[75] Ibid. [76] Ibid.

notice of French legal activity, including the French view on the proposed international copyright agreement.[77] These were likely notices that lawyers would not have had available from other sources. Thus, for the first time, a law booksellers' advertising provided not only useful information about new law books but new information about new developments in the law in France and Germany – thus the inclusion of the phrase "law intelligencer" in the title of the pamphlet. Certainly, the amount of added value for the reader of this pamphlet was not great; however, the pamphlet was sent free of charge. What Lea & Blanchard had clearly come to believe was that by increasing the utility of their advertising to the recipients, they would raise the likelihood that their advertising would be read. Several years later, as Chapter 6 discusses, John Livingston of New York carried this principle to even greater lengths.[78]

Law booksellers' use of mail advertising was only as effective as their ability to compile or purchase lists of likely purchasers of books to whom they might send their catalogues and advertisements. In this sense, mail advertising and catalogues were related, because the same list would be used for both. But how would the booksellers obtain the names of would-be recipients? A hint of one way this was done is provided by the Lea & Blanchard pamphlet. The following notice appears at the bottom of the first page:

> Gentlemen who receive this would oblige the Publishers by handing it to their friends. Lists of the names of Lawyers, Physicians and others with their address, will be thankfully received, to whom this publication will occasionally be sent.[79]

Thus, they solicited lists from those who already had their publication. And they offered an inducement, a "subscription" to future issues in exchange.

In fact, the law booksellers and publishers would seem to have exploited virtually every opportunity that could be found to advertise their wares. An example of such opportunistic advertising is the standard form of invoice used by most of the major houses. For the most part, booksellers, including those specializing in law, used preprinted invoice forms during most of the antebellum period. In the 1860s, W.C. Little of

[77] Ibid. [78] See Chapter 6. [79] *Literary News*.

New York City used a half-sheet on which was printed details of the shop, terms of sale and, in the top left corner, a list of twenty-eight law texts he had published.[80] T. & J. W. Johnson of Philadelphia exploited their preprinted invoice form even more.[81] Their form was a full sheet. On the top right were details of the firm. On the top left was a box containing a priced list of ten of their legal publications, indicating the binding, including *The Law Library*, and a general advertisement: "Together with all the Reports published in the different states, and a large stock of English and French Law."

In addition to their increasing use of the U.S. mails to send catalogues and advertising, legal booksellers and publishers also used both newspapers and periodicals to advertise their books. Newspaper advertisements, often only a paragraph or two, were used from an early date, when fuller catalogue listings were not. For example, in 1793, George Davis, a Philadelphia bookseller, advertised law books for sale in the *Pennsylvania Gazette*:

LAW BOOKS

George Davis ... respectfully informs the gentlemen of the bar and their students, in this and other states, that by the Camilla, just arrived from Dublin, he has received a Collection of Law Books, the titles of which will appear in our next catalogue.[82]

Newspapers could also be used for more detailed advertisements of a single book, complete with testimonials to the book's value. For example, Lucas advertised Virginia law professor Francis Gilmer's *Sketches and Essays* in the *Baltimore Patriot* for January 30, 1828. In this advertisement he not only spoke of the importance of the book to the public, but also quoted "extracts" from five letters praising Gilmer's works.[83]

[80] See www.antebellumlegalpublishing.org.

[81] See www.antebellumlegalpublishing.org.

[82] The *Pennsylvania Gazette*, May 1, 1793; it is interesting to note that law schools also used newspapers to advertise their courses; see, for example, the *Independent Chronicle & Boston Patriot* (January7, 1835), 4, column 6 for an advertisement for the Harvard Law School.

[83] *Baltimore Patriot and Mercantile Advertiser* (January 30, 1828), 1, column 6.

Law magazines, such as the *American Jurist* and the *American Law Magazine*, also provided a perfect vehicle for advertising new law books.[84] These journals regularly featured lengthy reviews of law books and also regularly included lists of new publications in the law, both domestic and foreign. For example, the July 1835 issue of the *American Jurist* contained reviews of six new law books and listed ten new European and five new American law books.[85] It also listed notices of two new American law books then in press.[86] Whereas a favorable review could do much to improve sales, a negative review might well have just the opposite effect. When a publisher–bookseller produced the periodical, as did Lea & Blanchard and later John Livingston, there was no risk of this happening. But independently produced periodicals like the *American Jurist* were not so safe. In the July 1835 issue, for example, the review the newly published *Supplement to Petersdorff's Abridgement of English Common Law Cases* began: This a mere bookseller's job, with hardly labor enough infused into it to save the copyright.[87] One may suspect that this review did not help sales. Although sellers of new and used law books and publishers of new ones dominated the antebellum law book trade, they did not monopolize it. Not all used law books were sold through the trade. A small amount of used law books were sold by a related, but separate merchant group: auctioneers. This specialized trade group is the focus of the Chapter 4.

[84] *The American Jurist* (Boston: Freeman & Bolles, 1829–1843); *American Law Magazine* (Philadelphia: T. & J.W. Johnson, 1843–1846).
[85] *The American Jurist.* [86] Ibid. [87] "Review," *The American Jurist* (July 1835).

Chapter 4
Bidding for Law Books

In autumn 1859, the United States was in a tumult. The South and the North were rapidly approaching a point of no return on the road to secession and civil war. Politicians were battling for the highest national office, and every American was preoccupied with what was soon to come. Yet amid this political and social turmoil, a young lawyer sat at his desk in New Hampshire writing his most intimate thoughts in his diary.[1] These thoughts were not of slavery or of gathering war clouds; they were about a book auction. Stephen Greeley Clarke, the son of the Attorney-General of the State of New Hampshire, had been a lawyer for only a few years on Sunday evening, November 20, 1859, when he added several pages to his journal/commonplace book. Like most young lawyers of his time and social standing, he was much concerned with building his personal and professional library. He confided to his journal that he had "been adding some" to his libraries "of late," especially from the "magnificent private library" of Rufus Choate. But his pleasure at purchasing these volumes was bittersweet:

> Have been adding some to my library of late – both my own and the Law L. of the firm – A portion of both came from the Libraries of the Late Mr. Choate – He had a magnificent private library – It made me feel bad to read the catalogue – and worse to see the books and realize how few of even those that I should most desire I could hope to possess –"[2]

[1] See www.antebellumlegalpublishing.org.
[2] See www.antebellumlegalpublishing.org.

For a young educated lawyer like Clarke, book auctions presented opportunities to purchase books, both rare and common, at prices they might never again see.

Auction catalogues have a great deal to offer both legal historians and historians of the book in America.[3] Law book auction catalogues are perhaps the best source for reconstructing private law libraries from the antebellum period. In a few cases, we still possess manuscript catalogues of such libraries, such as the hand-list of James Kent's library now at Columbia or Emory Washburn's manuscript catalogue now at the American Antiquarian Society, but these are unusual.[4] Many lawyers, even those who possessed important libraries either did not have catalogues made during their lifetimes; or, if such were made, they are now lost. Similarly, post-mortem probate lists, though useful when they exist, are often sketchy in details, so that any serious reconstruction of the library of the deceased is impossible.

There are difficulties in reconstructing libraries from auction catalogues. Often, auctioneers would add books to an auction that were not from the principal library for sale. Occasionally, there is also more than one catalogue of the auction of a single library, such as is the case with the library of Hugh Swinton Legare, and it is difficult to discover the precise parameters of the library or account for differences between the different versions of the catalogue.[5] It is also impossible to create a statistically valid sample from which to make sweeping generalizations. The number of such catalogues published during this period that are identifiable as law related is too small. Even with these problems,

[3] Historians have done work with English and European book auction catalogues; there now exists a substantial literature on these, but much remains to be done. A useful starting point is the December 1995 volume (89 [4]) of *The Papers of the Biographical Society of America*, ed. Roger Stoddard, which contains papers from the 1995 conference "Book Catalogues, Today and Tomorrow;" as is Robin Myers, Michael E. Harris, and Giles Mandelbrote, eds., *Under the Hammer: Book Auctions since the Seventeenth Century* (New Castle, DE: Oak Knoll Press, 2001) and see other books and articles cited.

[4] On Kent's library and his reading therein, see John Langbein, "Chancellor Kent and the History of Legal Literature," *Columbia Law Review*, 93 (1993): 547–94.

[5] See Hoeflich, 163, note 41. Another problem case is that of the library auction sale of Joseph Story's books. There are two catalogues extant, one from 1846 and the other from 1856. On these, see M. H. Hoeflich and K. Beck, ed. *The 1846 Auction Catalogue of Joseph Story's Library* (Austin: Jamail Center for Legal Research, 2004).

however, auction catalogues provide an incredibly rich resource for library reconstruction. Equally important, in regard to catalogues of law book auctions, it was not only the libraries of notable lawyers and jurists that were sold by auction, but also the smaller libraries of ordinary lawyers. Thus, we are able to discover much about not only the greatest law libraries of the antebellum period but also about the libraries of common lawyers in ordinary practice.

Law book auction catalogues are also of immense value for a second related type of research. These catalogues permit us to learn a great deal about the sale and distribution of law books in the antebellum United States, the subject of this book. The fact that a law bookseller lists a particular work in its catalogue as available is not necessarily evidence that the book was, in fact, available for sale. On the contrary, there is good evidence that law booksellers listed volumes for sale that they did not have in stock and may well not have been able to supply at will.[6] The presence of a book in an auction catalogue almost certainly means that the book was, indeed, owned by someone and that it was in circulation at the time in the United States. Again, one finds significant differences in the numbers of foreign books listed for sale by booksellers like Livingston or Little, Brown and those listed for sale in even the largest law book auctions. This may indicate either that booksellers listed books in the belief that they could obtain them, if ordered, but did not necessarily stock them or that many foreign books were kept in small quantities on booksellers' shelves but simply may not have sold.

A third significant fact that may be gleaned from the study of antebellum law book auction catalogues is the extent to which lawyers were willing to invest in their libraries. Information about the cost and value of law libraries during this period is hard to come by. Booksellers' catalogues can give us some indication of the cost of law books in the primary retail market, but they tell us nothing about how much lawyers actually invested in their libraries or what the secondary market for law books was like.[7] All of this can be learned to some degree through the study of law book auction catalogues.

[6] This would appear to have been the case, for example, in regard to John Livingston's law book catalogues; see Chapter 6.

[7] For example, Emory Washburn listed in his manuscript library catalogue, now at the American Antiquarian Society, that "... the prices set to the books are those for which

Finally, one occasionally comes upon an auction catalogue that provides, at least for the book historian, a remarkably exciting treasure trove of information. One such catalogue, found in the collection of the American Antiquarian Society, is a record of a sale of what was most likely the combined stock of two substantial law book publishers and booksellers' businesses in Philadelphia and New York. In this catalogue is exceptionally important information about the forms in which law books were produced and marketed, relative quantities of books available, and costs.[8]

Looking at the catalogue as a whole, several facts become immediately obvious about the sale of law books by auction during this period. First, auctions of law books in the United States clearly predate 1800.[9] Indeed, such auctions were an established part of the bookselling landscape during the eighteenth century. It is equally clear, however, that the "golden age" of law book auctions in antebellum America was the 1840s and 1850s, periods in which such auctions reached the double digits. As we have seen, this is also the period in which the antebellum law book trade reached maturity and in which the great houses like Little, Brown became truly national in the scope of their business

they were purchased when recollected and in no cases excluding the lowest catalogue prices of the bookstores – many of them are less than half price – as they were bought at auction," 1, note in *Catalogue of Books Belonging to the Library of Emory Washburn*, AAS call no. "Misc. Mss, Box 'W'".

[8] The study of these auction catalogues has been made significantly easier by several bibliographical resources. The first is George L. McKay's *American Book Auction Catalogues, 1713–1934*. This volume provides a union list of auction catalogues based on an extensive survey of contemporary sources, including newspapers and modern library catalogues. The volume also contains an extremely helpful list of American book auction houses and locations of catalogue copies in contemporary locations, when known. The original 1937 edition of McKay was supplemented in 1946 and 1948. The copy of McKay now at the American Antiquarian Society has itself been further annotated and updated by the AAS staff and includes several items not found in the 1948 supplemented edition. McKay is usefully supplemented for nineteenth century items, in particular, by Professor Morris Cohen's magisterial *Bibliography of Early American Law*; see Morris Cohen, *Bibliography of Early American Law* (Buffalo, NY: Hein, 1998). Although this catalogue lists fewer law book auction catalogues than McKay, it gives far greater bibliographical detail about those catalogues listed. These two published sources are, themselves, usefully supplemented by the catalogues of several contemporary collections, particularly those at the Library of Congress and the Harvard Law School. Taken together, although these bibliographical sources do not provide us with a complete picture of law book auctions in the United States in the nineteenth century, they do give us, at the very least, a good overview.

[9] See, for example, McKay, *American Book Auctions*, listing sales including law books.

activity. Second, it is clear that law book auctions, like the great law booksellers, tended to be located primarily in the major northeastern cities, particularly Boston, New York, and Philadelphia, although later in the century St. Louis also became a center for such sales.[10] Third, the law book auction trade was dominated by a few auction houses, similar to the law bookselling trade. Leonard & Company, for example, was the equivalent in the law book auction world to Little, Brown in the law bookselling and publishing world. Fourth, law book auctions were not limited only to the great law libraries or to antiquarian law books. One could purchase quite mundane law books from working lawyers' libraries at auction, often, as we shall see, at a significant price discount. In contrast, books owned by eminent lawyers and judges were in demand and no doubt sold, particularly when annotated, at a premium.[11]

For the most part, it seems that those libraries that were sold at auction tended to be those of deceased lawyers. One may speculate that many executors of lawyers' estates chose the route of selling their goods, including their libraries, at auction rather than by private sale or sale to a dealer. Again, although there is little hard information as to why this was the case, the reasons were probably the same then as they are today. To sell an estate library at auction was often more lucrative to the estate because most dealers would be willing to pay only a fraction of the open market value of books. This was probably especially true when dealing with books with valuable provenances. Further, it may well have been difficult for many retail booksellers to raise the capital sufficient to buy a large library en masse, whereas an auction would produce an immediate return to the estate.

It is also important to spend a few moments considering the printed catalogues produced for law book auctions. These could range in size and sophistication from a single-sheet broadside with little detail as to individual books to the very elaborate pamphlets published by the major auctioneers in connection with the sale of important law libraries.

[10] See McKay, *American Book Auctions*, pp. xvii–xxxi and the essay by Clarence S. Brigham, "History of Book Auctions in America," in McKay, *American Book Auctions*, 1–3.

[11] I base this judgement on the fact that annotated volumes listed in auction catalogues of libraries such as Justice Joseph Story's often list when a particular volume has annotations; see, for example, *Catalogue of Law and Miscellaneous Books, Belonging to the Library of the Late Mr. Justice Story* ... (Boston: A. Mudge, 1846), n. 7: "Littleton's Tenures 'autograph.'"

Again, it is extremely difficult to know how many catalogues were produced for the average sale and how far they were distributed. One may assume that a sufficient number were produced to satisfy the Bar in the city in which a sale was held as well as more distant dealers and interested parties. Certainly, by the 1840s, retail booksellers like Little, Brown in Boston were producing large numbers of catalogues and distributing them widely by mail. There is little reason to doubt that the sale catalogues of libraries such as those owned by Rufus Choate or Joseph Story were not similarly treated. Contemporary newspaper accounts confirm this.[12] Moreover, I own copies of the two 1855 sale catalogues of the Purviance library at Baltimore, Maryland.[13] These catalogues bear two indications that they were widely distributed. The first is the provenance mark on the cover of the law library catalogue. This indicates that the catalogue was in the Union College Library in upstate New York during the nineteenth century. The second indication of its distribution comes from an unusual preface appended to the law book catalogue.[14] This catalogue's preface is virtually unique among nineteenth-century law book auction catalogues because it bears printed values for the books, designed to provide bidders some idea of the retail market value of each title. The preface notes, however, that a secondary purpose in adding these prices was so that lawyers "in the interior of the country" might use this catalogue as a reference work to aid them in subsequent book purchases.[15] That the auctioneers believed it was possible that their catalogues would be retained and used by lawyers far removed from Baltimore would suggest that in their experience such catalogues had a far greater geographical distribution pattern than simply a local one.

Another significant fact about these law book auctions is that many of these sales included books that were not professional law books and,

[12] The ProQuest online data base contains the text of *The New York Times* from 1859 on; the following notice dated 12 September 1859, on p. 2 reads: "The Boston Journal is informed that the library of Rufus Choate will be sold at auction in October. It consists of 10,000 volumes, of which one-third are law books."

[13] *Catalogue of the Miscellaneous Library (Theological, Classical, etc.) of late Judge Purviance, of Baltimore* (Baltimore: James Young, 1855) [sold by Gibson & Co.]; *Catalogue of Judge Purviance's Common and Civil Law Library* (Baltimore: James Young, 1855) [sold by Gibson & Co.], McKay, 679 [hereafter "Purviance Law Catalogue"].

[14] *Purviance Law Catalogue*, 1–2.

[15] Ibid., 1.

indeed, not law books at all. This fact, too, is not at all surprising. Lawyers in antebellum America were not all narrowly educated and narrowly read people with little interest outside the law.[16] On the contrary, the typical American lawyer of the period had broad interests in politics and history, as well as the arts and humanities.[17] Some lawyers, like Rufus Choate, amassed major specialist libraries outside the narrow confines of the law. Choate's library was one of the greatest American antebellum classics libraries, rich in both Greek and Latin texts and the scholarship appurtenant thereto.[18] Other lawyers were quite catholic in their tastes. Gustavus Schmidt, one of the greatest figures at the antebellum Louisiana Bar, collected French novels and purchased by subscription one of the first sets of Audubon's *Birds* sold in the United States.[19] Judge Purviance's library sale required two catalogues and two sales. The first sale was of his general library, which was particularly strong in theology; the second sale was devoted specifically to his law books.[20]

Even the professional law books sold at these auctions were not solely those one would expect to belong to a narrowly trained lawyer and practitioner. Virtually every sale of a substantial library contained copies of case reports and legislative materials, as well as the standard English and American treatises on the Common law and its various specialties likes contracts or property of wills and trusts. But these library sale catalogues also reveal that American lawyers possessed books on foreign law, particularly Roman law and the laws in force in France and Germany at the time.[21] In part, these holdings reflect the great influence Roman and Civil law exerted on American law,

[16] See Chapter 1.

[17] See, for example, R. Ferguson, *Law and Letters in America History* (Cambridge, MA: Harvard University Press, 1984); and Chapter 1.

[18] The number of classical texts as well as the level of classical scholarship represented by them had few matches in contemporary private libraries.

[19] Gustavus Schmidt, *Catalogue of a Large and Valuable Library* ... (St. Louis, MO: Souls, Thomas & Wentworth, 1877); the unique surviving catalogue of this library is now at Tulane Law Library. See M.H. Hoeflich and Louis del la Vergne, "Gustavus Schmidt: His Life and Library," in *The 1877 Sale Catalogue of Gustavus Schmidt's Library*, ed. M.H. Hoeflich and Louis de la Verne (Austin, TX: Tarlton Law Library, 2005), 5–15.

[20] Schmidt, *Catalogue of a Large and Valuable Library.*

[21] From my reading of these catalogues over the past decade, I would estimate that perhaps 25 percent contain several or more works on Roman law and modern civil law.

especially in such areas as admiralty and commercial law. These holdings reflect, as well, the rather sophisticated notion commonly held by members of the American Bar that the law was a learned profession and that part of this scholarly heritage must be a serious interest in both legal history and comparative law.

The specific types of works found generally in these sale catalogues of private libraries provide some significant evidence of the interests of American lawyers in their professional activities. For example, one finds, generally, that lawyers owned the published case reports from their own jurisdiction as well as case reports from a few other jurisdictions, particularly those from New York and Massachusetts. The fact that one finds New York reports far more frequently than, for example, Connecticut reports in these catalogues suggests that the decisions of the New York courts were held in higher esteem outside New York than were Connecticut reports outside Connecticut. Also, one can gain some insight into the actual popularity of individual authors, both living and dead. It comes as no surprise, for example, that the works of Blackstone and Story were immensely popular, judging by their appearance in auction sale catalogues. What is perhaps more surprising, given the apparent scarcity of such items in the United States, are the numbers of pre-nineteenth-century law books printed in England and on the continent that also appear in these catalogues. The frequency of the appearance of such antiquarian texts, even in libraries of modest size, suggests that the importation of such treatises may have been even greater than suggested by the works of some scholars.[22] It also may suggest that lawyers who would have had very little practical use for such books in nineteenth-century America found some other value (i.e. prestige) in the ownership of such volumes, a supposition borne out by other evidence.[23]

[22] See Erwin C. Surrency, *A History of American Law Publishing* (New York: Oceana, 1990), 142.

[23] On the "prestige" value of law books for lawyers, see M.H. Hoeflich, "Lawyers, Books, and Pages," *Green Bag*, 5 (2, 2002): 163–72; see also Ann Fidler, "'Till You Understand Them in Their Principal Features': Observations on Form and Function in Nineteenth-Century American Law Books," *Papers of the Bibliographical Society of America* 92, no. 4 (1998): 427–42.

The best way to understand the nature and scope of the law book auctions that occurred during the antebellum period, and of the libraries that were sold at these auctions, is to examine a few of the sales closely.

One of the most interesting law book auction sales to take place during the antebellum period was held in Baltimore in October 1855. The sale was an estate sale of books belonging to a well-known local judge, John Purviance.[24] The sale catalogue was actually in two parts. The first part of the catalogue was devoted to the general library, which was advertised as being especially strong in works of theology and classical literature. The second catalogue, obviously designed for a specialized market, listed the contents of the judge's law library. The auctioneer was Gibson & Co., and the auction was held in their salesrooms on North Charles Street in the city. The general catalogue was divided into five sections: miscellaneous, classical, theological, church fathers, and American history and politics. The first section consisted of 385 numbered lots; the second, 164; the third, 343; the fourth, 16; the fifth, 128. Many of the lots comprised multiple items. The law book catalogue was divided into two sections. The first section, devoted to works on the common law, consisted of 889 numbered lots. The second section, devoted to books on the civil law, consisted of 169 numbered lots. Lots in both sections were arranged alphabetically.

The Purviance catalogues are unusual in several respects, but particularly because they contain a substantial amount of information about the auctioneers and the auction sales. First, a note in the first catalogue provides strong evidence that the auctioneers did not prepare the sales catalogue entirely on their own but rather used a list prepared by the administrator of Judge Purviance's estate (presumably as part of the probate process). That this was the case is confirmed by an introductory note to the law catalogue to the effect that the prices provided as guides to books listed in the common law section of the catalogue were, in fact, provided by the administrator who had first made up a priced list of these books in the hopes of making a private sale of the entire library.[25] The inclusion of such price guides was, as noted previously, quite unusual. One does find, on occasion, auction catalogues of this sort with prices inserted by hand by a participant in the auction, but pre-printed prices to be used by would-be purchasers as guides is very

[24] *Purviance Law Catalogue.* [25] Ibid., 12.

unusual in law book auction catalogues of this period.[26] Retail prices would not have provided exact values for purchasers because evidence suggests that auction prices were generally substantially lower on such books than retail prices. In contrast, such prices might well have served as guides for bidding, particularly to the upper limit of values because books could be obtained from retail book sellers at these prices.[27]

Both catalogues have information on how they might be obtained and how individuals unable to attend in person could still bid on items. The catalogues were available from not only the auctioneers but also other Baltimore booksellers who were prepared to act as agents for bidding at the auction. In addition, catalogues could also be obtained from the estate's lawyer as well as the estate administrator. The catalogues were offered postage paid. Finally, the note recommends that successful absentee bidders might want to use a particular freight company, Adams' Express, for the "safe transmission" of their purchases.[28]

The catalogues themselves were issued in pamphlet form, octavo with paper covers. The copy in my possession has the remnants of a postmark stamp on its rear cover, suggesting that it was mailed as is, without a wrapper or envelope. A note on the cover of the catalogue of the general library gives some indication of the order of sale: The general books were to be sold in the morning and the law books were to come under the hammer that evening, but changes in accord with "the views of purchasers" were said to be possible. One may assume that the auctioneers wanted to save the law books until the evening, when more lawyers, freed of their professional duties of the day, might attend.

[26] The use of book auction catalogues as price reference guides is of some antiquity, stretching back at least as far as the seventeenth century in Europe; see M. H. Hoeflich, "Bibliography in the Seventeenth Century: J. G. Graevius' Lectures," *The Library*, 32 (1977): 48f.; M.H. Hoeflich, "Two Heinsius-Related Volumes in the University Library, Cambridge," *Transactions of the Cambridge Bibliographical Society* (1975): 262ff.

[27] A printed note at the top of wrappers on the Harvard copy of the Purviance catalogue was a "reserve catalogue." This may indicate that the prices were included because there were auction reserves placed on the items up for sale. Without further information, however, it is impossible to know.

[28] *Purviance Law Catalogue*, rear cover; on The Adams Express Company, see Richard B. Kielbowicz, "Mere Merchandise or Vessels of Culture? Books in the Mail, 1792–1942", *Papers of the Bibliographical Society of America*, 82 (1988): 169–200.

The compilers of the sale catalogues did not hesitate to comment on particular aspects of the books or on the special desirability of certain volumes. According to Madeleine Stern, by the time of the Purviance sale, the cult of antiquarian books had spread to the United States, and antiquarian booksellers were to be found in several major American cities.[29] It seems that interest among some members of the Bar in antiquarian law books was also significant, enough so that such volumes were specially identified in catalogues like this.[30] The introduction to the law book sale catalogue takes pains to advertise the presence of several antiquarian volumes in the sale, including a *Provinciale* of 1505 and a copy of a 1585 Fitzherbert. The cataloguer also notes, however, as to the condition of these older volumes, that they had undergone "the mellowing influence of time."[31]

Individual lots are generally well described. Each volume is listed by title and author and both the place and date of publication are given when known. Occasionally one finds a note as to condition (i.e. "a fine copy").[32] One also finds special notes such as the cataloguer's comment that a copy of the 1686 London edition of Malyne's *Law Merchant* is a "scarce and valuable work."[33] These notes suggest that the catalogue was compiled with the assistance of someone familiar with the law – probably, in this case, the estate administrator.

Not all of the volumes sold at the auction were separately listed in the catalogue. A note in the general catalogue tells the reader that several unbound periodicals and other volumes not listed by the administrator of the estate, but found by the auctioneer, were to be sold.[34] Similarly, the law book catalogue notes that periodicals, pamphlets, and other

[29] Madeleine B. Stern, *Antiquarian Book Selling in the United States* (Westport, CT: Greenwood, 1985), vii–xviii.

[30] Not all lawyers thought antiquarian volumes were worth consulting; see [Wright], *Advice on the Study of Law with Directions for the Choice of Books, Addressed to Attornies' Clerks, with Additional Notes for the American Student* (Baltimore: E. J. Coale, 1811), 47, n. 1: "These ancient authors are not much read in our offices or used in our courts."

[31] *Purviance Law Catalogue*, 2. The comment is interesting because it suggests that condition was considered to affect both desirability and, presumably, price.

[32] Ibid., 30, note 457.

[33] Ibid., 29, note 436; see also 29, note 437: "Lyndewode's Provinciale ... Paris, 1505, (a rare work, printed in black letter, rubricated throughout, a fine specimen of early printing) ..."

[34] Ibid., 51.

works not found prior to compilation of the catalogue would be sold after the numbered lots.[35] Once again, we may assume that the auctioneers were working from a list provided by the estate's administrator when they compiled the auction catalogue but that they also found supplemental material that they intended to sell even though it had not been listed as numbered lots.

In terms of the library itself, Purviance's collection was quite remarkable. The law library alone numbered in the thousands of volumes, and the administrator estimated that it represented an investment of some $35,000 by Judge Purviance – during his lifetime, a remarkable sum.[36] Purviance's library was unusual, although not unique, because it contained so many foreign law books, including many in French, German, and Latin. The common law library was rich in reports and digests, as well as the myriad of specialist treatises one would expect to find in a comprehensive law library of the period. The library was rich in American imprints as well as books printed in London and Dublin. This was a working lawyer's library. Although there are antiquarian volumes listed in the catalogue, for the most part these were standard works of English law and not historical oddities. There are virtually no books listed in the law catalogue that would not have been of some use to a working lawyer and judge. Even the Civil law library represented a working lawyer's interests. It was rich in maritime law as well as international law, just the topics one would expect to be of interest to a lawyer in a major port city like Baltimore.

We have no evidence of the success of the Purviance sale or of the purchasers' identities. But the catalogues themselves can, as noted, provide a wealth of evidence about trade practices as well as collecting habits of the period.

Another one of the most celebrated antebellum auctions of law books took place in Boston in 1859. Once again, the sale was comprised of two parts and had two separate primary catalogues.[37] These were

[35] *Purviance Miscellaneous Catalogue*, 51. [36] *Purviance Law Catalogue*, 1.

[37] *Catalogue of the Law Library of the Late Hon. Rufus Choate to be Sold by Auction* ... (Boston: Leonard & Co., 1859); *Catalogue of the Valuable Private Library of the Late Hon. Rufus Choate* ... (Boston: Leonard & Co., 1859). McKay also lists an *Addition to the Law Catalogue* of three pages and seventy lots sold on November 9, 1859, a copy of which is owned by the New York Public Library; see McKay, *American Book Auction Catalogues*.

also estate sales. The owner of this great library had been Rufus Choate, one of the greatest lawyers the United States has ever known and, with Daniel Webster, the greatest of all antebellum Yankee advocates. Choate was far more than simply a courtroom lawyer, however. He was also a serious classical scholar who, had he not been so preoccupied with the daily tasks of a busy law office, might well have made a major contribution to classical scholarship.[38] Certainly, he was exceptionally well read in the classics, and he built up one of the premier classical libraries in the United States during his lifetime. But he was also a thorough and scholarly lawyer, and his law library reflected this.

The auction of Choate's books was conducted by Leonard & Company, one of the leading auction houses in Boston at the time. It was held at their auction rooms on Tremont Street (close to Little, Brown's retail establishment). The law books were sold on two days, November 8 and 9. The catalogue was issued in octavo in paper covers. It is arranged alphabetically by numbered lots, 463 in all. The library was a large one and its contents were typical for the period. It had the standard runs of reports and statutes as well as periodicals. Like Purviance, Choate also had a good selection of American, English, Irish, and European imprints. The collection was rich in volumes on maritime law and was also particularly rich in works on Roman law produced in Germany during the late-eighteenth and early-nineteenth centuries.[39] It is interesting to note that Choate seems to have been less interested in antiquarian volumes than was Purviance. Whereas Purviance owned a sixteenth-century edition of Fitzherbert, Choate owned a mid-eighteenth-century Dublin reprint. There can be no doubt that Choate had the opportunity to purchase pre-eighteenth-century Common law volumes for his law library had he wanted to. Thus, the absence of such volumes from the library might suggest a lack of interest. Indeed, his collection of works on Roman and civil law lacks

[38] See Jean V. Mathews, *Rufus Choate, The Law and Civic Virtue* (Philadelphia: Temple University Press, 1980), 105–46; Samuel Gilman Brown, *The Life of Rufus Choate* (Boston: Little, Brown, 1891), e.g., 97–98.

[39] This was a period in which Roman law scholarship flourished in Germany and in which German-American ties within the legal and scholarly communities also flowered; see M.H. Hoeflich, "Transatlantic Friendships and the German Influence on American Law in the First Half of the Nineteenth Century," *American Journal of Comparative Law*, 35 (1987): 599f; M.H. Hoeflich, "Savigny and His Anglo-American Disciples," *American Journal of Comparative Law*, 37 (1988): 17–37.

older antiquarian editions. Instead, Choate seems to have chosen the latest editions of works that he wanted to own. All of this suggests that Choate collected his books for practical use in his practice rather than for either antiquarian or legal historical purposes; thus, he chose more recent and less expensive copies. It may also reflect Choate's text-critical training and his preference for more modern, "scientific" editions, when available.

Although there is no evidence in the catalogue of the extent to which it was distributed or as to the attendance at the auctions themselves, some evidence of this is provided by the commonplace book kept by the young New Hampshire attorney Stephen Greeley Clarke, mentioned previously.[40] Even better evidence comes from a notice published in the *Boston Advertiser* for October 19, 1859:

> The sale of the miscellaneous library of the late Rufus Choate, began yesterday at Chapman Hall, by Messrs. Leonard & Co., and attracted a considerable collection of book buyers, besides an unusually large number by orders from a distance.[41]

This suggests that the auction did indeed attract at least regional attention and that the sale of Choate's collection was viewed by members of the bar as a major opportunity to acquire volumes for their own libraries.

Most of the private law libraries that came up for auction in antebellum America were not of the size or scope of Purviance's or Choate's. They were the libraries of working lawyers and judges: some filled little more than a page or two in a catalogue, and others numbered in the hundreds of lots and warranted a catalogue of their own. Some catalogues can give a good impression of the nature of these libraries and their sales. On October 22 and 23, 1828, for example, J. L. Cunningham, located at the corner of Milk and Federal streets in Boston, auctioned off the law library of Barney Smith, Esquire.[42] This library was advertised by the auctioneer comprising more than 3,000 volumes. The catalogue itself consisted of fifteen octavo pages, and lots

40 See p. 105.

41 *Boston Advertiser*, 19 October 1859; a clipping of this notice has been inserted in the copy of Choate's library sale catalogue in my personal collection.

42 *Catalogue of the Library of Barney Smith, Esq. Consisting of Nearly 3,000 Volumes ... Also a Collection of Valuable Law Books ...* (Boston: 1828) [McKay, 223].

were listed in two sections, miscellaneous and law. In the law section were listed 63 law books for sale. (Several law volumes were also listed in the miscellaneous section.) The majority of Smith's law books were the standard reports, statutes, and treatises one would expect to find in a working lawyer's library. But there were several other volumes as well. He owned some works on Roman law, for example. He also owned a copy of the *Code Napoleon* as well as Chief Justice Marshall's *Life of Washington*. It is interesting to note that he had a copy of Halshead's *Code of Gentoo Laws*, a work that appears in many library lists of the period.[43] Smith also owned a two-volume translation of Cicero's works on oratory, a strong reminder of the importance of Roman oratorical models to members of the antebellum Bar.[44] Finally, Smith possessed a "copying machine" that was auctioned at this time. We may suspect that this machine was like the one used by Thomas Jefferson and may well have been used by Smith in his practice.[45]

On July 5 and 6, 1848, Leonard & Cunningham, Boston book auctioneers, sold the library of Judge Hubbard, who had recently died.[46] This sale consisted both of the late judge's miscellaneous books and his law books, and the sale was so described. The sale was held in two days; the first day saw the auction of the nonlaw books. The catalogue consists of thirty octavo pages. There are no lot numbers, but the law book section covers pages 18–30 and consists of 336 titles. Of these titles, 136 were London imprints, strong testimony to the importance of London printed law books in the United States even at mid-century.

For the most part, Hubbard's library was a working judge's library. But, again, there are some interesting books in the collection. Hubbard, like Smith, owned a copy of the *Gentoo Laws*. Like many of his

[43] *Catalogue of the Library of Barney Smith*, 10; this was a compilation of translations by Halshead, a friend of Sir William Jones, of various Indian legal texts.

[44] See M. H. Hoeflich and L. Jenab, "Forensic Oratory in Antebellum America," *Kansas Law Review*, 51 (2004): 449–71; and see Stephen Botein, "Cicero as a Role Model for Early American Lawyers: A Case Study in Classical 'Influence,'" *Classical Journal*, 73 (1978): 313–21.

[45] On copying devices, see Silvio Bedini, *Thomas Jefferson and his Copying Machines* (Charlottesville, VA: University Press of Virginia, 1984); Barbara Rhodes and William W. Streeter, *Before Photocopying: The Art and History of Mechanical Copying* (New Castle, DE: Oak Knoll, 1999).

[46] *Catalogue of the Law Library of the Late Judge Hubbard ...* (Boston, 1848) [McKay, 773].

contemporaries he also owned a copy of a translation of Beccaria's work on criminal law, attesting to the importance of this Italian jurist's influence on the development of American criminal law and penology.[47] He owned several foreign imprints, mostly texts on maritime law with a few works on Roman law intermixed. Finally, Hubbard owned fifteen volumes of *The Law Library*, the pioneering Philadelphia effort to reprint English legal treatises in a format better suited for the American market.[48]

One year later, on December 14, 1849, M. Thomas & Sons of Philadelphia held an auction of the law library of another recently deceased lawyer, C. Wallace Brook.[49] The library itself was small; the catalogue consists of only eight octavo pages with unnumbered lots. But this is a particularly interesting sale catalogue nonetheless because it seems that the auctioneers were asked to sell the contents of Brook's law office, not just the library. Thus, it is likely that this catalogue represents both the library Brook actually kept in his office as well as equipment he used in his law practice. The library itself was typical of one owned by a successful practitioner. It contained the standard works as well as a few foreign works on maritime law. Brook also owned a copy of Beccaria. He, like Rufus Choate, did not collect antiquarian volumes, but he did own the 1846 edition of the *London Law Catalogue*, which he used, perhaps, to order London legal imprints.

The office equipment listed for sale in the catalogue gives an almost unprecedented insight into the material culture of the law during this period. He owned two seal presses, large and small, which he must have used to notarize and seal official documents (among his books was a three-volume treatise on notaries). He also owned a "marble office slate," a "patent bond docket or ledger," an engraved copper plate of the "Arms of the United States," and a case of "mathematical instruments," which we can suppose may have been of use in dealing with surveys or patent applications. These details of the office contents left by Brooks are simply invaluable, for they are found in no other sources.

47 Ibid., 2 [*Gentoo Laws*]; 21 [Beccaria].

48 Op. Cit, n. 54, *supra*, 22. On this series, see, E. F. Surrency, *A History of American Law Publishing* 167.

49 *Valuable Law Library by Order of the Executor of the Late C. Wallace Brook, Esq.* (Philadelphia, 1849).

Not all auctions of law books were of private law libraries. Indeed, it was common during the antebellum period to hold auctions either of imported books brought over specifically for the purpose or general trade auctions, which drew on many sources for the lots.[50] But we also find that, on occasion, auctions were held to sell off the entire stock of a single bookseller or publisher. One such sale was held on September 9, 1830, by M. Thomas at 87 Chestnut Street in Philadelphia.[51] This catalogue, as noted previously, is most likely of the law stock of the Carey law bookstore, which incorporated the remaining stock of Isaac Riley's law book operations from New York.[52] The sale catalogue consists of twenty-seven octavo pages filled with unnumbered lots. Although the sale contained many law lots, it also contained non-legal materials. Many of the lots contained multiple items. Often these items were in either sheets or various formats. There can be little doubt that this was a sale of a dealer's stock. The value of this catalogue is immense; it provides an insight into the typical stock of a publisher–bookseller of the period, and because the catalogue lists quantities and formats of books in each lot, it permits us to estimate the availability and, perhaps, even rough print runs for the works listed.

The value of this catalogue to legal historians is significant and may be illustrated by looking at one genre of law books: books on foreign law in translation. The extent to which American lawyers during the antebellum period were interested in foreign law has been the subject of much scholarly debate. This 1830 catalogue offers some vital evidence for this question. For example, on sale at this auction were six volumes of Azuni's treatise on maritime law bound in sheep, as well as 24 sets folded in sheets.[53] There were 247 sets of Burlamaqui's treatise on natural law available in sheets.[54] There were 10 sets of Pothier's treatise on obligations available bound in sheep and fifteen sets available in sheets.[55] There were 260 copies of Ingersoll's translation of the Italian jurist Roccus's treatise on admiralty law available in sheets and 29 sets

[50] See John Tebbel, *A History of Book Publishing in the United States. The Creation of an Industry, 1630–1865*, vol. 1 (New York: Bowker, 1972), 230 ft.

[51] *Extensive Sale of Books by Auction ... Catalogue of an Extensive Collection of Law & Other Books ...* (Philadelphia, 1830).

[52] See Chapter 3.

[53] Ibid., 6. On law book bindings in the nineteenth century, see Fidler, "'Till You Understand Them in Their Principal Features.'"

[54] See note 54, Catalogue. [55] Ibid., 16.

of Pothier's maritime law treatise available bound.[56] There were also 170 copies of volume three of Hall's *American Law Journal*, which contained Peter DuPonceau's translation of the work on admiralty law written by the seventeenth-century Dutch jurist Bynkershoek.[57]

The number of these texts available for sale at this auction in 1830 make it plain that these books were far from rare and that they were, in fact, readily available to American lawyers, a fact borne out by a study of private library and booksellers' catalogues. Another interesting fact is also revealed in this catalogue: The auctioneers hoped to attract individual lawyers to the sale as well as dealers. Therefore, they added a note to the catalogue that they had made arrangements to have any volumes purchased bound to order, if desired. The cost of such binding was forty cents in "best sheep" and seventy-five cents per volume in "best calf."[58]

One could also purchase law books at auctions of general books as well. Often a general library sale would contain several law volumes for sale as well. For example, Dorr, Howland & Company held a sale of "valuable school, classical, law, medical, theological, and miscellaneous books" in Worcester, Massachusetts, in 1829.[59] As part of that sale they offered five lots of law books: Davis's *Justice*, Goodwin's *Town Officer*, the *Laws of Massachusetts*, a treatise on patent law, and the texts of the United States and Massachusetts constitutions.[60] They also offered blank docket books designed for lawyers and sheriffs.

Just as interesting as the information one finds in these auction sale catalogues is the information that is often lacking. For example, there is rarely indication of the type of binding or condition of volumes to be sold. In part, this may be due to the auctioneer's assumption that would-be purchasers or their agents would inspect the books for sale

56 Ibid., 16 [Pothier]; 16 [Roccus].

57 Ibid., 12; on all of these translations, see M.H. Hoeflich, "Translation and the American Reception of Foreign Law," *American Journal of Comparitive Law*, 50, 753–75 (2002).

58 Ibid., Introduction; cf., Fidler, "'Till You Understand Them in Their Principal Features.'"

59 *Catalogue of Valuable School, Classical, Law, Medical, Theological ... Books* (Worcester, 1829).

60 Ibid., 9, 13, 18, and 3; see also J. A. Conley, "Doing It by the Book: Justice of the Peace Manuals and English Law in Eighteenth Century America," *Journal of Legal History*, 6 (1985): 257–98.

before the auction took place. But it is also possible that binding and condition were of less importance to lawyers purchasing at these auctions because they were not buying to add to collections designed to delight the eye and mind but, instead, were buying working books, and all that concerned them was the contents.[61] Or lawyers may have simply assumed that, unless otherwise noted, the books would be bound in the standard sheep or "law calf."

From all of this, what can we conclude about what information can be gained from the study of law book auctions in antebellum America? First, it should be clear that law book auctions were a significant source of books for the American Bar in this period. If one were to compare the books available at auctions held during the 1840s and 1850s, for example, with those available from booksellers' catalogues, one would notice several facts. In general, auctions were a better source for antiquarian and, in many cases, foreign texts, than were booksellers. This is not surprising. By and large the demand for antiquarian texts among members of the Bar was limited. The catalogues of the largest law booksellers offered a few such items, usually English reports or classic treatises.[62] Many auctions of law books offered few if any such texts. One may suppose, therefore, that there was a limited market for such books and that few booksellers were willing to invest in such stock. If one wanted to obtain such a book, one would be forced to either import it from a foreign bookseller or buy it from another collection, usually at auction. As to contemporary foreign books, although the major legal booksellers like Little, Brown or Banks, Gould did offer several foreign law books for sale in their catalogues, here, again, it seems that a wider variety of such texts, particularly those on more esoteric subjects, tended to be available at auctions rather than from booksellers' catalogues. Finally, auctions made large numbers of common and esoteric law books available more inexpensively than retail booksellers. This could be quite crucial for impecunious lawyers.[63]

What all of this adds up to is that law book auctions during this period provided a major source for certain types of law books in the

[61] See Fidler, "'Till You Understand Them in Their Principal Features.'"

[62] For example, the 1844 *General Catalogue of Law Books* offered by Little, Brown lists more than one thousand titles available, of which only 34 were published before 1700.

[63] See note 16.

United States. Lawyers seeking to purchase the New York Reports could obtain these easily enough from any legal bookseller, but if they wanted an esoteric work on Roman law or an early edition of a common law text, they would most likely either have had to arrange to purchase such a text abroad or find it at an auction. And, if they wanted bargains, an auction sale was ideal.

Law book auctions could only have served a relatively small portion of the law book market. At their height, according to McKay, there were rarely more than twenty auctions devoted specifically to law books in any year during the antebellum period. Even adding in catalogues not listed in McKay and others that may well have contained substantial numbers of law books, based on the owner's identity, the number of law book auctions probably rarely reached thirty in any year. There is simply no way that these auctions could have supplied the books needed by an ever-growing legal profession. To understand these auctions in the context of the law book trade in the United States during this period, one must understand them as supplementary to the main source of law books – the law booksellers discussed in Chapter 2.

Although what we learn from law book auction catalogues is of importance to the history of the law book trade in antebellum America, its importance in helping us reconstruct the intellectual milieu of the antebellum Bar is far greater. Here, again, it is necessary to sound a note of caution. The auction catalogues that most lend themselves to such a study are, for the most part, representative of the Bar's elite, of those lawyers who amassed substantial enough libraries to warrant such sales and be of significant historical interest. Nevertheless, there is value to knowing what the elite lawyers of the period were reading and what they were willing to purchase. We discover, for example, that many lawyers did own books on foreign law, particularly in such subjects as admiralty and commercial law. Through the study of the auction sale catalogues of individual lawyers' libraries, we can reconstruct the sources they drew on in their writing and in their advocacy.

Chapter 5
Risk, Subscriptions, and Status

Law book selling, book publishing, and book binding, as discussed in previous chapters, were often all performed by the same individuals or small publishing consortia in the period from 1770 to 1830.[1] Most printers and law booksellers lacked the substantial capital to undertake expensive publishing projects without some form of subsidy, unless the book was assured sales because of either an author's reputation in the Bar or the importance of the subject of a new book. Until the introduction and widespread use of stereotyping in the second quarter of the nineteenth century, a technique that created economies of scale by freeing up expensive lead type, the risk of producing books without an assured market was high. Unusual volumes, or those with limited markets, were unlikely to be published or distributed by normal trade methods.

Law books posed a particularly risky form of book publishing and selling precisely because they were, for the most part, only going to be bought by lawyers. Legislative printing was probably the least risky, because it generally carried an exclusive copyright in one printer or printers' group and often also had guaranteed sales. But legal treatises had no such advantages. Unless the treatise was of a general nature – such as Blackstone's *Commentaries*, which were widely purchased by nonlawyers, and the many quasi-legal texts designed for farmers, businessmen, or others who might have need of legal sources – treatises

[1] See Chapters 2 and 3.

generally could only be expected to sell to lawyers.[2] The more specialized the subject, the far fewer purchasers could be expected.

Law books were also often quite expensive to produce. Legal writers, though not commanding the astronomical fees of authors like Fenimore Cooper or Longfellow, still expected to be well compensated for their labors. The cost books of Carey & Lea, one of the most prominent of antebellum Philadelphia publishers, provide evidence of production costs. In 1825 they published the fourth American edition of Chitty's *Pleadings*.[3] Under the Copyright Act of 1790, they were not required to pay the British author or publisher a royalty, but they still had to pay their American editor, Edward Ingraham.[4] He received $200 for his work.[5] Production costs for 1,500 copies overall were $4,578.[6] That same year, they published Chitty's *A Practical Treatise on Bills of Exchange*. For this, they paid an editor $150, and total production costs were $1,494 for 750 copies. They sold the book at a trade price of three dollars and fifty cents.[7] It is obvious that although the profit margins could be high, the risk of loss was also high. This was particularly true because the publishers could not expect to sell all the volumes at the suggested trade price, nor could they hope to sell out an edition quickly. Often, especially in the case of expensive treatises, the publisher might be required to wait years to sell out an edition. In these two cases the risk was somewhat reduced because Chitty was one of the best-known and best-selling English legal authors used as much in the United States as in Britain. Regardless of the risks, antebellum American lawyers needed law books, American or Americanized law books, which would provide them with the tools necessary for competent practice. It was left to printers and booksellers to find a means to produce these without taking risks that might bankrupt them.

One of the most important methods adopted by law publishers and booksellers to deal with the risks of producing and selling law books

[2] And see "Doing It by the Book: Justice of the Peace Manuals and English Law in Eighteenth Century America," *Journal of Legal History*, 6 (1985): 257–98..

[3] D. Kaser, ed., *The Cost Books of Carey & Lea 1825–1838* (Philadelphia, 1963), 22.

[4] Ingraham was a prominent Philadelphia lawyer and author and editor of several important legal works; see, J. G. Wilson and J. Fiske, eds., *Appleton's Encyclopedia of American Biography* (New York: D. Appleton & Company,1898), vol. 3, pp. 350–51.

[5] See Chapter 3. [6] Ibid. [7] Ibid., 21.

early in the antebellum period was the subscription method.[8] As Donald Farren, the leading expert on subscription bookselling has observed, Americans of the antebellum period were quite used to subscriptions as a means of raising money.[9] They subscribed to library associations, periodicals, and insurance, among others. The subscription sale of books was also not uncommon; it had been used in England since the seventeenth century.[10] Lawyers would also have been used to seeing subscription publishing schemes for English law texts.[11]

The subscription method was relatively simple in conception if not in execution. A printer, bookseller, or combination thereof would decide to seek subscriptions for a particular work. This could be a book already in circulation abroad, new work, or new edition of an existing work. The printer would then advertise its intention to produce this work. This could be done by broadside; by advertisements in newspapers, periodicals, or other books; or even through the use of book agents, a practice that became popular in the early nineteenth century and will forever be associated with Parson Weems, the biographer of George Washington and book agent extraordinaire.[12] A good early example of a broadside advertisement of an American subscription

[8] Subscription sales and other types which guaranteed the publisher a ready market were called "forced sales" see, R. Remer, *Printers and Men of Capital* (Philadelphia: University of Pennsylvania Press, 1996), 125–30.

[9] Donald Farren, "Subscription: A Study of the Eighteenth-Century American Book Trade," unpublished doctoral dissertation, Columbia University, 1982. 9–10; see also F. E. Compton, *Subscription Books* (New York; New York Public Library, 1939); see also Michael Hackenberg, "The Subscription Publishing Network in Nineteenth-Century Book Publishing," in *Getting the Books Out: Papers of the Chicago Conference on the Book in 19th-Century America*, ed. M. Hackenberg (Washington, D.C.: Center for the Book, Library of Congress, 1987), 45–75; see also Hall and Amory, *The Colonial Book in America*, 80–81, 243–246 [on subscription law publishing in colonial Maryland], 284–287, 427, the last of which refers to the importance of growing "bodies of the learned" to the success of subscription publishing in specialized fields.

[10] Ibid.

[11] See, for example, James Huntingford, *Proposal to Print 'A Digest of the Statute Laws, with Subscribers List & Terms* (London: R. B. Scott, 27 Clements Ln. & 378 Strand, 1801), listed for sale in the auction catalogue of Thompson, Ruddick & Medcalf, 21 August 2008, lot. No. 179.

[12] Lewis G. Leary, *The Book-Peddling Parson: An Account of the life and Works of Mason Locke Weems, Patriot, Pitchman, Author, and Purveyor of Morality to the Citizenry of the Early United states of America* (Chapel Hill, NC: Algonquin Books, 1984); Hackenberg, "The Subscription Publishing Network in Nineteenth-Century Book Publishing."

scheme is that produced by the Philadelphia printer and bookseller, Robert Bell, to announce his intention to publish an edition of Blackstone's *Commentaries* in 1770.[13] This was one of the first and most successful American subscription law publications and eventually had more than 1,500 subscribers. At the time of publication, Pennsylvania was still a colony under British colonial rule and Blackstone was *the* newest and best treatise on law for not only lawyers but also anyone with interests affected by the law.

The method Bell adopted was typical of that used for selling subscriptions. The broadside announced the proposed publication and gave details of the books. It also stated the expected publication price ("eight dollars") and pointed out that this price was substantially below the cost in Philadelphia of a copy imported from England. It also stated that the production of the first of four volumes would not begin until at least 200 subscriptions had been received and that the remaining volumes would be published within six months of the first. Another feature of this broadside was the promise that subscribers' names would be printed in the fourth and last published volume. This is particularly significant, as it indicates that Bell believed that publication of the names of subscribers would be a selling point. His understanding, undoubtedly correct, was that inclusion of subscribers' names would be viewed as a source of prestige, not only for the subscribers, but also for the publication itself. Indeed, Bell, like other subscription law publishers, endeavored to obtain subscriptions from prominent men, with whose names others of less prominence would be pleased to have theirs.

Finally, Bell's prospectus also reveals one other aspect of subscription publishing during this era: It states that Bell was prepared to receive subscriptions at his office and, further, that "all the booksellers and printers in America" would also accept subscriptions. It would appear that booksellers and printers routinely worked with one another to sell these volumes.[14] One that accepted a subscription for a book published by another would receive compensation, either in cash or in stock.[15]

[13] Edwin Wolf II, *The Book Culture of a Colonial American City: Philadelphia Books, Bookmen, and Booksellers* (Oxford: Clarendon Press, 1988), 157; Farren, "Subscription: A Study of the Eighteenth-Century American Book Trade," 125–36.

[14] Ibid. [15] Ibid.

Although the subscription method was relatively simple, it was not without risks for both buyer and seller. The greatest risk for buyers of a subscription book was that they would be asked to pay some portion of the purchase price in advance and then the book would not be published. By the end of the nineteenth century this had become so common, particularly with subscriptions sold by book agents, that the whole method came to be viewed with distrust by potential buyers.[16] When Bell promised to begin publication after receiving only 200 subscriptions, he was, in effect, promising to publish the volumes at a loss, if no further subscriptions were received. Bell, perhaps, might have been able to accept such a loss. Others who offered subscription books could not. Joshua Montefiore, a scion of the great Anglo-Jewish legal family, who came to the United States at the beginning of the nineteenth century and became a successful legal author, attempted to sell his *Synopsis of Mercantile Laws* himself.[17] He obtained forty-one subscribers, all from New York City.[18] At this point, Montefiore became ill and was no longer able to carry the subscription scheme forward. Rather than simply default, he sold the rights to the book to a New York publisher, G. & C. & H. Carvill, who eventually published the book in 1830 and included the list of subscribers obtained by Montefiore in the back of the volume.[19]

In addition to all of the normal risks of producing a new law book, subscription publishing also introduced another risk: During the subscription period a competitor might foster negative rumors, either that the book would never be published or that there was a problem with the text. This seems to have been what led Little, Brown to include a remarkable statement in an 1854 advertisement for their subscription edition of the English Equity Reports. Little, Brown felt it necessary

[16] Farren, "Subscription: A Study of the Eighteenth-Century American Book Trade," 183.

[17] Joshua Montefiore, *A Commercial Dictionary Containing the Present State of Mercantile Law, Practice and Custom* (Philadelphia: Printed & Sold by James Humphreys), 1804.

[18] Ibid., xiii.

[19] Joshua Montefiore,. *Synopsis of Mercantile Laws with an Appendix, Containing the most Proved Forms of Notarial and Commercial Precedence, Special and Common, Required in the Daily Transaction of Business by Merchants, Traders, Notaries, Attornies, & C.* (New York: G. & C. & H. Carvill, 1830).

to assure the profession, that the statement industriously circulated that these Reports will be soon discontinued is untrue. In the face of a most determined opposition, and against the most unscrupulous detraction and misrepresentation, they have gained a circulation which places the enterprize beyond the possibility of failure.[20]

It seems that American law bookselling had become quite cutthroat by the 1850s.

This intense competition for subscribers gave rise to another risk that the subscription bookseller encountered: resistance to proposed prices for books by subscription. This seems to have been the problem faced by the publisher of *Shaw's Reports*, Chauncey Goodrich, law book publisher and seller in Burlington, Vermont. Goodrich published several important law texts, including a reprint of George Crabb's *History of English Law in 1831*.[21] He also undertook to publish the Vermont law reports edited by Shaw. In 1840 Goodrich circulated a notice to potential subscribers to *Shaw's Reports*:

A few individuals having said to the subscriber, that they thought the price of the volume to be too high; the subscriber would respectfully state, that the Volume is lower; when its size and execution are considered, than any Volume of Law Reports published at any time . . .[22]

Chauncey also attempted to justify his price over his competitors by assuring his subscribers that their books would arrive safe and on time:

. . . the Publisher, on his part, will spare no pains . . . by having them [the books] stored in various places, that they shall not meet the fate of many books by accidents of fire . . .[23]

The subscription method could be used by both professional printers and booksellers as well as individual authors who sought self-publication, as did Joshua Montefiore.[24] It was especially useful for books that were either particularly expensive to produce; of limited appeal, even among lawyers; or especially risky for some other reason. Although the total number of law books sold by subscription during the

[20] *Advertisement*, Little, Brown & Co. (1857), in the author's collection.

[21] George Crabb, *A History of English Law . . . 1st American edition . . .* (Burlington, VT: F. C. Goodrich, 1831).

[22] Advertising circular in the author's collection, titled: Shaw's Reports, Vol. 1 (Burlington, 1840).

[23] Ibid. [24] See the section "Joshua Montefiore's *Commercial Dictionary*," 137.

antebellum period in the United States was not large, it was a significant method in these cases and an important part of the law bookselling and publishing industry.[25] The full extent of the method and its importance, not only as a means of risk reduction for law booksellers and printers, but also for modern legal historians, can be best understood by an examination of several representative subscription books sold during the period.

BELL'S BLACKSTONE

The publication of Sir William Blackstone's *Commentaries on the Laws of England* marked a turning point in law publication both in Britain and the United States. Not since the publication of Lord Coke's *Institutes* had a law book attracted the audience that Blackstone's attracted.[26] Indeed, while Coke's work was written primarily for lawyers and those with a professional interest in English law, Blackstone's *Commentaries* appealed to a wider audience of anyone interested in the law, whether professionally or otherwise. From their initial appearance in print, the *Commentaries* became the first legal bestseller of the modern era.

Very soon after the *Commentaries* were published in England, copies began to be imported into the American colonies. These books suffered from certain disadvantages, most notably price and availability. Edwin Wolf, the great historian of the Philadelphia book trade, noted that David Hall, a leading Philadelphia bookseller, offered individual volumes of the English edition in 1769 for £1.6s. each, a rather steep price.[27] It seems that these problems of availability and cost prompted Robert Bell, one of Hall's competitors, to undertake the Blackstone subscription publication project. Without documentary evidence, one can only speculate that his reason for adopting the subscription method was his insecurity, at this early date, of whether there would be a sufficient American market to justify the publication of these four volumes. It may also be possible that Bell feared that the publication of an English law book in 1770, just as the winds of revolution were

[25] On what Farren refers to as the "patterns of practice" in subscription selling generally, see Farren, "Subscription: A Study of the Eighteenth-Century American Book Trade," 181–85.

[26] Wolf, *The Book Culture*, 159. [27] Ibid., 156.

beginning to swirl around the colonies, might be especially risky. Whatever his reason, Bell did choose to take the subscription route. If anything, he underestimated the demand for the book by specifying a needed subscription base of 200. By the time the book was on the market, Bell had sold more than 1,500 copies.[28] The subscription list, included in the fourth volume, contains 837 names, an indication that Bell received almost half of his subscriptions during the latter part of the publishing process, which may also suggest that the popularity of the book and buyers' willingness to subscribe increased as the risk that the project would fail decreased.

The subscription list itself is of enormous legal historical and bibliographical significance. Each subscriber is identified by name and address and many also by profession.[29] The list is divided into two parts. The first part lists eminent personages who had subscribed: the governor of Virginia, the governor of New Jersey, the governors of Bermuda and the Bahamas, the lieutenant-governors of Pennsylvania and East-Florida, and the deputy-governor of Connecticut. The inclusion of these high office holders in a special introductory section hearkens back to the early modern practice of dedicating books to noble patrons.[30] It was also good advertising for the book, both to subscribers who might wish to be included in a list containing these people and to others who might be inclined to purchase the books later based on the implicit recommendation witnessed by these subscribers' names.[31]

The second, a far longer section, contains the list of ordinary subscribers. (One may wonder whether those included in the first section actually paid for their sets.) Of these, 102 identified themselves either as attorneys-at-law or barristers-at-law. A further 21 are identified as either judges or court clerks, 2 are listed as sheriffs, and 12 identify themselves as law students. Thus, altogether, a total of 137 of the listed subscribers, or roughly 16 percent, listed a professional affiliation with the practice of law. This is rather surprising that so small a number of the listed subscribers identified themselves as lawyers. It testifies to the general popularity of Blackstone. It may also indicate either that most lawyers were

[28] Ibid. [29] See also Amory & Hall, *The Colonial Book in the Atlantic World*, 481–82.

[30] Sir William Blackstone, *Commentaries on the Laws of England in Four Books*, vol. 4 (Philadelphia: Printed for the subscribers by Robert Bell, 1771–1772).

[31] See Farren, "Subscription: A Study of the Eighteenth-Century American Book Trade," 165–67.

unwilling to invest a large sum in advance for a relatively new work or, perhaps, a recognition that the English text of Blackstone, without American notes, would be of limited value to them.

If lawyers and judges did not constitute the majority of subscribers, who did? The answer is quite important; a detailed analysis of the subscriber list indicates that the vast majority of subscribers identified themselves either as merchants, printers, or booksellers, strong evidence that these subscribers subscribed to the Blackstone not for their own use but for resale. Indeed, some of these subscriptions were for multiple copies, another indication of the intent to resell. The use of the subscription method as an alternate to the formation of publishing consortia among booksellers was a common device used for many literary works, as Donald Farren has suggested. Farren has also suggested another possible reason for the use of the subscription publishing format, which seems particularly likely in the case of Bell's Blackstone[32]: A subscription program could be used as a means of "preempting" a potential market for a work. In the case of Blackstone's *Commentaries*, Bell must have been aware that other printers and booksellers would rush to either import editions from abroad or publish their own. He was able to print his proposal broadside and publish his newspaper advertisements far more quickly than he could publish the actual texts. By acquiring subscribers to the work, he was able to tie up a substantial number of would-be buyers before any competitor might be able to have substantial numbers of Blackstone's work available on the American market. Indeed, soon after Bell undertook his Blackstone project, David Hall published his own inexpensive octavo edition of the *Commentaries*.[33]

In addition to both the subscribers who bought for resale and those who identified themselves as part of the colonial legal profession, there was also a significant number of other individual subscribers. There were several British military officers serving in the colonies at the time. There were several subscribers who simply identified themselves as "gentlemen" and others as farmers, plantation owners, or similar titles. These, too, are of interest, as Blackstone's original lectures, on which the *Commentaries* were closely based, were given at Oxford and

[32] Farren, "Subscription: A Study of the Eighteenth-Century American Book Trade," 183–84.

[33] Wolf, *The Book Culture*, 159.

intended for an audience of gentry and landowners who would need knowledge of the law as Justices of the Peace, Members of Parliament, and others with legal or governmental functions rather than for would-be lawyers. These colonial gentlemen and farmers were much the same type. There are also some subscribers whose presence on the list gives rein to fascinating speculation. There was a "comedian," several clerics, a cordwainer, and a shoemaker. There were also several "scriveners," perhaps men who aspired one day to a legal career. Several institutions, including the Philadelphia Library Company and the Wilmington Library Company, also subscribed for at least one set.

The subscription lists also give an important clue as to the distribution of the books geographically. Mail service in the colonies and the early republic was expensive and often uncertain. Yet the Blackstone subscriber list, and the placement of Bell's advertisements as far as the Danish Virgin Islands, makes it clear that colonial booksellers could and did have geographically extensive markets for their books.[34] Of course, Blackstone's work would have had relevance to anyone interested in law throughout the British colonial empire, unlike many more local legal tomes. Nevertheless, the sheer size of the subscriber area is impressive. Subscribers are listed from Pennsylvania, New York, Massachusetts, New Hampshire, Connecticut, Delaware, Maryland, New Jersey, Rhode Island, Virginia, Georgia, South Carolina, North Carolina, East Florida, Barbados, the Bahamas, Nova Scotia, Jamaica, and Bermuda. Also, interestingly, two of the three largest multiple subscribers were in South Carolina and North Carolina, testimony, perhaps, to the difficulty of shipping these volumes from Philadelphia to the deep South. The largest multiple subscriber, who subscribed for 200 sets, was James Rivington of New York City, evidence of both the size of Rivington's bookselling enterprise and the size of the colonial New York Bar.

KIRBY'S *REPORTS OF CASES* AND ZEPHANIAH SWIFT'S *SYSTEM OF THE LAWS OF CONNECTICUT*

In 1789, Collier & Adam, printers of Litchfield, Connecticut, issued Ephraim Kirby's *Reports of Cases Adjudged in the Superior Court of*

[34] See Farren, "Subscription: A Study of the Eighteenth-Century American Book Trade," 133.

the State of Connecticut.[35] Six years later, John Byrne of Windham, Connecticut, printed the first of Zephaniah Swift's *System of the Laws of the State of Connecticut*.[36] Both were printed for the authors and both were sold by subscription. Both were also of great importance in the legal community of the time. Kirby's *Reports* were the first published reports of a court of general jurisdiction in the United States. Swift's *System* was one of the first attempts by an American lawyer to provide a systematic analysis of the whole of the law.

Kirby's book had a subscriber list of 226, of whom the vast majority listed themselves as lawyer, judge, or law student, and came from Connecticut. A minority of the subscribers were from the neighboring states of New York and Vermont. The size of the subscriber list is relatively small and the geographic and professional diversity of the subscribers quite limited. This may well account for the use of the subscription method. It also is not at all surprising. Kirby's *Reports* would have been of primary interest to lawyers and judges in Connecticut and neighboring states. In 1789, there were still substantial local variations in the law, so that lawyers in other jurisdictions may well have believed that Connecticut reports would be of little value to them professionally. Further, because Kirby's was the first publication of American reports from courts of general jurisdiction, he may well have worried that many lawyers would be slow to purchase what was then an innovative publication.

Swift's work in two volumes was somewhat different. There were almost twice as many subscribers: 466. The subscribers also were far more geographically diverse. The largest number, not surprisingly, came from Connecticut. But substantial numbers of subscribers came from Massachusetts, Rhode Island, New York, New Jersey, Pennsylvania, and Virginia. Smaller numbers listed New Hampshire, Delaware, Maryland, North Carolina, South Carolina, Georgia, and Kentucky as their homes. Unfortunately, the subscriber list published in

[35] Ephraim Kirby, *Report of Cases Adjudged in the Superior Court of the State of Connecticut: From the Year 1785, to May 1788; with Some Determinations in the Supreme Court of Errors* (Litchfield, CT: Printed by Collier & Adam, 1789); for background to this publication, see Farren, "Subscription: A Study of the Eighteenth-Century American Book Trade," 66–79.

[36] Zephaniah Swift, *A System of the Laws of the State of Connecticut. In Six Books* (Windham, CT: Printed by John Byrne for the author, 1795).

volume 2 of the work does not include the professions of the subscribers but, even without identification, the names themselves are a roster of the greatest lawyers of the period; therefore, it is clear that the book did well in selling to lawyers and judges. Several subscribers took two copies; these may have been merchants. Several also subscribed for institutions.

It is difficult to know precisely why Kirby's work had so many fewer and less diverse subscribers. In part, it may be that a treatise was of greater interest than reports. It may also be that Swift's reputation in the Bar was greater than Kirby's. Or, it may be that Swift did a better job of marketing. It would seem, from remaining evidence, that Kirby concentrated his marketing efforts in Connecticut and the surrounding states. The answers to this are lost in time.

VON MARTENS'S *SUMMARY*

In the same year Swift produced the first volume of his *System*, Thomas Bradford, one of the leading Philadelphia printers and booksellers, published George Von Martens's *Summary of the Law of Nations*.[37] Von Martens's work, first published in Europe, was certainly of contemporary importance. The new republic was just entering into the global family of nations, and its diplomats, lawyers, and traders would all need guidance in this new era. Indeed, Bradford thought it fitting to dedicate the work to George Washington. The work itself was translated into English by William Cobbett, an English expatriate and a resident of the United States, who was trying to make his living through literary endeavors.[38] The idea for the translation was not Cobbett's, but Bradford's, who sought Cobbett out with the project. Bradford paid Cobbett twenty-five cents per page or just under one hundred dollars for the entire book.[39] Bradford, perhaps following Carey's lead, chose to sell the book by subscription.

[37] George F. Von Martens, *Summary of the Law of Nations, Founded on the Treaties and Customs of the Modern Nations of Europe: with a List of the Principal Treaties Concluded since the Year 1748 down to the Present Time, Indicating the Works in which They Are to Be Found*, trans. William Cobbett (Philadelphia: Published by Thomas Bradford, Printer, Bookseller, and Stationer, 1795).

[38] On Cobbett, see *The Life and Letters of William Cobbett in England and America* (London: J. Lane, 1913), 2 vols.

[39] Ibid., vol.1, 90.

The subscription list published at the end of the work lists the subscribers' names and addresses. It does not list their professions. At the end of the list, however, is a quite interesting note that helps us reconstruct the marketing of the books. The note, from the publisher, laments the fact that many of the "subscription forms" that had been sent out to various places had gone astray because no returns had been made. This makes it clear that Bradford, at this relatively early date, had used forms to sell copies rather than simply advertising for them. Based on other examples, one may speculate that these forms were sent to booksellers, merchants, and post offices. The use of these forms, even if some did indeed get lost, was successful, at least in geographical terms. The list contains the names of 211 subscribers, among them some of the leading American lawyers, including James Kent and Aaron Burr. The subscribers listed their home states as New York, Pennsylvania, New Jersey, North Carolina, South Carolina, Georgia, Rhode Island, Connecticut, Virginia, Delaware, Massachusetts, Kentucky, Maryland, Vermont, and the Southwest Territory (later Tennessee). Several were multiple subscribers. The two largest were booksellers. George Keatinge of Baltimore took 12 copies. James Rivington of New York took 200, as he had done two decades earlier with Bell's edition of Blackstone.

Once again we see a book published by subscription with a relatively small subscription list by even contemporary standards. Although Von Martens's work was not inherently local in nature, as was Kirby's, it was nonetheless a foreign work in translation that might well have appeared rather esoteric and impractical to the typical small-town lawyer concerned with the minutiae of everyday life, who rarely encountered problems of international law.

JOSHUA MONTEFIORE'S *COMMERCIAL DICTIONARY*

Joshua Montefiore, mentioned earlier, the scion of one of England's most prominent Jewish families, was born in London in 1762 and died in St. Albans, Vermont, in 1843. He led what can only be described as an extraordinary life. He graduated from Oxford, read law, and was admitted a barrister in 1784. Seven years later, he became the military leader of a group of English "adventurers" who failed to establish a British colony on an island off Africa. He returned to England and became the first Jewish commissioned officer in the British Army. After several more adventures worthy of the fictional Flashman, he immigrated to the United States and began a literary life. One of his first literary endeavors in his new country was to author an American version of a book he had published earlier in England, the *Commercial Dictionary*.[40] This work was published by James Humphreys, a printer and bookseller in Philadelphia. The volume was sold by subscription. Unlike the other books so far discussed, the *Commercial Dictionary* was a law book designed primarily for nonlawyers. It contained several hundred short articles on various aspects of trade and commercial law (including a special article on Madeira written for the American market). Thus, unlike the other books already discussed, its potential market was far larger than books aimed exclusively at lawyers. The subscription list reflects this broader market.

The subscription list, which appears at the back of Montefiore's book, is divided into two sections. The first section consists of ten subscribers' names, highlighted because of their importance. What is interesting is that these subscribers were neither prominent citizens nor well-known lawyers. On the contrary, these ten subscribers were banks, such as the Bank of the United States, and insurance companies, such as the Phoenix Insurance Company of Philadelphia. This initial list sets the tone for the regular subscribers, most of whom were not attorneys. There are 210 regular subscribers listed. Scattered throughout are the names of a few lawyers, such as Peter S. Du Ponceau and William Rawle, but the majority of the subscribers were undoubtedly merchants, who purchased the volume for their own use. Again, this is not surprising because most practicing lawyers would have found Montefiore's work far too elementary to be of much use. In addition to the merchants who purchased the book for their own use, there were also several subscribers who purchased for resale. Most notable of these was Joseph Conrad & Company, a bookseller of Philadelphia, who purchased 150 copies of the work.

Conrad & Company's subscription for such a large number of copies has great significance on several counts. First, Conrad & Company was not known as a law bookseller, and the purchase of so many copies further emphasizes that the market for the book was primarily

40 Montefiore, *A Commercial Dictionary*.

nonlawyers. Second, Conrad & Company was one of the pioneers in Philadelphia of publishing consortia. Conrad had a regular arrangement with five other Philadelphia booksellers to publish works in consort.[41] It seems quite probable that Conrad & Company's subscription to so large a number of copies of a work published by another Philadelphia bookseller, who was part of Conrad's regular consortium, indicates that this subscription was, in fact, nothing more or less than a co-publishing agreement.

Unfortunately, the subscription list does not list professions, although the use of the term "Esq." after the names of a small number of subscribers, many of whom are known to have been lawyers, helps in some respects. Others, who were merchants, can be identified from contemporary business directories. The list does give locations for the subscribers. They came from a widely diverse pool: New York, Pennsylvania, South Carolina, Virginia, New Hampshire, Georgia, the District of Columbia, Maryland, and Nova Scotia.

The question is why was the subscription method was chosen for this publication, particularly when it had the potential for attracting a larger market? The answer seems to be, first, that Montefiore, as a recent immigrant, was not well known as an author at the time of publication, and second, that the book had originally been written for the English market, although with major American additions, may have been perceived by buyers as not useful. At any rate, the publication scheme succeeded.

AND SOME VARIATIONS ON THE THEME . . .

Not all subscription law publishing followed the standard model already described. There were also variations on the theme. The first of these was the routine printing of legal and law-related pamphlets by the application – that is, subscription – of private groups. The second variation was the subscription monograph series established by John S. Littel in Philadelphia and carried on by several others published under the series name *The Law Library*.[42]

[41] John Tebbel, *A History of Book Publishing in the United States*, Vol. 1 (New York: R. R. Bowker Co., 1972), 214.

[42] See Chapter 3.

To take the latter first, the antebellum period was literally awash in pamphlets: political tracts, sermons, eulogies, celebratory addresses, university lectures, and legal texts. They were cheap, were easy for even a small job printer to produce, and fed the almost unquenchable public thirst for printed materials. Many of these pamphlets had a legal aspect. Lawyers were often the subject of eulogies, for example. More important, many of the pamphlets printed during this period had a limited audience and were, as a result, printed at the instigation of a specific group – people who, in effect, were subscribers to these works. From the printer's perspective, this was a risk-reducing device. From the buyers' perspectives, it was often the only way to ensure that a particular text was printed.

An excellent example of such a pamphlet is the *Memorial of Ambrose Spencer* printed by Joel Munsell in Albany, New York, in 1849. Munsell was one of the most important antebellum New York printers and publishers.[43] Ambrose Spencer, a brother-in-law of Governor DeWitt Clinton, served in a variety of legal and political posts in New York State, including congressman, New York attorney general, mayor of Albany, and chief justice of the New York Supreme Court. His death in 1848 was marked by a series of tributes, including resolutions of the Bar and state legislative bodies, as well as eulogies and memorial sermons. In 1849, Munsell gathered these various texts together and issued them in pamphlet form together with a portrait frontispiece of Spencer. What is notable about this publication, in particular, is how Munsell came to print it. The title page of the work carries the following imprint:

> ALBANY;
> Printed for the Friends of the Deceased,
> By Joel Munsell
> 1849

Later, on the verso of the table of contents, a printer's note indicates that "the following collection . . . has been printed for distribution among his [i.e. Ambrose Spencer's] friends, to whom, it is hoped, it will afford an agreeable reminiscence . . ."

[43] On Munsell, see David S. Edelstein, *Joel Munsell: Printer & Antiquarian* (New York: Columbia University Press, 1950).

The use of this variant form of a subscription scheme made a great deal of sense in this context. Although Spencer was well known, it is hard to believe that the pamphlet would have been a bestseller. Yet, Munsell printed 500 copies of the pamphlet.[44] Presumably, he did so because he was assured that a substantial number of copies would be purchased by the various groups whose texts were included and by family and friends who wanted a keepsake of Spencer's death. Although there is no list of subscribers included in the pamphlet, there can be little doubt that this was the meaning of the imprint and the printer's note.

A second example of this type of arrangement being used to ensure the publication of a text is the pamphlet publication of Daniel Mayes's *Address to the Students of Law in Transylvania University* published by Thomas Pew in Lexington, Kentucky in 1833. Mayes was the first of a line of prominent law professors at Transylvania, whose law school was a serious rival of Harvard in the antebellum period. The speech itself is of great importance in the history of legal education in the United States, as it contains one of the first statements of the need for a national and broadly scientific legal education, as opposed to the more parochial form of legal education offered by the apprenticeship system. That it has been preserved in printed form is due to the students who heard the speech: The produced version, like Spencer's memorial, was printed at the express request of the auditors.

Unlike the Munsell work, the printed version of Mayes' speech includes neither an indication of the subscription nature of the piece nor a printer's note to this effect. On the verso of the title page, however, is found a transcription of two letters, one from the students asking Mayes for a copy of the lecture so that they might have it printed and a second, from Mayes, agreeing to do so. Even more significant, however, is the list of the fifty law students in the class, complete with their home addresses and, where appropriate, the name of their preceptor at Transylvania. This list is, in effect, a subscription list.

Another interesting feature of the printed version of Mayes's lecture is the note on the verso of the last leaf of the lecture. This note gives the date at which the next term of the law school would meet along with the

[44] Ibid., 146; the number of copies published is taken from *Bibliotheca Munselliana*, cited in Edelstein, p. 146.

charges for attendance at the lectures (twenty-five dollars) and the matriculation and library fee (five dollars). The presence of this note may be a witness to some subsidy provided for the printing of the lecture by the university, in addition to whatever the students had paid.

Perhaps the most important, and certainly the longest-lived, law subscription publishing scheme in antebellum America was *The Law Library*, initiated by John S. Littel of Philadelphia in 1833.[45] *The Law Library* was, in most cases, an exact reprint of English legal texts without change or additional American material. By 1860, there were 104 volumes in six series that had been printed. The scheme itself was a hybrid between a standard subscription publication scheme and a periodical. Subscribers were asked to commit and pay in advance for one year of books, initially at a price of ten dollars. According to an early advertisement for the series, the originals of the reprinted texts would have cost a subscriber sixty dollars. The texts were issued on a monthly basis, although there is evidence that they were actually sent out quarterly. Each text carried a date stamp of month and year (e.g., "November 1834").

Although the series was issued in monthly installments, it was not a periodical. It was also not an issuance "in parts" as became common for certain literary works, a method pioneered by Charles Dickens and his English publishers. On the contrary, each text published was complete in itself. J. G. Marvin, in his 1847 bibliographical guide, indicates that the purpose of issuing the books in this monthly arrangement was to ensure that the books could be sent by mail as cheaply as possible under the then restrictive mailing laws. Indeed, in his 1834 advertisement, Littel adverts to this purpose by stating that the monthly texts, "of about 200 pages" would "be sent by mail to any part of the United States."

The series was originally edited by Lowber and Sergeant, two Philadelphia lawyers well known for their editions of case reports published by Carey. In June 1834, these two were replaced by John Purdon, another Philadelphia lawyer. In fact, the task of editing was minor: The texts were exact reprints of the English originals. What was notable about the series, aside from its low price, was that it reached for completeness. Over the course of twenty-six years, the series reprinted

[45] See also Chapter 3.

more than 100 English legal texts, a substantial number by any measure. Most of the standard English legal works of the first half of the nineteenth century were included.

The absence of American notes was a significant disadvantage, as contemporary reviewers frequently remarked. Indeed, the publisher of the series recognized this disadvantage but touted the volumes for their ability to "enlarge the science of jurisprudence and elevate the character of the profession." The publisher also stressed the difference in availability of such books in the states on the eastern seaboard and in the "interior" of the country. The low cost of the series combined with the delivery by post was deemed to be a great advantage to practitioners in the interior who might, thereby, be put on a footing equal to that of their colleagues on the coasts.

In spite of the limited practicality of the reprinted works, the series seems to have been at least somewhat successful, judging by its continuance for a quarter century. In 1860, John Campbell, a Philadelphia bookseller, listed the series in his catalogue. The original first series, of seventy-three volumes, had sold out and was out of print.[46] The remaining thirty-one volumes of the series were available at a price of ninety-three dollars, almost three times what they had cost by original subscription.

CONCLUSION

Although not the primary form of law book publishing or selling during the antebellum period, sale by subscription was an important phenomenon in the law book world. It offered substantial risk reduction to printers and booksellers and often substantial price savings to buyers. It was used for a variety of different types of law texts and was itself subject to variation in method. In addition, subscription arrangements could be used as an alternative to publishing consortia and were particularly useful for interstate distribution of law books. Subscription publishing and selling was significant, and its history provides another key part of the overall history of law bookselling and publishing in antebellum America.

[46] John Campbell, *Catalogue of Law Books* (1860).

Previous chapters have discussed the principal aspects of the law book trade in the United States from 1770 until 1870. We have analyzed the various ways law books could be published, financed, and distributed. We have seen the development of markets for new and used law books and for domestically produced works by American authors, American reprints of English works, and the importation of English works produced in England or pirated in Ireland. In telling this narrative, we have mentioned many law book publishers and sellers and have seen how the trade started with a number of smaller firms and came to be dominated by a few national firms like Little, Brown and Banks, Gould. But even when these great national firms were at their height in the 1850s, it was possible for a single entrepreneurial lawyer and book seller to succeed on a national scale. For example, in John Livingston, the first great law bookselling entrepreneur and innovator in providing services to the American Bar, we have a story in which we can see all of the various aspects of the antebellum law book trade come to fruition in one man's remarkable enterprise. We turn to this subject in Chapter 6.

Chapter 6

John Livingston, Esq.

Law Bookseller as Cultural Entrepreneur

Although we know little of John Livingston's private life, there is much material from which a history of his professional career may be written.[1] Livingston was involved in several major business and legal activities during his career (in addition to practicing law).[2] His first major activity was as the editor and publisher of the *U.S. Monthly Law Magazine*, which under his leadership became *Livingston's Monthly Law Magazine*.[3] His second major business activity was the editorship and publication of *Livingston's Law Register*, a predecessor of today's Martindale-Hubbell.[4] His third major business venture was the publication of a series of biographical encyclopedias, including the *Biographical Sketches of Eminent American Lawyers*, published in ten parts, and *Livingston's Portraits and Memoirs of Eminent Americans*, a broader series of biographies printed in several issues of two and three volumes each.[5] Livingston was also instrumental in the organization

[1] A search of various New York City archives has turned up virtually nothing on Livingston, though he is listed in Gould's *New York Diaries* for several years.

[2] See *U.S. Monthly Law Magazine* (New York: Livingston, 1850) [USMLM]; Erwin Surrency, *A History of American Law Publishing* (New York: Oceana, 1990), 204–5.

[3] See Surrency, *A History of American Law Publishing*, 205–6. [4] Ibid.

[5] Livingston published several versions of his biographical sketches in book form: J. Livingston, *Biographical Sketches of Eminent American Lawyers Now Living*, 10 parts (New York: Livingston, 1852) [published monthly]; J. Livingston, *Portraits of Eminent Americans Now Living* (New York: Livingston, 1853) [published in two volumes]; J. Livingston, *Portraits of Eminent Americans Now Living* (New York: Livingston, 1854) [published in three volumes]; J. Livingston, *American Portrait Gallery, Containing Portraits of Men Now Living* (New York: Livingston, 1853–54)

and operation of the North American Legal Association in 1849 as well as the Merchants' Union Law Company in 1866.[6] Finally, in the 1870s, Livingston was actively engaged in representing shareholders in the Erie Railroad, as well as publishing memorials in their favor in conjunction with the proposed reorganization of that railroad.[7] During all these years Livingston remained an active member of the New York Bar. Livingston was the first great lawyer–entrepreneur the United States had produced.

Livingston's first great enterprise, and one that all others built on to some degree, was his monthly magazine. The *United States Monthly Law Magazine* began publication with volume 1, number 1, in January 1850. Livingston (giving as his address 54 Wall Street, New York) identified himself as its editor in the preface. In this introductory piece, he related that he had long been sought to begin a monthly legal periodical, but that it was only with the coming of 1850, with a sufficient number of advance subscriptions in hand that he was willing to commence such a publication.[8] He stated that one of the purposes of the publication was:

> [T]o gather from, and diffuse among the members of the Bench and Bar of the United States, such decisions and legal intelligence as may be the most useful and interesting.[9]

He promised to provide "condensed reports" of cases as well as articles on subjects interesting to the professional reader. In publishing such a legal journal, Livingston was not a pioneer. Several such periodicals had been published in the United States before 1850.[10] Further, many general circulation periodicals, like the *North American Review*, also carried articles of legal interest. What was new about Livingston's

[published in four volumes; volumes 1 and 2 bear the publisher's imprint of Comish, Lamport & Co.].

[6] See J. Livingston, *Letter to Merchants and Manufacturers Throughout the Union* (New York: Office of the Merchants' Union Law Company, 1866).

[7] See J. Livingston, *Analysis of the Erie Reorganization Bill, prepared for and at the request of Holders of More than $15, 000 Erie Railroad Shares* (New York: 1876).

[8] *USMLM*, l (I; l850), 1. [9] Ibid.

[10] See Surrency, *A History of American Law Publishing*, 7, 25–26, 30; F. L. Mott, *A History of American Magazines* (Cambridge, MA: Belknap Printing, 1957); M. Bloomfield, Bloomfield, *American Lawyers in a Changing Society* (Cambridge, MA: Harvard University Press, 1976), 306, notes that there were ten legal periodicals in existence in the United States in 1850.

periodical, however, was that Livingston aimed it at not a local audience but the national market, and that it was part of a broad collection of related legal businesses. He understood that to succeed in his publishing venture, he also needed to succeed in other businesses. His new magazine was not cheap; subscription costs were five dollars per year, a considerable sum in 1850.[11]

Livingston's publishing career actually began in 1849 with his first *Law Register*. The *Law Register* continued to be published intermittently into the 1860s and was one of the earliest attempts to provide a national law directory.[12] The structure of Livingston's work was ingenious. He provided the name of every lawyer known to him by state, county, and town, giving their full postal address when known. It seems that he built his directory on what we would now call a database, constructed through extensive correspondence with lawyers and postmasters throughout the United States. Livingston seems to have realized that the rise of a national commercial economy and businesses with interests in more than one state was going to require them to locate reputable lawyers in each jurisdiction in some systematic manner.[13]

The publication of the *Law Register* in 1849 was crucial to the commencement of the *United States Monthly Law Magazine* precisely one year later because it provided Livingston with a ready-made list of potential subscribers. Indeed, we may suppose that the primary purchasers of the advance subscriptions mentioned in the preface to volume 1 were lawyers who had been listed in the 1849 *Law Register*.[14] Livingston's genius was to realize that he not only needed a product to

[11] *USMLM*, 1 (1; 1850), 2. It is interesting to note that the price of the magazine subscription was reduced to three dollars by January 1854, or with the "*Law Register* for 1854," the price was four dollars. The single issue price was twenty-five cents.

[12] See Surrency, *A History of American Law Publishing*, 205–6. According to the bibliographical note given in The Harvard Law Library catalogue (which agrees with information contained in The National Union Catalogue of Pre-1956 imprints), the *Law Register* was published annually until 1854. It was published inconsistently from 1854 until 1858, then published in 1859, 1860, and 1866. It seems to have ended publication in 1868.

[13] We recall such a "national" economy in law was created by Justice Story's decision in *Swift v. Tyson*, 41 U.S. 1 (1842); See M Horwitz, *The Transformation of American Law* (Cambridge, MA: Harvard University Press, 1977).

[14] Indeed, the *USMLM* carried "updates" for the *Law Register;* see *USMLM*, 1 (1, 1850), 103.

sell (i.e. his magazine), but also a market for that product. By developing the *Law Register*, he created, in effect, a database from which he could develop the market for his new publication ventures. The other important aspect of this new enterprise was that Livingston had the vision to look beyond state and regional boundaries to create a publishing and bookselling venture that was truly national in scope and in design. In this he followed the models established already by the great national houses like Little, Brown.

By the middle of the nineteenth century, the United States, as we have seen, had begun to develop a national identity. More important, it had also begun to develop, albeit on a small scale at first, a national commerce. In 1849 the discovery of gold in California ensured that this state would develop rapidly and draw thousands of immigrants. The railroads were expanding as well. In every aspect of life the nation was on the move, and the transformation of the original thirteen colonies into a vast, continent-spanning nation was in full swing.

Lawyers, whose activities had been very much limited by distance during the first part of the century, soon found themselves faced with the possibility of taking advantage of this national transformation. As the nation expanded, so did its economy and the opportunities for lawyers. But to take full advantage of this opportunity, lawyers needed to keep abreast of the law in not only their own jurisdiction but in others where they might transact business. They also needed contacts with other lawyers in other jurisdictions so that they might form alliances for such work as collections or trans-jurisdictional litigation.

Livingston realized all of this and designed his business enterprises to serve this national legal market. The *Law Register* not only provided a necessary database, it also assisted lawyers, bankers, and merchants in finding lawyers in other jurisdictions. The *United States Monthly Law Magazine* was a means by which to provide reports of cases on a national scale to its readers. Livingston's bookselling business, so closely tied to the magazine, was another effort to profit from the need for law books by lawyers across the nation, providing access to law books in many places that lacked local law booksellers. The biographical publications served to feed lawyers' need for publicity and recognition, and they were also a thinly disguised method of national advertising for the lawyers whose biographies were featured. The Merchants' Union Law Company was simply an extension of the earlier North American Legal Association. Both were attempts to forge a loose national alliance of lawyers who would serve the increasing needs of banks and merchants for legal services. John Livingston was a visionary who understood the impact that Manifest Destiny and the national transformation of the original colonies would have on the legal profession in America.

THE *LAW REGISTER*

Our endeavor has been to make [the Law Register] contain the name and address of every lawyer in the United States, and denote who are practicing, and who have retired from practice, and who are on the bench.[15]

When John Livingston began to publish the *Law Register* in 1849, he began an enterprise which continues today through its successor, Martindale-Hubbell. The *Law Register* was both visionary in scope and peculiarly modern. It was conceived as an annual publication to be sold both by subscription and at booksellers.[16] Designed to be used by lawyers, it was also for "bankers, merchants, manufacturers, insurance companies – in short, to all whom are employed in active business."[17] To give the *Law Register* maximum utility, Livingston realized that it had to be comprehensive. To achieve this, Livingston devised an ingenious method for gathering names. He contacted the postmasters for every post office (more than 1,800) and asked each to send the names and addresses of their local attorneys.[18] This was a break from standard practice, which would have been to publish the names only of those attorneys who subscribed to the periodical.[19] But to limit his list in this manner would have seriously reduced its value to its readers. By

15 *Law Register*, 1853, 13.

16 The *Law Register* for 1853 states, "This Work will be sent by mail to any part of the United States on the receipt of One Dollar by the Publisher." The title page indicates that it was "for sale by all booksellers." One dollar was the additional price for annual subscribers to the *USMLM* if they wanted to include the *Law Register* in the cost of their subscription.

17 *Law Register*, 1853, 13.

18 Ibid. Livingston used this same method to gather names for his North American Legal Association in 1849 as well; see *Manual of the North American Legal Association*, 6. It may well be that he solicited for both of these enterprises at this time.

19 *Law Register*, 1853, 13. This was the method traditionally used to sell books by subscription; see Chapter 5.

1853, its fourth year of publication, the *Law Register* listed more than 25,000 individual attorneys.

The bulk of the volume of each *Law Register* was taken up by the listing of attorneys, by state and county. Attorneys were indexed by city, village, and post office. Also listed were all of the counties of each state as well as each county's seat. The *Law Register* contained a list of the judges of the highest courts of each state (with their salaries). It contained a list of county sheriffs and recorders. Finally, the *Law Register* contained a brief summary of the usury laws of each state.

The contents of the *Law Register* are absolutely consistent with its primary purpose of being a desk-side reference work for lawyers, bankers, and merchants who might need to find a lawyer or legal official in a state not their own. Even the cover illustration of the *Law Register* is consistent with promoting this objective. Livingston chose to illustrate each cover with a complex design using traditional symbols of the law and the nation. Thus, the cover illustration contains Blind Justice surrounded by a shield of stars and stripes, the lamp of wisdom and books, with a classical building in the Greek or Roman tradition, and a pyramid in the background.[20] All of these were symbols attached to the ideals of the new republic.

Livingston was also aware of the scope of the readership for the *Law Register*. He made this clear by including an advertisement for his own practice as a lawyer, notary public, and "Commissioner for every State in the Union" at the end of the preface.[21] Livingston appreciated the commercial value of the *Law Register*'s national scope and used it not only for his personal practice but also for his other publishing endeavors. He advertised the *United States Monthly Law Magazine* on the back cover of the 1853 *Law Register*.

Even if John Livingston had done nothing more than publish the *Law Register*, he would still stand out as one of the first major legal entrepreneurs of nineteenth-century America. He did do much more; however, it must be understood that the *Law Register* was the basis for much of his other activities and was the source of all his future mailing lists. Therefore, it is not surprising that Livingston published the

[20] Ibid. at cover page. On the significance of the Pyramid see John Fabian Witt, *Patriots and Cosmopolitans* (Cambridge, MA: Cambridge University Press, 2007).

[21] Ibid., 16. Livingston also adds that "He takes depositions with accuracy and despatch [sic], and on reasonable terms."

Law Register for nearly a decade, even though standing alone it was not profitable.[22] Its price of one dollar per annual issue was not unreasonable. It seems that the primary reason why the publication was not profitable during its early years was because too few lawyers and others subscribed to it. We may surmise this lack of subscribers was owed to the very novelty of Livingston's effort. As with any visionary project, the public is often the last to realize its value. Whatever financial losses Livingston may have suffered in publishing the *Law Register*, its value to him and his other enterprises was sufficient to guarantee its continuation.

THE NORTH AMERICAN LEGAL ASSOCIATION

At the same time that Livingston was preparing the *Law Register* for publication, he was also busy organizing the North American Legal Association (also known, in some sources, as the "American Legal Association"). The Association was intended to bring together lawyers from different counties and states to form a loose organization for referral purposes. Livingston published a circular outlining the purposes of the organization and distributed this "to the postmaster of every county town, together with a letter requesting that the same should be placed in the hands of some trustworthy lawyer."[23] Several months later, Livingston did the same for county clerks throughout the United States.

The notion underlying the formation of the Association was much the same as the *Law Register*. Livingston realized that the transformation of commerce into a national activity would produce the need for lawyers throughout the nation and that this need presented an opportunity for an entrepreneur. The *Law Register* was intended to provide a ready reference for those seeking a lawyer; the Association took this idea one step further: It would publish a list of all member lawyers, and the members of the Association were expected to "give preference to their fellow members in transaction business at distant points."[24] The bylaws of the Association established that members would be expected to share proceeds from any business transacted by agreement and that

[22] Ibid., 13. "Having for three years published this work at considerable personal loss . . ."
[23] *Manual of the North American Legal Association*, 6. [24] Ibid., 12.

members were expected to pay a minimum referral fee of twenty-five percent unless otherwise agreed.[25]

The next evidence of the subsequent history of the Association comes in the January 1851 issue of the *United States Monthly Law Magazine*. Appended to the end of this issue is a prospectus under the heading "United States Monthly Law Magazine Advertiser" for the "American Legal Association" with a "Catalogue of Members."[26] The president of the Association is listed as James M. Buchanan of Baltimore, Maryland. Livingston is listed as secretary. Thirty-two men are listed as members of the Board of Directors. The Association's members came from every state, as well as from the Minnesota and Oregon Territories, and two from Great Britain. According to this 1851 publication, membership in the Association cost five dollars for two years.

The Association was a bold enterprise and foreshadowed the development of corresponding law firm associations a century later. It may have been true that the existence of the *Law Register* condemned the Association to fail from the start. Any law firm looking to find a referral entity needed only to look to the Law Register. There appears to have been little value added by joining the Association and no value to a possible client in choosing an Association member firm. However, the Association promised national advertising and claimed to provide a screening function to guarantee a high level of expertise.[27] These factors may have helped to sustain the Association; nevertheless, there is little further publication after 1851, and it failed several years later.[28] Regardless, the Association was not a major misstep for John Livingston or his growing enterprises. For Livingston, his most important and lasting venture was started in 1850, the *United States Monthly Law Magazine and Examiner*, which became *Livingston's Monthly Law Magazine*.

[25] Ibid. [26] *USMLM*, 3 (1; January 1851): i–iii, following 140.

[27] Ibid. Stating "it is believed that all [members] will be found not only intelligent and worthy, but faithful and competent men, upon whom the business public and the profession can safely rely, and who will always be found at their posts, ready to give prompt and efficient attention to such matters as may be entrusted to them."

[28] See Bloomfield, *American Lawyers in a Changing Society*, 321, stating that the Association failed in 1854.

THE UNITED STATES MONTHLY LAW MAGAZINE

In January 1850, *The United States Monthly Law Magazine and Examiner* made its appearance on the American scene. The cover carried an illustration designed to convey the importance of the magazine. The center was a glass-fronted bookcase, within which the shelves were filled with heavy tomes of the law. At its top was the bust of a man in the classical style. At its bottom, on a pedestal rested a statute of Blind Justice accompanied by a bust of Athena, Goddess of Wisdom, and by her side, the lamp of wisdom. More law books were scattered on either side of the pedestal.[29] On the pedestal where Blind Justice stood were inscribed the words "New York, John Livingston, 52 Wall Street." At the very bottom of the cover were the date and the price: "Terms, Five Dollars a Year, Invariably in Advance."

Three years later, the publisher changed the title to *Livingston's Monthly Law Magazine*. The cover was also changed, now reflecting the same illustration that was used for the *Law Register*. In addition, the place of publication changed to 157 Broadway. In spite of these surface changes, Livingston's periodical continued in publication throughout the 1850s and into the mid-l860s. The magazine appeared at a time when few new legal periodicals were introduced, although some already existed, having been part of the first wave of legal periodical publication that took place just after the turn of the nineteenth century.[30]

Livingston explained the purpose of his new publication in the first volume published in January 1850. He said that he had been solicited by many to start such a periodical and had done so because he had sufficient subscriptions at hand. We may wonder whether this was true

[29] The use of books as a symbol for learning was quite common at this period; see A. Fidler, "'Till You Understand Them in their Principal Features': Observations on Form of Function in Nineteenth-Century American Law Books," *Papers of the Bibliographical Society of America*, 92 (4, 1998): 427–42.

[30] See Surrency, *A History of American Law Publishing*, 203–4; Mott, *A History of American Magazines*. Most of these law periodicals were short-lived, although during the antebellum period there were more than two dozen at one time or another. On one such, Timothy Walker's *The American Jurist*, see Walter Theodore Hitchcock, "Timothy Walker: Antebellum Lawyer," unpublished doctoral dissertation, University of Michigan, 1980.

or simply a statement of entrepreneurial bravado. Whatever the case, in the preface Livingston promised his readers that he would publish:

> [A]ccurate and condensed reports of such cases, civil and criminal, as comprehend judicial decisions or interpretations of importance to the practicing lawyer.[31]

He also promised that each issue would contain "one or more articles of interest to the professional and general reader."[32] He also promised that the magazine would contain reports of cases not otherwise reported, reports of cases in advance of their publication by other reporters, and digests of both American and British decisions.[33]

Even more important from the historical perspective, in an appendix to the first volume of his new magazine, Livingston stated categorically that the magazine "would contain matter from, and is intended for circulation in, every part of the Union."[34] Indeed, as an added inducement to get his readers to subscribe, Livingston offered to send new subscribers a free copy of the *Manual of the North American Legal Association*. The appendix provides evidence of the importance of Livingston's vision – to provide a legal periodical that would cover the whole country, from Maine to California and all territories in between. Livingston's desire to create a series of interlinked legal enterprises is obvious here. This is an early example of what today we describe as "convergence."

Livingston's plan for his new magazine was aggressive. He was going to publish as many reports of significant commercial cases as he might find in the reports of all the states of the Union. In so doing, he intended to appeal to those lawyers practicing around the country whose practices involved them in interstate activities and who either could not afford or did not have access to all of the various state reports. Of course, Livingston was also operating in a world made by Justice Story's decision in *Swift v. Tyson*, so he was going to have to publish not only state cases, but any new federal case reports that might have a bearing on commercial practice. His understanding of the growing demands on commercial practice is illustrated by the inclusion of British cases, clearly intended to attract those lawyers who were actively

[31] *USMLM*, 1 (1;1850), 1. [32] Ibid. [33] Ibid., 1–2. [34] Ibid., 104.

engaged in the growing trade between the United States and Great Britain.[35]

Livingston had higher aspirations for his new journal than simply being the most comprehensive source of commercial law reports. During the early years of publication, Livingston filled the magazine with what we would today call "feature" articles. In volume 2, he published extracts from John Anthon's work, *The Roots of Common Law*.[36] In volume 3, he published an essay on the "Nature and Method of Legal Study," which was a review of the Harvard Law School Catalogue for 1850–51.[37] In April 1851, he published a rather unusual piece on "What Are the Organic Prerequisites for a Lawyer" by "A Phrenologist."[38] This essay explored those aspects of the legal character and bodily constitution deemed necessary by a phrenologist.[39] In volume 3, Livingston also published the inaugural address of Professor Carruthers, recently installed as the professor of law at Cumberland University in Tennessee.[40] Volume 5 of the magazine is filled with legal biographies, for the most part drawn from his biographical works. In the November 1855 issue, Livingston published David Dudley Field's "Address to the Graduating Class of Albany Law School,"[41] and in the March issue of that year, he republished an article from the *London Law Review* on comparative jurisprudence.[42]

It seems reasonably obvious that Livingston was aiming his magazine for a broad section of the profession, for both those who saw it as a practical business as well as those who saw it as a learned one; those interested not only in the minutiae of practice and commerce but also in broader questions of method, education, and even comparative jurisprudence.[43] In so doing, Livingston was following in the steps of the earlier publishers of the *American Jurist* and *Law Magazine* and similar

35 Particularly important at this time were the bi-national commissions on losses related to the War of 1812.

36 *USMLM*, 2 (1851): 6. 37 *USMLM*, 3 (1851): 379–95. 38 Ibid., 466–72.

39 See M. H. Hoeflich, "Lawyers and the Science of Character," *The Green Bag* (2003): 253–64 for an account of nineteenth-century lawyers' fascination with phrenology.

40 *USMLM*, 3 (1851): 539.

41 *Livingston's Monthly Law Magazine (LMLM)**, 5 (1855): 675. Note that by this time the name of the magazine had been changed to *Livingston's Monthly Law Magazine*.

42 *LMLM*, 5 (1855): 678ff.

43 On the law as a "learned profession," see, above all, P. Miller, *The Life of the Mind in America: from the Revolution to the Civil War* (San Diego: Harcourt Brace Janovich,

periodicals. But Livingston was also a businessman determined to succeed and turn a profit, and it seems that the success of his magazine venture was never really assured. In issue after issue, he advertised for subscribers. He did not hesitate to offer special prices to attract them, and it seems he did not hesitate to change the format of his magazine in response to subscriber criticism. In the February 1853 issue, Livingston published the following notice to his readers:

> Biographical, obituary, or miscellaneous notices are not what subscribers want: what they want is law – and we promise as much of it as can be condensed in our pages.[44]

Although the magazine continued to carry scholarly articles and articles on practical subjects, biographies of lawyers and related texts disappeared after this issue. However, Livingston continued to include engravings of prominent lawyers, perhaps because he already had them available from his biographical publications. He may well have been attempting to get the maximum use of such portrait engravings because they were quite costly: $200 each.[45]

Given the high aspirations Livingston had for the magazine, its production was not easy. Certainly it is hard to imagine that one man, even one so energetic and entrepreneurial as John Livingston, could possibly have produced all these endeavors by himself. In part, the problem of text was solved by the fact that Livingston published very little original material in the magazine. Most of what he published was reprinted from other sources, including his own biographical publishing venture. Much of the scholarly material came from pamphlets and other American and British reviews. But this still left an enormous amount of effort that needed to be expended on the case reports.

1965); see also Bloomfield, *American Lawyers in a Changing Society*, 137–90; see also M. H. Hoeflich, "Lawyers and the Science of Character," note 39, for the contrary view.

[44] *LMLM*, 1 (February 1853): 160ff. In the February 1853 issue, Livingston printed a letter from a New York subscriber, David Depue, in which Depue asked Livingston to print "more and fuller" case reports. Livingston again made such a promise in his February 1855 issue of the *LMLM*.

[45] *LMLM*, 2 (January 1854): 90; see also 92, where Livingston printed that he had spent $10,000 in printing the *Law Register* for 1854. This would indicate that Livingston had well over $50,000 invested in just his publishing enterprises at this time.

Livingston solved the problem of case editing in much the same way that modern publishers do. He hired two young brothers, both lawyers, referred to only by their last name, "Abbot."[46] According to Livingston, these young lawyers were "men of much promise." Apparently they were responsible for "collecting and condensing" case reports. Livingston was clearly aided by his location in New York City, where there were plenty of young lawyers just starting out in practice who would be glad for the remunerative work. In addition, New York City was rich in law libraries, an excellent place to obtain the most recent reports from throughout the United States and Great Britain, as well as the most current law periodicals within which an editor could easily find material suitable for reprint.

LIVES OF EMINENT LAWYERS

Livingston published his *Biographical Sketches of Eminent American Lawyers*, issued in ten monthly parts, during 1852. He also published several multivolume editions of his *Portraits of Eminent Americans, Now Living* during 1853 and 1854. Although these latter sets did not contain lawyer biographies exclusively, lawyers made up the majority of biographical subjects (the remainder were primarily bankers). Taken together, these biographies published by Livingston over a three-year period numbered close to one hundred.

Livingston's purpose and method in publishing these biographies were quite significant. The motto that he appended to these was "Philosophy Teaching by Example."[47] In the prefaces to the various volumes he explained that his purpose in providing the biographical essays was to provide "examples for emulation."[48] In fact, the publication of these biographies served several purposes for the legal profession as well as their readers. For the profession, these biographies provided the general reading public with exemplary stories of distinguished lawyers. The reader of these volumes comes away from them with a distinctly positive

[46] *LMLM* (February 1853): 160. "We are much indebted to the Abbot brothers of this city for assistance in collecting and condensing the cases in this number. They are young men of promise, and cannot fail to succeed at our Bar."

[47] In fact, this motto appears on the spine of each bound volume in gilt lettering.

[48] See for example, J. Livingston, *Portraits of Eminent Americans, Now Living* (hereafter *PEA NL*), vol. 3 (New York: Livingston, 1854), v.

view of American lawyers. From the reader's perspective, the biographies do, in fact, present life stories after which readers might model their ambitions and activities. They also are designed to enlighten the reader, in much the same way as earlier clerical biographies.

Another interesting aspect of Livingston's biographies is the method and style in which they are written. Unlike many of his contemporaries, Livingston did not attempt to write most of the biographies himself. Instead, he solicited biographical memoirs from the subjects themselves as well as their friends and colleagues.[49] Thus, the biographies, though somewhat uneven in style and substance, provide a truly representative portrait of the legal profession, albeit painted by members of the profession and their supporters.

These were intended to be instructive, and their readers understood that purpose. It was the whole point of didactic literature.[50] They were also repetitive precisely because the authors of these books and essays had a firm notion of what the life and character of a good lawyer was and should be. This paradigm of a good lawyer forms the template for these biographies. What is particularly interesting is that this literary template of the good lawyer's life was so firmly established that so many of the biographies of the period used it. By reading through Livingston's legal biographies one can get a clear picture of the paradigm of the good lawyer promoted by the legal profession and its allies during the nineteenth century.

In Livingston's biographies, the typical lawyer's life was one of hard work, strong body and mind, commitment to success, and eventually success. The biographies have three consistent themes. First, many of the lawyers featured did not come from wealthy backgrounds, in fact, many of those that did come from prosperous backgrounds were often depicted as having reversals in family fortunes that forced them to begin their legal careers without substantial assets.[51] Whenever possible, the

[49] Thus, it would be more accurate to classify some of these biographies as "autobiographies."

[50] See, above all, S. Caspar, *Constructing American Lives* (Chapel Hill: University of North Carolina Press, 1999).

[51] See for example, *PEA NL*, "James P. Simmons, of Georgia." 79: "No early advantage of wealth, or even a sufficiency requisite for the necessary and ordinary pursuits in life, or the assistance of valued friends, were at his command"; see also Bloomfield, *American Lawyers in a Changing Society* 312–13.

biographies portrayed the lawyer as having overcome hardships early in his life or career.[52] A second theme was used to point out that the many of the lawyers portrayed had to teach school for a year or more before they could afford to enter the legal profession.[53] Again, the idea was that these lawyers needed to earn money to enable them to study law. This theme may also have been employed to infer that they were sufficiently well educated to allow them to teach school.

A third theme is that many of the lawyers were forced to migrate (usually west) to find a community where they could earn a decent living.[54] Several facts may affect this third theme, but undoubtedly the migration westward was a common experience for not just lawyers but many individuals in the eastern states. The frontier West was the land of opportunity and economic promise, echoing the call of Horace Greeley's advice to "Go West."

Aside from historical accounts of lawyers' lives, Livingston's biographies also express the ideological belief of the day that law was a relatively democratic profession. Virtually anyone could qualify as a lawyer and anyone so qualified could, if he were willing to be mobile, succeed in his profession. The democratic aspirations of success through hard work are a consonant theme throughout. The biography of Timothy Boutelle of Waterville, Maine, states:

[52] Many of the lawyers whose lives are included also suffered from ill health or other infirmity at some time; see, for example, *PEA NL*, "Timothy Boutelle, of Maine," 114: Mr. Boutelle, when young, had a feeble, delicate constitution, which unfitted him for the labors of a farm; and this circumstance, together with a love for study and the early indication of mental vigor and acuteness, induced his father to give him a public education.

[53] See, for example, *PEA NL*, "Hon. Peter Hitchcock, Late Chief Justice of Ohio," 183: "The pecuniary circumstances of his father limited, so much so, that in order to acquire the means of defraying the expenses of an education, he was compelled to rely measurably upon his own exertions. For this purpose he spent his vacations, and occasionally some portions of the college terms, in teaching school."

[54] See, for example, *PEA NL*, "Gen. Ver Planck Van Antwerp, Late Commissioner of Public Works of Iowa," 341: "For a year or more after his admission to the bar, Mr. Van Antwerp practised as an attorney in Albany, in co-partnership with his father-in-law, Mr. Yates; but soon the prevailing spirit of emigration reawakened his love for the West, and he readily obeyed the impulse. Accordingly, in the summer of 1832, he went out to Ohio." This theme of migration may well be part of a broader theme of social mobility on which, see Bloomfield, *American Lawyers in a Changing Society*, 313.

In a few years his talents, legal knowledge, industry and integrity, being known and appreciated, he found himself possessed of an extensive and lucrative practice.[55]

In addition to hard work, knowledge and skill as a speaker were important to a lawyer. The biographer of Franklin Pierce, writing of his pre-presidential career as a lawyer, observed:

Legal knowledge, ready to be used at a moment's warning, self-possession, experience of human nature – all the energies of a well-stored and well-poised mind are called into constant requisition in every important trial.[56]

But eloquence and strength and knowledge were not enough. Just as men like David Hoffman and George Sharswood insisted that the lawyer also exercise independent moral judgment in regard to his client's cause and limit his actions accordingly, so too did these various biographies point out as positive attributes that there were certain legal tactics and techniques to which their subjects would not stoop.[57] In Livingston's biography of John McHenry of Hartford, Kentucky, the biographer says:

[H]e scorned to lend his aid to malignant and vexatious prosecutions, and to waste the time of the court in frivolous and unimportant questions.[58]

An anecdote about Franklin Pierce makes the point of the importance of this gate-keeping function by the lawyer even more strongly:

Fully recognizing the principle that his profession could only be used for moral purposes, Mr. Pierce was always anxious to prevent litigation where the ends of justice could be gained without this resort.[59]

But, if the cause was just, then the lawyer, here again Pierce, would be a zealous advocate for his client:

The defense of the innocence – the assertion of right – the exposure and punishment of fraud – and the redress of wrong – these were the occasions which roused to the utmost the energies of his mind and furnished full scope for the exhibition of his uncommon power as an advocate. At such times, when the full exertion of his strength was demanded, his eloquence rose with the occasion

[55] *PEA NL* 41. [56] Ibid., 211.

[57] M.H. Hoeflich, "Legal Ethics in the Nineteenth Century: the 'Other Tradition,'" *University of Kansas Law Review* 47 (1999): 793.

[58] *PEA NL*, 416–17. [59] Ibid., 212.

in power and energy, and bore along with its irresistible torrent the convictions of his hearers.[60]

A good memory was another characteristic possessed by the paradigmatic good lawyer:

Mr. McHenry's great excellence as a lawyer consists in his retentive memory, by which he takes hold of and retains a long and complicated chain of facts and circumstances in a cause, his presence of mind and cool deliberation, clear, discriminating judgment, and thorough knowledge of the law.[61]

One extremely interesting aspect of these legal biographies is that although the lawyers were generally said to be well educated and knowledgeable in the law, this did not mean that they attended one of the elite, university-affiliated law schools. Indeed, the vast majority of the men profiled in these volumes were not university or law school graduates. Instead, for the most part they were trained by the traditional apprenticeship model, having "read the law" with one or more distinguished lawyers and practitioners.[62] In fact, these biographies take great pains to provide the educational genealogies of the men studied. The reader is told, often in detail, the names and places of practice of each of the lawyer's teachers. Clearly, the identity of one's "master" in the law was deemed to be of primary importance. The more distinguished the master, the more prestige enjoyed by the pupil.

The amount of text devoted to the biographical subject's legal instruction also provides an interesting sidelight on the success of university affiliated legal education by the 1850s. Although Harvard Law had been in existence since 1817 and Transylvania since 1799, the overwhelming majority of American lawyers were still trained in law offices.[63] Thus, although proponents of university-affiliated law schools were attempting at this time to establish their own graduates as the intellectual elite of the American bar, they had not yet succeeded in this by the early 1850s, as Livingston's biographical volumes attest. Again, Livingston may have been upholding the democratic ideal that any man, not just the wealthy

[60] Ibid., 211. [61] Ibid., 417.

[62] On the system of apprenticeship, see, generally, P. Hamlin, *Legal Education in Colonial New York* (New York: Da Capo Press, 1970).

[63] See P. Hamlin, *Legal Education in Colonial New York*. I would like to thank "B.J.," the Archives Director at Transylvania University in Lexington, Kentucky, for providing the date for the inception year of the law school there.

elite, could be a good and successful lawyer through hard work and determination.

One other aspect of the legal professional is highlighted by the biographical sketches. Although the greatest part of most antebellum lawyers' practices was litigation, the biographies praise the lawyers' interest in and skill at the use of arbitration and settlement rather than litigation. In the case of Pierce, he is praised for his "habit of advising his clients to settle their disputes by conciliation and mutual agreement" rather than by a full-blown trial.[64]

Finally, one last aspect of lawyers' activities that finds its place in these biographies is benevolence. Individual lawyers are praised for their willingness to work for the deserving poor on a pro bono basis. For example, James Simmons of Laurenceville, Georgia, is commended in his biography for never having "left a client because he was poor."[65] Ironically, just a few lines later in his biography he is also praised for the fact that he never had trouble collecting his fees.[66]

The overall portrait of the good lawyer that emerges from Livingston's collective biographies is of a man who is strong in body and in character, exudes integrity and intelligence, knows the law but is not a pedant. These are biographies that would have been well received by both those written about and those who knew the subjects. Indeed, they would have been well-received by any lawyer wishing to confirm to himself or those around him of the positive character of the legal profession.

From the business viewpoint, these were biographies that were of interest to the legal profession. By publishing literally hundreds of these biographical sketches, Livingston assured himself of a ready market. Through these biographies, he also acquired the reputation of a man who understood and who promoted the legal profession, a useful reputation for a legal entrepreneur.

LIVINGSTON'S SELECT LAW LIBRARY

Livingston's success as a legal entrepreneur depended, in part, on his ability to forge useful links between his various businesses. For example, the magazine reprinted biographical sketches from the biography series.

[64] *PEA NL*, 212. [65] Ibid., 87. [66] Ibid.

The North American Legal Association and the magazine both shared the mailing list developed by the *Law Register*. It is not at all surprising, therefore, that Livingston decided that another venture that made sense for him was that of bookselling.[67] Within a few years, *Livingston's Monthly Magazine and Law Register* was national in both scope and subscribers.[68] Indeed, one of the strongholds of the magazine was California.[69] As has already been described, by the 1850s, the great law book houses, like Little, Brown and Banks, Gould had already become firmly established as national in scope. For the most part, these booksellers were, like Livingston himself, based in the Northeast.[70] For the many lawyers who migrated and found themselves practicing west of the Mississippi, acquiring a serious law library was not an easy or affordable task and required recourse to catalogues. Livingston also realized that one of the great disadvantages of the apprentice system was that lawyers trained in this way rarely had access to a major law library and often had very little guidance as to what books, at a minimum, ought to comprise their personal law library. They turned to law booksellers' catalogues for assistance. Livingston was in the perfect position to come to the aid of lawyers seeking to acquire a library. Once again, his New York City location was a great advantage, as this put him near to most of the law book publishers. It also made it relatively easy for him to import foreign law texts himself or purchase them from the larger booksellers in New York. His proprietorship of the magazine was also a clear advantage, because this gave him an easy forum for advertising. In fact, *Livingston's Monthly Law Magazine* carried reviews of new and important law books, a significant advantage because he could then offer these

[67] The linkage between bookselling and periodical and book publishing was not unique to Livingston. It was the utility of just such linkages that moved the Harper brothers to found *Harper's Monthly* in 1850; see K. Price and S. Smith, eds., *Periodical Literature in Nineteenth-Century America* (Charlottesville: University Press of Virginia, 1995), 169.

[68] See *LMLM*, 5 (August 1855): 530ff. Among the listed subscribers were Caleb Cushing of Washington, D.C., J. L. Petigru of South Carolina, and two lawyers in Montreal, Canada.

[69] See *LMLM*, 5 (January 1855): 96: "We should be very ungrateful not to thank the bench and bar of this golden state [California] for their patronage. *With scarcely a single exception, they are our subscribers;* and we now send over five hundred copies to California alone." (emphasis in original).

[70] See Surrency, *A History of American Law Publishing*, 211.

volumes for sale to his readers. In effect, he could create demand for new law books simply by reviewing them.

Interestingly, Livingston seemed not to abuse this privilege. Rather than simply provide positive reviews of each new book, thereby encouraging sales, he made it clear that the reviews in his magazine would be objective. In one issue, Livingston recounted the following:

> One of the publishers of this little work [The Legal and Commercial Commonplace Book] complained of the manner in which it was noticed in the August number of the Magazine. He was surprised that considering his liberality in sending us a copy, we had spoke so disparagingly of it ... This journal will contain reviews of books, speaking of them as they may deserve, but no puffs manufactured to order will be inserted therein[71]

Nevertheless, when a book was well reviewed, Livingston was in the perfect position to sell it.

A further advantage was that Livingston was intimately familiar with the postal regulations of the United States and, was in fact, expert at mailing books and magazines throughout the country. Thus, he was in an excellent position to begin a nationwide mail-order law book company just at the time when the postal regulations had changed to make this possible.[72] To compete with the great houses, Livingston had to use every means available to him in his bookselling business and offer to his would-be clients catalogues as useful as those they might obtain from others in the book trade. So Livingston, like Little, Brown and others, used Simon Greenleaf's old list of recommended law books as the basis for his own catalogue.[73] He actually went a step further than the other booksellers and titled his catalogue after Greenleaf's list. In the catalogue he provided his readers with titles, places of publication, and retail prices. He did not tell his readers the origins of his list, which may suggest that neither Greenleaf nor other booksellers who had earlier used the list had agreed to Livingston's use of it. However, he did tell his readers which of the listed books were absolutely critical for a practitioner's library and which could be acquired as enrichment

[71] *USMLM*, v. 6, p. 100. [72] See Chapter 1.

[73] See, for example, J. Livingston, *Catalogue of a Select Law Library* (New York: Livingston, March 1856); see also, "Catalogue of Modern Law Books," *Legal Reference Service Quarterly*, 13 (1994): 127–41, has reprinted this list.

texts.[74] He also offered his readers a substantial discount from what they might pay at a more traditional bookstore.[75]

Livingston's catalogue offered a wide variety of books. His list of a select law library included not only the standard English and American reports, but also a large number of treatises including several on foreign and civil law.[76] The lawyer who actually ordered even the small, most select library would have been required to pay $1,000 – a large sum for any lawyer in the 1850s.[77]

LIVINGSTON THE LAWYER

Throughout the period in which he managed his various enterprises, John Livingston never forgot, or let his readers forget, that he was also a lawyer. In virtually every issue of his magazine he also advertised his legal services:

> John Livingston,
> Counsellor at Law, Notary Public
> Commissioner, Resident in New York,
> Appointed by the Governors of Every State in the Union, to Take Testimony,
> Affidavits and Acknowledgments, to be Used Therein.
> Office, No. 157 Broadway, (up stairs,) New York,
> Having Been Appointed
> Court of Claims Commissioner
> •••
> New York Law and Collecting Agency
> John Livingston
> 157 Broadway, City of New York
> Established for the Use of Lawyers, Merchants, and Bankers
> Collections Made Through the United States[78]

Here again, we see synergy at work among his various enterprises. The practice specialties he outlines in these advertisements tie directly to his other activities. Both his collection work and his work as a lawyer taking oaths, affidavits, and acknowledgments were related to the national scope of his other activities. Presumably, he hoped to get referrals for work in New York from those who were his subscribers

[74] J. Livingston, *Catalogue of a Select Law Library*, 3. [75] Ibid., 1.
[76] Ibid., 10. [77] Ibid., 1–10. [78] *LMLM*, 6 (January 1856): final page.

elsewhere and work outside New York for those who would use his national contacts for collection of interstate debts.

At times, Livingston seems to have taken on partners. In the September 1855 issue of *Livingston's Monthly Law Magazine*, he advertised his legal services with the firm name of Livingston & Bradley.[79] Livingston is referred to as the "senior partner." Included in the advertisement is a list of references and clients. They came from New York, London, Alabama, Arkansas, California, Connecticut, Delaware, the District of Columbia, Florida, Georgia, Illinois, Indiana, Iowa, Louisiana, Maine, Maryland, Massachusetts, Michigan, Mississippi, Missouri, New Hampshire, New Jersey, North Carolina, Ohio, Pennsylvania, Rhode Island, South Carolina, Tennessee, Texas, Vermont, Virginia, and Wisconsin.

In the January 1854 issue of his magazine, Livingston solicited his readers for another kind of legal work:

> Law libraries in villages are generally small and opportunities for consultation with books limited. As the Editor has connected with his office, two members of the bar, who transact much of his ordinary business, he finds ample time to prepare briefs upon questions of law, which he is willing to do for his professional brethren in the country for reasonable compensation.[80]

Presumably, the two lawyers to whom he refers are the Abbot brothers mentioned earlier.[81] Livingston's offer to do briefs for country lawyers who were far from an extensive law library is quite significant. We know that it was not uncommon to find lawyers in New York City who subsisted on work given them by other lawyers. These were usually men who had failed to build up a practice of their own. C. C. Langdell, before he became dean of the Harvard Law School, was among their number.[82] But it was Livingston's entrepreneurial instinct that led him to extend this practice to a mail-order business by which rural lawyers might obtain the benefit of his services. Livingston knew that many of his subscribers were not near substantial law libraries – thus the initiation of his book selling business. He expanded on their lack of access to law books by offering his professional services as a lawyer.

[79] *LMLM*, 3 (9; September 1855): inside front cover.
[80] *LMLM*, 2 (1; January 1854): 90. [81] *LMLM*.
[82] C. Warren, *A History of the Harvard Law School and of Early Legal Conditions in America* (New York: Da Capo Press, 1970), 175–82.

Presumably he had gained something of a positive reputation through his publishing endeavors, and he attempted to capitalize on this reputation through the offering of brief-writing services. We do not know how many lawyers sought his services in this area, but whatever his actual success, this venture, like so many of his others, was the first of its kind and a precursor of modern practices.

Livingston continued to find opportunities for his law practice. In the January 1854 issue of his magazine, he also placed a "Notice to All Persons Having Unadjusted Claims Against the British Government":

> We invite the attention of persons having claims to be adjusted under the mixed commission instituted by the governments of Great Britain and the United States, to the following notification. The Editor will send a brother to London about the first of March next, on business relating to unclaimed estates belonging to the heirs in this country and is willing to take charge of any matter of this kind, It will be seen that every claim must be presented on or before the 15th of March 1854.[83]

Livingston saw an opportunity and the magazine gave him the perfect forum in which to advertise his services to a large number of lawyers across the nation.

It seems that Livingston was involved in, and may well have been the founder of, another legal association somewhat like the failed North American Legal Association in the period immediately following the end of the Civil War. In December 1866, Livingston published a six-page circular on behalf of an organization called the Merchants' Union Law Company, based at 128 Broadway, of which Livingston was the secretary.[84] The purpose of this circular was to alert merchants and bankers throughout the United States of potential legislation, supported by the secretary of the treasury, the effects of which would have been quite negative on banks outside New York City. The circular consists of a detailed explanation of the proposed legislation plus a reprinting of portions of a report presented to Congress by the secretary of the treasury on December 3, 1866. In his explanation, Livingston stated that "eminent counsel have been retained at Washington" and that he had been obtained in New York.[85] He sought assistance from his

[83] *LMLM*, 2 (1; January 1854): 95.
[84] See Livingston, *Letter to Merchants and Manufacturers Throughout the Union.*
[85] Ibid., 1.

intended readers in the form of letters to congressmen, petitions, and other actions. In effect, it seems that the Merchants' Union Law Company was a lobbyist organization. Livingston's role was one he was well-suited to play – namely, to contact those bankers, merchants, and lawyers that he knew from his publications and other activities, and seek their help in defeating the proposed bill in Congress. His participation in this effort was quite opportunistic. The circular is dated the same month as the secretary presented his report requesting the disputed legislation. I have found nothing more about the Merchants' Union Law Company after this circular, so it may well be that Livingston created the "Union" as a lobbying device after he was retained by parties opposed to the legislation.

THE LAST DAYS

Little is heard from Livingston after the late 1860s. His publishing ventures seem generally to have ceased and there are no historical records of other activities until 1875.

At that time, Livingston again appears in the record, this time involved in one of the greatest legal controversies of the day: the Erie Railroad reorganizations. Between 1866 and 1870, a vast battle for the control of the Erie Railroad and, in fact, control of parts of the significant American securities and commodities markets took place. Involved were some of the greatest financiers and robber barons of the era: Daniel Drew, Jim Fisk, "Diamond" Jim Brady, Cornelius Vanderbilt, and Jay Gould, as well as leading legal luminaries such as David Dudley Field. Also involved, but of more dubious legal reputation were Judges George Barnard and Albert Cardozo (the father of United States Supreme Court Justice Benjamin Cardozo).[86]

During the late 1860s and early 1870s, a series of corporate and legal skirmishes changed the face of American corporate finance and American law. Much of the action took place in New York City and the state of New York. Thus, it is not surprising that Livingston saw in these legal battles another business opportunity. Livingston does not seem to have been a principal player in the major battles for control of the Erie line. His

[86] K. Farmer, "The Formation of the Bar of the City of New York," unpublished, May 2000.

name does not appear in the standard histories of the scandal. But in 1875, three years after the close of the main battle, Livingston seems to have been involved. In 1875, he wrote a critical history of the Erie battles and a legal analysis of the various steps taken by the lawyers, financiers, judges, and legislators.[87] In 1876, he produced a short pamphlet titled "An Analysis of the Erie Reorganization Bill," which was an attack on the receiver of the Erie Railroad appointed by the courts in 1872 and the legislation proposed to reorganize the railroad.[88] In this pamphlet, submitted to the New York Legislature in March 1876, Livingston notes that he has written and published the work at the request of Erie stockholders. At the conclusion of the preface to the pamphlet, Livingston signs himself "counsel for Erie Railroad stockholders."[89] From all indications it seems that during the mid-1870s, Livingston had found employment in clearing away the mess that the Erie railroad and its various owners had created in the years before. Here again, Livingston's primary function seems to have been less as a typical lawyer and more as a writer, publisher, and lobbyist. No doubt his earlier publishing and lobbying ventures made him seem an appropriate person for the task at hand.

Nothing more is known of John Livingston after this final pamphlet of 1876. He effectively fades into the shadows of history, neither seen nor heard from again. And yet, John Livingston was a remarkable individual who had a spectacularly interesting career from the mid-1840s until the mid-1870s. He did not achieve the kind of lasting renown lawyers such as David Dudley Field achieved, but he was in a true sense a pioneer as a legal entrepreneur. He may well have been one of the first America lawyers to see the business potential in the growing national market for legal services. Certainly his understanding of the role synergy can play in creating related businesses was groundbreaking and, in many ways, not to be duplicated again until the end of the twentieth century.

[87] J. Livingston, *The Erie Railroad: Its History and Management from April 24, 1832 to July 13, 1875* (New York: J. Polhemus, 1875).

[88] J. Livingston, *Analysis of the Erie Reorganization Bill.* [89] Ibid., 4.

Chapter 7
Conclusion
Selling the Law in Antebellum America

In one sense, this book has been about the growth of what may be called a "support industry." Lawyers were, and are, bookish creatures by both inclination and professional necessity. At the very beginnings of our republic, there were few lawyers and relatively few law books being published in the United States. For the most part, American lawyers depended on imported English texts, which had to be transported across the ocean, a time-consuming and expensive process. But when they reached the United States, for most of these books, the travels were far from over. In the beginning, there were few specialized law booksellers and these, for the most part, were located in larger urban centers. General booksellers might well stock a few law books and, on occasion, even receive a shipment consisting primarily of legal texts, but the fact is most American lawyers before 1800 had relatively small law libraries, consisting mainly of local laws and case reports and the occasional English legal treatise.

By the outbreak of the Civil War, this situation had changed dramatically. In 1860, there were more than a dozen major law book houses, companies that published law books, sold their own and others' legal publications, often did binding and specialized legal printing, and had built a national network of customers whom they serviced through large and learned catalogues. In effect, the American system for the distribution and sale of law books and related texts and equipment grew from its infancy to maturity in a space of approximately sixty years. In this book, I have attempted to trace the outlines of this growth and to provide the details of the most important aspects of this new industry.

In another sense, however, this book is about far more; it is about a different way of looking at the history of law and the legal profession in the antebellum period. Rather than focus on the development of doctrine or the relationship of law to society, it focuses on the way legal ideas are transmitted. The story of antebellum America is a story of growth: the growth of a nation southward and westward; a profession from a small cadre of ill-trained craftspeople to a professional elite with aspirations to learning, public service, and social prominence; and an entire complex industry involving importers, paper makers, printers, binders, publishers, authors, and booksellers. This story touches on the development of transportation and media in the United States; the shipping industry by canal, road, and railroad train; and the growth and maturity of the U.S. Postal Service into the primary means by which to convey information across the newly enlarged nation. This book is a work of business, professional, and intellectual history, and in it I hope I have shown readers the importance of the mundane necessities of life without which high theory can come to nothing. Just as kingdoms proverbially may be lost by a horseshoe, great doctrinal developments in the law may be advanced or impeded by nothing more glamorous than a decent postal route. This said, there are some aspects of the narrative I have set forth that merit a final summation.

FACTORS AFFECTING GROWTH

There were several factors affecting the growth of the American legal publishing and bookselling business in the antebellum period that I have attempted to explore in this book. Among the most important was the growth in the number of American lawyers; the spread of lawyers to the West as the population moved westward; the strong desire by the leaders of the antebellum American Bar to establish themselves as a learned profession; and the development of university-affiliated law schools, which stressed the "scientific" aspects of the law as a basic theme of their instruction;[1] the Federalist political agenda of the first quarter of the century and its dependence on authorship,

[1] See M.H. Hoeflich, *The Gladsome Light of Jurisprudence: Learning the Law in England and the United States in the 18th and 19th Centuries* (Westport, CT: Greenwood Press, 1988), intro.

publication, and dissemination of law treatises; the development of a transportation and shipping infrastructure throughout the United States, which linked larger and smaller cities across the nation;[2] and, finally, the growth of the U.S. postal system and the evolution of postal regulations, which made using the mails to send books secure and dependable after 1851.[3]

At the time of the Revolution, the number of lawyers practicing in the United States was relatively small. This meant that the market for specialized law texts was also small, because only lawyers – and the occasional library – were likely to purchase such texts. Printing, publishing, and distribution costs for law books were generally high. Thus, until a critical mass of lawyers in the population could be reached, few, if any, domestically produced law books would find their way into the mainstream of commerce in this country. Thus, during the earliest decades of the new nation, the books that tended to be available for purchase were imported, of local use (e.g., J. P. manuals) and were distributed locally, or works with broader appeal, such as Sir William Jones's *Essay on the Law of Bailments*,[4] which would also have appealed to businesspeople, and the several translations of Beccaria's *Dei Delitte e de la Pene*, whose appeal was universal to all reform-minded citizens.[5] Even such fundamental works as Sir William Blackstone's *Commentaries on the Laws of England* were first offered by subscription, a technique designed to reduce the financial risk to the publisher and bookseller.[6] Only after the success of the first subscription publication did other publishers venture new American editions.

One problem was that American law and English law began to diverge with independence. Further, each state of the new union began to develop its own laws, which often were different from each other. The social, physical, and demographic conditions of the new American republic were, in many cases, quite different from those of

[2] See, for example, Charles H. Ambler, *A History of Transportation in the Ohio Valley* (Glendale, CA: Clark, 1932), 107–209.

[3] See Chapter 1. [4] See note 25.

[5] Translations of Beccaria's work were published, for example, in Philadelphia in 1793 by William Young, in 1809 by William Farrand (with Voltaire's commentary), and in 1819 by Philip Nicklin (with Voltaire's commentary and translated from the French by a Philadelphia lawyer and legal writer, Edward Ingraham); in New York City in 1819 by Stephen Gould; and in Boston in 1809 by Farrand & Mallory.

[6] See Chapter 5.

England. And, of course, the wounds of the Revolution, reopened by the War of 1812, remained. Many American patriots of the Revolutionary generation and the succeeding generation were loathe to continue to use English statutes or cases. Thus, the demand grew for American texts or, at least, English texts adapted to the American market. As soon as the legal profession reached a size sufficient to make the risk of law book publishing and selling acceptable, printers, publishers, and booksellers appeared to meet the demand. By the early 1800s, this was already occurring in the large Eastern cities, particularly New York, Philadelphia, Boston, and Baltimore. By the middle of the 1820s, the profession was growing quickly enough that urban law book publishers and booksellers began to think about a national market. By the 1830s, this national market had become a reality, and the great houses, such as Little, Brown in Boston; Voorhies and Gould, Banks in New York; and T. & W. Johnson and Lea & Blanchard in Philadelphia had assumed positions of dominance.

One of the most important cultural and sociological factors affecting the growth of the antebellum law book trade was the increasing aspiration of the organized legal profession in the United States to be seen as a "learned" profession. From its humble beginnings in the colonial years, after the Revolution, the legal profession made enormous efforts to upgrade its social standing and to set itself apart from the "tavern lawyers" and pettifoggers who had brought the profession into disrepute. The most important means of achieving these ends were to raise the intellectual level of the profession and make it seen as a learned profession with all of the prestige associated with this idea. The surest route to creating a learned profession, or at least the appearance of one, was to create a "bookish" profession.

Throughout the history of the modern English Bar, lawyers were associated with books. This association was not always positive; the *Microcosmographie*, a satirical seventeenth-century tract, portrays lawyers as dry as dust, much like the bindings of the law tomes that lined their shelves.[7] But this association of lawyers with books in England could not last long in the United States without a

[7] John Earle, *Microcosmographie, or a Piece of the World Discovered: Essays and Characters* (Cambridge: Cambridge University Press, 1903), 92–93; see also M.H. Hoeflich, "Lawyers, Books & Papers," *The Green Bag* (Winter 2002): 163–71.

commercial infrastructure by which the lawyers could be supplied with texts.

Perhaps the most important development in the legal profession's antebellum drive for prestige was the founding of university-affiliated law schools at Harvard, Transylvania, Columbia, and elsewhere. These served to provide an alternative to the apprenticeship system for a small but elite group of lawyers. They offered a "scientific" approach to the law, which not only furthered the professional aspiration for social and intellectual prestige but also, as shown by Dan Hulsebosch, fostered the Federalist legal agenda. This form of education produced lawyers who could claim to be conversant with not only how to fill out forms and plead in a local court but also understanding the underlying rules and logic of the law wherever it might be practiced in the Common law world.[8] As noted in Chapter 1, this allowed Daniel Mayes at Transylvania Law School to declare he would teach his students in such a way that they would be as comfortable in the law courts at Westminster as they were in those of their own home towns.[9]

By the end of the antebellum period, more than a dozen such university-affiliated law schools had been established throughout the United States. The professors who taught at these schools, men like Joseph Story and Simon Greenleaf at Harvard, James Kent at Columbia, Daniel Mayes at Transylvania, David Hoffman at Maryland, and others elsewhere all viewed authorship of legal texts and articles as part of their professional responsibility. They not only lectured from texts, they also usually wrote the texts from which they lectured. These books they produced helped to create a native American legal literature that could be not only published by American law publishers but sold by American law booksellers to American lawyers.

The creation of this new genre of legal literature (i.e. a native American legal literature) also played to the patriotism of the American Bar in the antebellum period. American literature in the period following the Revolution lived very much in the shadow of England.[10] Native offerings were, for the most part, fairly scarce and

[8] Hoeflich, *The Gladsome Light*.

[9] D. Mayes, "An Address to the Students of Law in Transylvania University (1834)," in Hoeflich, *Gladsome Light*, 154.

[10] The attitude of the British critics to the nascent American literature is illustrated by the review of *Selections from American Poetry* (Dublin, 1834) printed in *The Edinburgh Review* (April 1835), 12–21.

those American productions that did appear, such as the work of the "Hartford Wits," tended to be imitative of English writers.[11] One of the few areas in which Americans excelled was the law and legal writing. England had no match for Story; indeed, Justice Story was consulted by the English when they sought to reform their own system of legal education.[12] Law was seen in antebellum America as a literary genre, and the growth of American law writing and law book publishing was viewed both in the United States and abroad as a source of American pride.

Book publishing and bookselling of all sorts, including law book publishing and bookselling, was condemned to being a localized industry until the United States developed a system of transportation and the infrastructure to permit the shipping of goods across the new nation and to the newly opening territories in the West. At the time of the Revolution there was very little infrastructure and virtually no transportation industry. But this situation soon changed. First came the toll roads and bridges; then the canals and the development of steamships, which could traverse the rivers and lakes of the new nation; and then, finally, toward the middle of the century, the development of railroads. The growth of national law book publishing and bookselling depended on the demographic expansion of the market. Other forms of literature, such as novels, could appeal to a large number of potential nonspecialist readers, so that even local markets might support a publisher or bookseller specializing in this genre. But technical law books, such as treatises, only appealed to lawyers and would-be lawyers. Thus, the pool of potential lawyer–readers had to expand. This pool could expand in only two ways: First, the number of lawyers in the United States had to increase, and second, the ability to reach as many American lawyers as possible had to become a reality. So long as the U.S. Postal Service made shipping books by post insecure, undependable, and expensive, private transportation was

[11] The best known of these Connecticut poets was Joel Barlow, a lawyer; see James Woodress, *A Yankee's Odyssey. The Life of Joel Barlow* (Philadelphia/New York: Lippincott, 1958). Barlow's best known poem was "The Columbiad," whose style was derivative of Pope. On the Wits, see, generally, Leon Howard, *The Connecticut Wits* (Chicago: University of Chicago Press, 1943).

[12] See M.H. Hoeflich, "The Americanization of British Legal Education," *Journal of Legal History* (1987), 244–59 (1989).

necessary.[13] The success of the trade depended on making transport reliable and the costs of transporting books low if nationwide distribution was to become a reality. As the various means of transportation developed and as private transportation companies, like Adams' Express Company, grew to take advantage of these new transportation networks, law booksellers and publishers could grow as well and develop a national business. By the late 1840s and early 1850s, this had become a reality, and entrepreneurs like John Livingston were able to exploit the situation to the fullest.

The difficulty of sending books through the United States mails until 1851 was a serious impediment to the growth of law book distribution in the United States. This forced booksellers to use private transportation companies and slowed the growth of a national law book market. When the prohibition was finally lifted in 1851, the last serious restraint on the growth of a national market for law books had disappeared. Of course, this also meant that the elite eastern booksellers, such as Little, Brown, would be able to gain an even more dominant position in the industry at the expense of local publishers and booksellers, but this was inevitable. Further, as great urban centers like Chicago and San Francisco grew in midcentury and later, these cities, also transportation hubs with large lawyer populations, also fostered the founding of law publishers and booksellers, like Callaghan and Bancroft-Whitney, which increased competition for the established elite of the Northeast.

One of the most important developments in American law during the antebellum period was the growth of a "national" law and legal literature, one of the primary goals of the Federalist jurists. When the nation was first founded, it consisted of thirteen colonies joined by a relatively weak federal government and a federal court system with little precedent and uncertain jurisdictional boundaries. It was possible that American law could develop on thirteen different models, each state with its own definite notions of private law and its own precedents that governed its jurisprudence. Indeed, given the great differences among the regions and the differing social and geographical conditions, such a system built on state law diversity might well have been likely. In some areas, such as slave laws, there were radical differences in the laws,

[13] See Chapter 2.

among not only northern and southern states but even states within the same region.

During the colonial period, when English law remained always not far in the background, some degree of uniformity was guaranteed among the various colonies, because English law and English legal literature served as the common, unifying thread. But when English law lost its authority after Independence, had each state developed its own legal literature and native law publishing and bookselling regimes, it is likely that this unifying feature of the colonial period would have been replaced by a much more diverse system. That it did not was, in part, due to the combined efforts of Federalist jurists, like Joseph Story and James Kent, who aspired to create an "American" jurisprudence whose basic tenets would be common to all states' systems and taught in the university-affiliated law schools like Harvard and Transylvania.[14]

Although it seems relatively clear that jurists like Story quite consciously attempted to create a distinctively American jurisprudence in cases like *Swift v. Tyson*[15] and in his various treatises on private law, it seems equally likely that the various law booksellers and publishers were more concerned with the economic benefits of an American jurisprudence than the ideological advantages to be gained therefrom. As has been noted several times here, the success of law book publishers and sellers depended on their reaching a large enough number of potential buyers to make a market sufficient to generate profits. Only a few jurisdictions, such as New York and Massachusetts, had a large enough number of lawyers in the first decades of the nineteenth century to support the publication and sale of books limited to the discussion of a single state's law. Other, less populous states simply did not have enough lawyers to justify the publication or sale of such state specific texts. Thus, law book publishers and sellers found it necessary to publish and sell books that were more generalized, teaching legal principles that would be useful in all American jurisdictions. To do this, they had to create a literature of American law. Thus, one finds relatively few

14 See M.H. Hoeflich, "How Justice Story Saved the Rule of Law in America," lecture delivered at the 2007 Meeting of the American Society for Legal History.

15 41 U.S. 1 (1842); and see R. Kent Newmyer, "Harvard Law School, New England Legal Culture and the Antebellum Origins of American Jurisprudence," *Journal of American History* 74, (3; 1987): 814–35.

reprinted English texts with state notes. On the contrary, what was produced and sold were English texts with "American notes." Treatises like Story's *Commentaries* described American law and cited both English cases and American cases (i.e., federal cases and cases from all of the American states).

The effect of the publication of these books, which offered their readers particular views of American law, was to help create modern American law. Their use in law schools and by practicing lawyers helped to bring the law of the various American jurisdictions closer together and thereby make practice across state lines far more feasible. In so doing, they helped to make real the aspirations of men such as the Federalist jurists, including Joseph Story, who believed that the greatness of the United States as a nation depended on its possessing a distinctive national jurisprudence in which there would be state-level variations, but such variations were just that: exceptions to more general, national rules. In this way, the development of a national trade in law books directly aided the nationalist agenda of Story and his compatriots.

There could be no American legal literature without American legal writers. The development of a cadre of American legal writers could not proceed until such writing became a viable economic activity. A few early American legal writers, like Joseph Story, did not need to support themselves through their writing, but most could not afford to take time off from practice to devote themselves to the profession of authorship until this activity could produce income sufficient to justify its time demands. Thus, for example, Rufus Choate, though he often spoke of writing books, never did so, because he could not give up his lucrative law practice.[16]

Legal writing became an economically viable activity only when a sufficient number of law book publishers and sellers could commission lawyers and jurists to write texts and pay them for their efforts. A few brave souls attempted to make a living by self-publishing through subscription, but this was a difficult path to follow as Joshua

[16] Choate long planned, but never executed, a study of Greek history, for which he accumulated source materials throughout his life; see Jean V. Matthews, *Rufus Choate: The Law and Civic Virtue* (Philadelphia: Temple University Press, 1980), 108–9.

Montefiore discovered.[17] Thus, it was no coincidence that the golden age of antebellum American law writing began precisely at the time, the late 1820s and early 1830s, when the law book trade was finally becoming established in the new nation. Men like Edward Ingraham, a Philadelphia lawyer, made a good living preparing notes to English treatises and editing case reports. As the market for law books expanded and publishers sought out new material to publish, American lawyers increasingly turned their hands to writing and editing as a means of earning a living.

The rise of university-affiliated law schools in the United States was closely intertwined with the rise of law publishing and law bookselling. As noted previously, law schools differentiated themselves from the traditional apprenticeship system of legal education by stressing the scientific, or principled, nature of law school legal education. The fundamental basis for such an education was instruction by lectures based on set legal texts. University-affiliated law schools like Harvard advertised that they offered their students a curriculum based on the best legal texts available and made these texts available to their students in their libraries. In short, American law school legal education in the antebellum era was "law-book centered." Apprenticeship education, in contrast, was "practice-centered." Apprentices might read law books, although rarely very many or in a systematic fashion. The primary educational experience of apprentices was attendance in court and law office, observing the ways in which the masters carried on their practice. The proponents of law school legal education derided apprenticeship as parochial and incomplete, a craftsman's, not a professional's, education. Law schools needed law books to teach from, and thus, early law professors like Story, Greenleaf, and Kent were prolific legal authors. All were associated with one or more law publishers and booksellers. Greenleaf's list of recommended law books became a frequent component of law booksellers' catalogues.[18] To a large extent, the ultimate victory of law school legal education in the United States could not have been achieved without the growth of legal publishing and bookselling. It was a symbiotic relationship that benefited both.

[17] See Chapter 5. [18] See Chapter 3.

THE IMPACT OF THE GROWING TRADE IN LAW BOOKS ON AMERICAN LAW

The history of the antebellum law book trade in the United States is, in many respects, typical of the history of most of the industries in the new American nation. Its growth was slow. At first it was a local industry and could not become national in scope until national markets were opened by the growth of a transportation infrastructure. It required legislative assistance. The ascent of the law book trade in the United States was indebted, in part, to the early protective copyright laws and the loosening of postal regulations. Without these legislative initiatives, the industry might well have failed to take root. The law book trade also needed product – in this case, texts that came from England at first but gradually domestically produced, as law school professors began to write for their classes and law book publishers began to commission lawyer authors to create saleable texts. Finally, like other early American industries, the law book trade gradually spread westward following the westward moving emigrants. Thus, New York, Boston, and Philadelphia were soon joined by Cincinnati and, eventually, San Francisco as law book publishing and selling centers.

Slow as it was, however, the trade's growth was crucial to the growth of American law, as previous chapters indicate. One could give many examples of how newly published editions of key legal texts supplanted earlier editions, both domestic and foreign. One can show, as well, how newly published translations of foreign works took root in the United States and introduced new ideas into American law. To do this thoroughly would require a second volume. Nevertheless, several examples may suffice to give at least some idea of the impact the growth of law book publishing and distribution had during this period. The first example is the widespread distribution and use of Thomas Cooper's edition and translation of Justinian's *Institutes*.

This tome was published in Philadelphia in 1812[19] and reprinted twice thereafter.[20] It was the first American edition of a translation that

[19] Thomas Cooper, *The Institutes of Justinian with Notes* (Philadelphia: P. Byrne, 1812).
[20] In New York in 1841 by Halstead and Voorhies and in 1852 by Voorhies.

was based upon George Harris' earlier work.[21] Cooper's American version found an immediate audience and became a staple of antebellum American booksellers' catalogues. It was, for example, offered for sale by Little, Brown in its 1856 catalogue, and John Livingston in his 1856 catalogue as well. It was offered for sale by John Campbell & Sons of Philadelphia in their 1872 catalogue. As a result of its easy availability and utility, it also found its way into numerous public and private law libraries. Thomas Jefferson owned a copy before 1814. The library of the University of North Carolina had a copy before 1830. The American Philosophical Society owned a copy before 1824, as did the University of Virginia by 1828. Peter Du Ponceau had a copy in his library, as did Joseph Story and Rufus Choate.

The widespread distribution of Cooper's *Justinian*, as it was called, was evidenced also by its frequent citation in reported decisions of the period.[22] For example, in South Carolina in the case of *Gregg v. Thompson*, a suit on a promissory note concerning the sale of a slave, the court quoted a passage from "Cooper's Justinian." In another South Carolina case, *Milledge v. Lamar*, Cooper's work was cited once again, along with the works of Vinnius and Voet. Cooper's text was cited in four Virginia cases between 1826 and 1838 in suits on a warranty in a sale of a sick slave, the partition of an intestate's estate, the proper division of profits in a partnership, and trover. The work was cited, as well, in Vermont in three cases between 1849 and 1865; in Texas in five cases between 1856 and 1867; and in five cases in Tennessee between 1824 and 1838. In fact, between 1812 and 1872, Cooper's Justinian was cited more than one hundred times in twenty-one states and the federal courts from the district level to the Supreme Court of the United States.[23]

This ownership and citation history of Cooper's edition and translation of Justinian's *Institutes* stands as strong evidence of the success of the law book publishing and distribution networks that developed in the period under study. Much the same results can be shown with

[21] On Harris's translation and the distribution of Cooper's edition, see M. H. Hoeflich, "Vinnius and the Anglo-American World," *Zeitschrift der Savigny-Stiftung fur Rechtsgeschichte. romanistiche Abteilung*, 114 (1997): 360–65.

[22] See Hoeflich, "Vinnius and the Anglo-American World," 366–68.

[23] This statement is based on a search done on the Lexis database.

hundreds of other law books published and sold in the United States during this era.

Time and time again during the antebellum period, we also see locally published and distributed legal texts replaced by a national text. Perhaps there is no more dramatic example of this than the printing and distribution history of one of the primary antebellum texts on the law of bailments: Sir William Jones's *Essay on the Law of Bailments* and its replacement by Joseph Story's *Commentaries on the Law of Bailments*. The publishing history of these two books in the United States draws together many of the historical trends described throughout this book.

Sir William Jones published his *Essay on the Law of Bailments* in London in 1781.[24] At the time of its publication, Jones was a young man, but one who had already achieved a measure of fame for his scholarship and writing in several subjects.[25] The book itself was quite different from earlier treatises. First, it was one of the first to treat law as a science to be derived from general principles.[26] Second, it was strongly comparative in nature, drawing not only on the English Common Law but also Roman, Islamic, and biblical, and even Hindu legal principles.[27] Within a short period of the appearance of the first edition, the work gained renown. It was reissued in a second edition with notes by John Balmanno, a barrister of Lincoln's Inn, in London in 1798. But American lawyers did not have to search out imported editions of Jones's work. In fact, Jones's *Essay* was one of the most frequently reprinted law books in the early Republic. It was first published in 1796 in Boston. It was reprinted, with Balmanno's notes, in 1806 in Albany, New York, and Brattleboro, Vermont in 1807. Moreover, it was reprinted at Brattleboro in 1813 and 1818, an indication of how much in demand the book was. It was reprinted in

[24] Sir William Jones, *An Essay on the Law of Bailments* (London: Dilly, 1781). This essay has been reprinted with explanatory notes and introduction: Sir William Jones, *An Essay on the Law of Bailments*, ed. David Ibbetson (Bangor: Welsh Legal History Society, 2007).

[25] The best biography of Jones is Garland Cannon, *The Life and Mind of Oriental Jones* (Cambridge: Cambridge University Press, 1990).

[26] See Jones, *Bailments* (2007 ed.), 195, note 202; D. Ibbetson, "Introduction," 26–29.

[27] See, especially, David Ibbetson, "Sir William Jones. Comparative Lawyer," in *Sir William Jones, 1746–1794: A Commemoration*, ed. A. Murray (Oxford: Oxford University Press, 1998), 19–42.

New York City in 1828 and in Philadelphia in 1836 with additional American notes by Halsted, which almost overshadowed the original text.[28]

Copies of Jones's *Essay* are listed for sale in virtually every American law bookseller's catalogue of the period and in every private law library catalogue as well. It was frequently cited in American courts as well. It was, very possibly, the first American legal bestseller since the reprinting of Blackstone's *Commentaries* by Robert Bell.[29] One may speculate as to the reasons for its success. It was scientific in its approach and, therefore, would have appealed greatly to Federalist jurists like Story and Kent.[30] It dealt with a subject of great practical significance and was the first volume published in the United States to do so. Finally, Jones's reputation as a model of the learned literary lawyer and the literary allusions in the text would have appealed to the American elite Bar.[31]

By the middle of the 1830s, however, Jones's work lost much of its popularity. This happened for one simple reason. In 1833 Little, Brown published Joseph Story's *Commentaries on the Law of Bailments*. This was the first of several major works to come from Story's pen. It was also, to a large degree, based on Jones's work, although it far exceeded it in both length and juristic accomplishment. After Little, Brown published Story's work and began to offer it nationally through its catalogues, the book rapidly came to replace Jones's and became the mainstay of the American law of the subject for decades to come.[32] The English authored text gave way to the native American production. The locally printed and distributed text gave way to the product of one of the great national houses. Thus the history of these two volumes is, in many respects, a microcosm of what was happening throughout the period in the United States.

[28] See Ibbetson, "Introduction," 60. [29] See Chapter 5.

[30] See Ibbetson, "Introduction," 65–68; James Oldham, "The Survival of Sir William Jones in American Jurisprudence," in *Objects of Enquiry: The Life, Contributions and Influences of Sir William Jones (1746–1794)*, ed. Garland Cannon and Kevin R. Brine (New York: New York University Press, 1995), 92–101, especially 95.

[31] See Robert Ferguson, "The Emulation of Sir William Jones in the Early Republic," *New England Quarterly*, 52 (1979): 3–26.

[32] See Hoeflich, "Vinnius and the Anglo-American World," 358–59.

A FINAL BRIEF NOTE

I do not pretend that this book is comprehensive. Many of the sources discussed here appear in print for the first time. Much more work in this field remains to be done and should be done. Ideas do not simply spread by magic. Lawyers do not absorb concepts and doctrines from the ether. Lawyers learn by being taught through observation, hearing, and reading. One cannot understand the circulation of legal ideas without understanding the circulation of the physical artifacts in which those ideas are to be found. For the period 1770 to 1870, those artifacts were law books. If we are fully to understand the history of American law in the antebellum period, we must understand the history of American lawyers' reading in this period – of which the history of the antebellum book trade is an essential part. This book is, I hope, a first step to that understanding.

FINIS
IN PIAM MEMORIAM
MAGISTRORUM MEORUM
GODDEFRIDI ELTON
JOHANNI CROOK

Index